Theology *and the* Crisis of Engagement

Theology *and the* Crisis of Engagement

Essays on the Relationship of Theology and the Social Sciences in Honor of Lee Cormie

Edited by
JEFF NOWERS
and
NÉSTOR MEDINA

☙PICKWICK *Publications* · Eugene, Oregon

THEOLOGY AND THE CRISIS OF ENGAGEMENT
Essays on the Relationship of Theology and the Social Sciences in Honor of Lee Cormie

Copyright © 2013 Wipf and Stock Publishers. All rights reserved. Except for brief quotations in critical publications or reviews, no part of this book may be reproduced in any manner without prior written permission from the publisher. Write: Permissions, Wipf and Stock Publishers, 199 W. 8th Ave., Suite 3, Eugene, OR 97401.

Pickwick Publications
An Imprint of Wipf and Stock Publishers
199 W. 8th Ave., Suite 3
Eugene, OR 97401

www.wipfandstock.com

ISBN 13: 978-1-62032-779-1

Cataloging-in-Publication data:

 Theology and the crisis of engagement : essays on the relationship of theology and the social sciences in honor of Lee Cormie / edited by Jeff Nowers and Néstor Medina ; Foreword by Gregory Baum.

 xx + 198 pp. ; 23 cm—Includes index.

 ISBN 13: 978-1-61097-992-4

 1. Cormie, Lee. 2. Christianity and the social sciences. 3. Christianity and culture. I. Nowers, Jeff. II. Medina, Néstor. III. Baum, Gregory, 1923–. IV. Title.

BR115 C8 T45 2013

Manufactured in the USA

Contents

Foreword—Gregory Baum   vii

Introduction—Jeff Nowers   xi

List of Contributors   xix

Part One: Historical and Methodological Issues

1. Biblical Interpretation as Political Practice—*Ched Myers*   3
2. Christian Ethics, Social Sciences, and Moral Imagination —*Marilyn J. Legge*   25
3. The Social Gospel and the Social Sciences —*Robert C. Fennell*   41
4. Washing His Hands of the Enlightenment: A Critique of John Milbank—*Christopher Craig Brittain*   58
5. Discerning Movements of the Spirit: The World Social Forum and the Work of Theology—*Janet Conway*   77

Part Two: Contextual and Constructive Proposals

6. ORiginAL Voices: Eradicating the "Fearful Asymmetry" or Power Imbalance between Indigenous and Western Thought in History and Theology—*Carmen Lansdowne*   93
7. Accompanying el Señor de los Milagros: The Early Processional Theology of Diego Irarrázaval —*Mario DeGiglio-Bellemare*   110
8. The Church and Indigenous Cultures: Beyond the Violent Encounter with "Modernity"—*Michel Andraos*   128
9. U.S. Latina/o Theology: Challenges, Possibilities, and Future Prospects—*Néstor Medina*   141

Contents

10 *Chi* and Holy Spirit: Towards a Korean North American Theology—*Grace Ji-Sun Kim*   161

11. Fossil Fuels and Apocalypse: Theology for "A New Dark Age"—*Harold Wells*   176

Index   193

Foreword

Gregory Baum

THE PREFERENTIAL OPTION FOR the poor is a hermeneutical principle, a reflection of the preaching of Jesus, that has affected the thinking and acting in the Christian Church in an irreversible manner. First formalized systematically by Latin American liberation theology, the preferential option has influenced the World Council of Churches and the Latin American Catholic Bishops Conference at Medellín (1968) and Puebla (1979). It subsequently affected the wider Christian Church. To read Scripture and society from the perspective generated by solidarity with the poor and oppressed has been a cognitive venture undertaken by Christians in all parts of the world, even occasionally by Catholic bishops.

Lee Cormie is one of the few North American theologians whose entire work has been produced by a commitment to the preferential option. Writing a foreword to the present *Festschrift* in his honor gives me great pleasure. We first met in the 1960s when he was a student and I a professor at St. Michael's College of the University of Toronto, and we subsequently become friends and theological allies.

Lee Cormie realized very early that in addition to economic exploitation and exclusion are other forms of domination and that, for this reason, the social analysis of oppression demands careful attention to the complexity of the historical situation. The "Theology in the Americas" conference held at Detroit in 1975, which Lee and I attended, demonstrated this complexity in dramatic fashion. The three teams of theologians invited to present their reflections became involved in a heated, yet very instructive debate. The Latin American theologians asked the black theologians why they offered no critique of capitalism, while the black theologians wondered why the Latin Americans present were all white and seemingly unconcerned about

Foreword

racism on their continent. Saying a *pox* on both your houses, the feminist theologians showed that the two teams, Latin American and black, were totally indifferent to the subjugation of women. The Detroit Conference had a profound effect on progressive theologians: it made them realize that to understand social oppression, one must take into account at least three forms of domination.

More than any other theologian Lee Cormie has immersed himself in the social and political sciences to produce empirically verifiable analyses of the unjust structures that humiliate and damage human beings in their respective historical context. While it is quite legitimate to denounce oppression and discrimination in general, Lee Cormie has never done this. He has always assumed the social-scientific task of clarifying the various factors—social, economic, political, and cultural—that inflict injustice and undeserved suffering on sectors of the population.

Liberation theology in its various forms also inquires what the divine promises implicit in the Christian gospel mean for the victims of oppression. Lee Cormie is permanently haunted by this question. As a man of faith he believes that God's presence in history as Word and as Spirit summons forth resistance to empire and movements of social reconstruction. In the apocalyptic passages of Scripture, Cormie hears God's promise that another world is possible. With great sensitivity he searches in church and society for signs of renewal, for new ideas and alternative practises. He studies these countervailing currents with great attention. If he finds them inspired by justice, he defends them in his academic writings and, if possible, supports them by his action. This is what the life of faith means to him.

At the same time, Lee Cormie is not a starry-eyed radical. For one, he does not believe God's gracious presence in history guarantees that the movements of resistance and reconstruction will eventually lead to a totally reconciled global society. He does not share the evolutionary faith of liberals or Marxists or Teilhard de Chardin. God summons forth people's engagement in critical movements and blesses the personal and social transformation they generate, yet—Lee Cormie insists—God tells us nothing about the end of history. To foster love, justice, and peace redeems, even if it cannot destabilize empire.

Moreover, Lee Cormie does not embrace the countervailing movements uncritically. He examines them in the light of the gospel and evaluates their ends and means in terms of justice. Since humiliation and social exclusion may produce feelings of hatred and revenge, resistance to empire

Foreword

is vulnerable to fanaticism and, thus, is in constant need of renewing its commitment to reason, measure, and equity. Lee Cormie is a radical thinker, yet a sane one, a critical one, a believing one.

Lee Cormie recognises that the majority of secular activists are not interested in the relation of faith and justice and prefer that religion not be mentioned in the joint struggle. This observation has been confirmed by his experience as a participant in the World Social Forums and the movement for an alternative globalization. Secular activists tend to look upon religion as a culture that defends the status quo; they also fear that talking about religion divides people into believers and non-believers. Liberationist Christians, only too often ignored in the churches, also receive little attention from secular intellectuals and activists. The contribution of Christian liberationism is hardly ever mentioned in the literature of the political Left. Lee Cormie has tried to change this. He explores the meaning of the biblical promises in dialogue with social and political science and adopts a discourse that can be understood by secular people troubled by inequality and committed to social justice. He is a pioneer in this enterprise and a pace-setter for the liberation theology of the future.

Introduction

Jeff Nowers

IN THE LONG COURSE of its development, Christian theology has weathered many episodes of crisis—moments, events, and experiences of emotional and intellectual upheavel that provoke imperative decision. The first century, for instance, witnessed St. Paul and his followers move away from the view that Jesus Christ's second coming would be imminent, to the position that certain conditions would necessarily usher in the "day of the Lord."[1] One way to account for Paul's apparent shift of perspective is to view him as re-evaluating his eschatology in order to mitigate the crisis of delayed expectation. The upshot for the earliest Christians was thus a gradual migration of focus from heavenly to earthly reality.[2]

There were other serious crises to follow in the succeeding centuries. Questions concerning the full deity of Jesus provoked the councils of Nicea and, subsequently, Chalcedon. Then, in the early seventeenth century, Galileo dropped a cosmological bomb: he offered unsettling evidence, informed by Copernicus, that the earth in fact revolved around the sun, not vice versa. Galileo was tried for heresy in Rome, banished from society, and his writings were censured. This ultimately engendered a difficult and fragile relationship between the church and the ongoing development of modern science, one that continues to the present, notwithstanding Pope John Paul II's 1992 vindication of Galileo's findings.[3]

---

1. Cf. 1 Thess 4:13–18 *contra* 2 Thess 2:1–8.

2. The so-called "delay of the *parousia*" has not always been interpreted in terms of crisis, as I am doing here. For alternative perspectives, see David E. Aune, "The Significance of the Delay of the Parousia for Early Christianity," in *Current Issues in Biblical and Patristic Interpretation*, ed. Gerald F. Hawthorne (Grand Rapids: Eerdmans, 1975); and Richard J. Bauckham, "The Delay of the Parousia," *Tyndale Bulletin* 31 (1980) 3–36.

3. See *L'Osservatore Romano*, November 4, 1992.

Introduction

In more recent times, another crisis emerged. In the 1970s, the independent and simultaneous irruption of theological voices from Latin America, Africa, Asia, and U.S. black church communities gave stern notice that theology was not simply a white, male, Western enterprise. These emerging "liberation theologians" often claimed political allegiances with such revolutionaries as Salvador Allende in Chile, Daniel Ortega and the Sandinistas in Nicaragua, and Malcolm X in the U.S. Methodologically, they drew upon a range of social-scientific theory in their theological reflection and construction of an "option for the poor." Marxist thought, in particular, frequently became a critical tool with which to assess the contemporary circumstances of the world. It is just this sort of *avant-garde* approach to theology that has been met with considerable resistance from traditional theological powers. The Roman Catholic Church's theological watchdog, the Congregation for the Doctrine of the Faith (CDF), has moved to "silence" certain liberation theologians whom it deems a threat. As recently as 2006, for example, the CDF issued a "notification" on two significant books by Jon Sobrino—*Jesus the Liberator* and *Christ the Liberator*—now judged to be at odds with the faith of the Church.[4]

These examples of crisis illustrate the ongoing challenge of theology's navigation of and engagement with its own historical situatedness and with other developments of thought in science, history, economics, political theory, and so forth. How then—and to what extent—should theology engage knowledge emanating from these various disciplines? That fundamental question forms the *raison d'être* of this volume as a whole, and it serves as the basic point of departure for all the volume's essays. This book is also a fitting *Festschrift* for Professor Lee Cormie, a scholar of theology and the social sciences, who has taught in the Faculty of Theology at the University of St. Michael's College and the Toronto School of Theology for over thirty years.

The relationship between theology and the social sciences has been an abiding theme of Cormie's academic career since his 1977 PhD dissertation on "The Social Sciences and the Problem of Religion in the Modern World: Durkheimian and Freudian Perspectives." While completing his doctorate, Cormie became involved in the "Theology in the Americas" gathering in Detroit in 1975. This groundbreaking event brought together key Latin American liberation theologians, leading representatives of Black

---

4. For the full text of the Notification, see www.vatican.ca/roman_curia/congregations/cfaith/documents/rc_con_cfaith_doc_20061126_notification-sobrino_en.html.

Introduction

Theology, and emerging feminist theologians for critical dialogue, reflection, and cooperation. For Cormie personally, his involvement inaugurated a longstanding commitment to learning from and teaching about what he calls "new voices" in theology. Cormie, however, has never been interested in detached observation and commentary: his connection to theologies of liberation has fueled a concern to integrate social-scientific theory with faith-based practices and to participate directly in movements of social change. This has culminated recently in his participation in the World Social Forum and more local fora that it has inspired. Cormie's concretized emphases in theological education have made him resistant to univocal readings of history that reenvision pluralities and differences in monolithic terms. He is thus always sensitive to the distinctives of any movement or "new voice," a sensitivity that ever impels him to read more and think more about the points of intersection between theology, social theory, and movements for change.

In view of Cormie's longstanding interests in theology and the social sciences, the essays in this book each provide examples of how the relationship or points of intersection between these two areas might be investigated. The five essays that comprise Part I each tackle historical and methodological issues, while Part II contains six essays which present constructive proposals for how theology might pursue social-scientific engagement in various ethno-cultural contexts.

Since theology is almost always, in varying degrees, dependent on Scripture as a key source, the first chapter of this volume deals with the Bible. In an essay titled, "Biblical Interpretation as Political Practice," Ched Myers reflects on the uses of Scripture for kindling social change. Myers discusses the development of socio-political hermeneutics vis-à-vis the rise of liberation theology. He then turns his attention to Isaiah 56 and Mark 7, reading these two biblical texts analogously with actual contemporary struggles of marginalized people for emancipation. His reading is a clarion call for Christians and their churches to be houses of radical hospitality, wherein every dividing wall is dismantled. Accordingly, his essay illustrates how theology can employ social theory in constructing a biblical hermeneutic that engenders praxis.

Marilyn Legge's essay stands in continuity with Myers, but from a more theoretical perspective. Legge presents a vision of Christian ethics as grounded in the power of imagination and animated by critical social theory. She probes why critical social theory is so crucial to Christian ethics

Introduction

and how the moral imagination of "justice-love" can shape the way in which critical social theory is engaged. She then explores the United Church of Canada's "intercultural church" initiative as a constructive example of what can happen when imagination and critical social theory jointly inform Christian ethics.

In the third chapter, Robert Fennell examines historically how the so-called Social Gospel movement in North America engaged the social sciences in its quest for societal transformation. Fennell discusses the emergence of the Social Gospel and its chief protagonists before analyzing how political and economic theory and sociology came to inform the movement. He argues that the application of these sorts of social-scientific disciplines to the Social Gospel resulted in "imprecise and idiosyncratic amalgams" with the religious sensibilities of certain exemplars of the Social Gospel itself. Fennell's essay thus illustrates that not every theological engagement with social theory results in the sort of harmony of ideas for which Myers and Legge hope.

Based on the conclusion of Fennell's case-study, it could be argued that theology and the social sciences should have no collaborative relationship. Indeed, John Milbank, a major protagonist of "radical orthodoxy," holds that all social theory is a form of anti-theology proceeding from an ontology of violence. Christopher Brittain's essay offers a careful critique of John Milbank's position. Whereas Milbank insists that theology contains its own tradition of resources for responding to all the issues that social theory attempts to address, Brittain disputes this thesis by showing that Milbank's arguments are mired in inconsistency on several fronts. Brittain argues that Milbank's theology is hostile to all that stands outside the Christian tradition. As a corrective, theology can benefit from constructive engagement with the social sciences as a means of assisting Christian communities to avoid those patterns of violence and exclusion to which the Christian tradition has been perennially susceptible. Brittain thus shows that theology can be helpfully augmented by social theory.

The fifth chapter by Janet Conway explores the theological import of the World Social Forum, an annual event that facilitates connections between movements and organizations pursuing the possibility of another world, one not defined or governed by neoliberalism. Conway interprets the World Social Forum in theological terms as a "movement of the Spirit," one which, in fostering convergence, paradoxically affirms difference and plurality. In this sense, the World Social Forum represents something of

Introduction

a new Pentecost, a time when theological reflection ought to inspire the broadening of solidarity and inclusion. Conway's essay is unique in that it explores not how theology can be augmented by social theory, but rather how social theory, particularly sociology and political science, can be enhanced by theology.

These five historically and methodologically oriented chapters lay the ground for the second part of the volume, which contain contextually driven essays of a more constructive character. In the sixth chapter, Carmen Lansdowne confronts the inadequacy and hegemony of Western academic categories of oral tradition and oral history. Writing as a First Nations theologian, Lansdowne introduces the idea of "ORiginALity" as a means of correcting the widespread academic misunderstandings of indigenous oral epistemologies. She argues that "ORiginALity" is defined by a politics of spatiality that is rooted in land. She further contends, drawing on the work of Paul Tillich, that such a politics extends to the academy, where indigenous oral epistemologies must claim their rightful place. Lansdowne's essay is ultimately an exercise in decolonial theory, with a view to constructing an emancipatory indigenous epistemology and a more deeply indigenous First Nations theology.

Mario DeGiglio-Bellemare's essay focuses on Peru and the "early processional theology" of Diego Irarrázaval, a liberationist colleague of Gustavo Gutiérrez. Bellemare examines an important 1977 text of Irarrázaval and argues that Irarrázaval made a pioneering breakthrough by utilizing a social-scientific approach in his interpretation of popular religion. In his extended study of the popular *Milagros* feast, Irarrázaval identified four typologies for understanding the feast but argued finally that the feast must be approached on its own terms, an approach that "accompanies those who are accompanying the processional Christ." Bellemare concludes that Irarrázaval broke new ground with his social-scientific and non-romanticizing emphasis on the actual hopes and aspirations of the popular masses. Bellemare's essay thus highlights a creative example of how the social sciences have been imaginatively engaged theologically and why such engagement regarding popular religion holds promise for today.

In keeping with Bellemare's Latin American focus, Michel Andraos is concerned with recent cultural encounters between the Catholic Church and indigenous peoples in Chiapas, Mexico. Andraos chronicles the episcopal career of Samuel Ruiz Garcia, bishop of the region from 1960-2000, during which Ruiz came to see the Church's missionary exploits among

Introduction

indigenous peoples as destructive to their culture. The missiology that emerged from this realization has paved the way for the emergence of indigenous ecclesial communities that retain their cultural distinctives. It has also birthed an open dialogue between indigenous religious thinkers and theologians representing Church hierarchy. Andraos concludes that these developments open a "horizon of hope" for imagining a new way of intercultural relations. His essay is thus a helpful illustration of how anthropology and theology can be mutually illuminating.

The ninth chapter by Néstor Medina shifts attention to the U.S. in dealing with the "Challenges, Possibilities, and Future Prospects of U.S. Latina/o Theology." Employing the bio-cultural category of *mestizaje*, Medina explores some of the contributions of U.S. Latina/o theologians, particularly their theological method of responding to racism and their hermeneutics of understanding popular religion. He then highlights some of the challenges that U.S. Latina/o theology face in accounting properly for its present contextual situatedness, and concludes that U.S. Latina/o theology occupies a unique space because of the way it uses social-scientific theory to develop a theological method of ethno-cultural identity. Medina's essay stands in helpful juxtaposition to the contributions of Bellemare and Andraos in showing how social theory functions somewhat differently in U.S. Latina/o theology vis-à-vis Latin American theology.

Representing a different context altogether, Grace Ji-Sun Kim develops a Korean North American pneumatological response to the "clash of civilizations" that Samuel Huntington has famously described.[5] Kim's response, which she intends to elicit liberative action, draws equally on the Asian concept of *Chi*—the life-force of all that is—and Christian understandings of the Holy Spirit, while utilizing the resources of postcolonial theory. Kim explores the phenomenon of hybridity and suggests that it is constitutive of the Korean North American immigrant experience. In formulating a response of pneumatological praxis, Kim emphasizes the qualities of balance and harmony that lie at the heart of *Chi* and which complement a Christian vision of the Holy Spirit's agency. This kind of pneumatology can provoke action that confronts structural power imbalances in today's world.

In the final chapter of this volume, Harold Wells contemplates theology for a new "dark age," a phrase drawn from James Lovelock[6] and also Jane

---

5. Samuel P. Huntington, *The Clash of Civilizations and the Remaking of World Order* (New York: Simon & Schuster, 1996).

6. See James Lovelock, *The Revenge of Gaia* (London: Lane, 2006) 11.

Introduction

Jacobs.[7] Wells links the onset of "darkness" to unremitting global warming trends aggravated by an inexorable dependence on fossil fuels. He proposes a renewed "theology of the cross" to respond to such pressing reality. In so doing, Wells welcomes the social and physical sciences as sources that can augment the church's teaching and preaching. He also calls for a rethinking of God not as "almighty" but as self-limited, one who loves and suffers *with*. Such a theology will evoke an ethic of self-discipline and self-limitation, wherein the world's resources are used prudently and sparingly for the good of all, especially the poor and dispossessed.

These essays are written by colleagues, friends, or former students of Professor Lee Cormie, and each essay reflects interests and areas of research to which he has devoted much attention inside and outside the classroom. The essays are offered in appreciation and recognition of Cormie's long-standing service to theological education and his tireless advocacy of "new voices" in theology.

LeRoy Francis Cormie was born in 1943 into a Roman Catholic family and grew up in Utica, New York. After completing high school, he matriculated at the University of Toronto, where he graduated with a degree in mathematics. He remained in Toronto at St. Michael's College to pursue an MA in theology, graduating in 1967 with a New Testament thesis on Matthew 17:24–27. He then moved to the University of Chicago Divinity School, earning his PhD in 1977 under the direction of Don Browning. In 1979 Cormie returned to Toronto to assume a teaching post with an emphasis on theologies of liberation. He has remained there to the present day. Along the way, he has mentored many graduate students and supervised many theses and dissertations. The contributors to this volume pay tribute to him as teacher, colleague, and friend.

This *Festschrift* has been a project of several years. Everyone involved has shown exceptional patience throughout the entire process—from the first days when this book was a mere idea, to its eventual publication by Pickwick. Grateful appreciation is extended to the editorial team at Wipf & Stock, to David Johnson for compiling the index, to Alison Hari-Singh and Samia Saad for their steady encouragement, and to Emmanuel College and the Faculty of Theology of the University of St. Michael's College for financial assistance along the way. Now that the volume has achieved publication, we hope that it will further the conversations that Lee Cormie has worked so diligently to enliven between theology and the social sciences.

7. Jane Jacobs (1916–2006) was an urban theorist and prolific author based in Toronto; her last book was *Dark Age Ahead* (New York: Random House, 2004).

Contributors

MICHEL ANDRAOS is Associate Professor of Intercultural Studies and Ministry at the Catholic Theological Union, Chicago.

GREGORY BAUM is Professor Emeritus in the Faculty of Religious Studies at McGill University.

CHRISTOPHER CRAIG BRITTAIN is Senior Lecturer in the School of Divinity, History and Philosophy at the University of Aberdeen.

JANET CONWAY is Canada Research Chair in Social Justice and Associate Professor of Sociology at Brock University.

MARIO DEGIGLIO-BELLEMARE teaches in the Department of Humanities, Philosophy, and Religion at John Abbott College, Montreal.

ROBERT C. FENNELL is Associate Professor of Historical and Systematic Theology at Atlantic School of Theology, Halifax.

GRACE JI-SUN KIM is a visiting researcher at Georgetown University.

CARMEN LANSDOWNE is a PhD candidate at the Graduate Theological Union, and Director of Operations at Alliance for Climate Education, Oakland, California.

MARILYN J. LEGGE is Associate Professor of Christian Ethics at Emmanuel College in the University of Toronto.

NÉSTOR MEDINA is Assistant Professor of Theology and Culture at Regent University School of Divinity.

CHED MYERS is an educator, activist, and co-director of Bartimaeus Cooperative Ministries in southern California.

Contributors

JEFF NOWERS is a pastoral associate at St. James Cathedral, Toronto, and adjunct lecturer in the Toronto School of Theology.

HAROLD WELLS is Professor Emeritus of Systematic Theology at Emmanuel College in the University of Toronto.

Part One

Historical and Methodological Issues

1

Biblical Interpretation as Political Practice

CHED MYERS

THERE HAVE BEEN FEW North American theologians in the past three decades who have seriously attempted to bridge the longstanding gulf that exists between the seminaries, the sanctuaries, and the streets. Of those few, Lee Cormie stands out as one of the most passionate and exemplary. As our paths have crossed at conferences, demonstrations, and ecumenical services, I have always appreciated conversations with Cormie, whose grounded theological perspectives and active commitments to social analysis and strategic action are encouraging and clarifying. It is in this integrative spirit, and in deep appreciation for Cormie's work and witness, that I offer the following reflections on the uses of Scripture for engaging social change.

SOCIO-POLITICAL HERMENEUTICS AND LIBERATION THEOLOGY

During the 1970s Christian liberation theologies percolated throughout Latin America, Africa, and Asia, as well as among Third World communities within First World countries.[1] These diverse theologies generally shared

1. See Alfred Hennelly, ed., *Liberation Theology: A Documentary History* (Maryknoll,

PART ONE—Historical and Methodological Issues

three characteristics: (a) a grounding in practices of popular education and pastoral work among the poor; (b) reflection generated from contexts of violence, poverty, and oppression; and (c) alignment with social movements of service to the marginalized, advocacy, and sometimes revolutionary engagement. During this same period a variety of "political theologies" and Christian-Marxist dialogues emerged in North Atlantic countries.[2] Lee Cormie has been one of North America's most diligent and faithful translators and promoters of this theological tradition. His writing and his activism around struggles for social change at home and abroad have inspired a generation of both students and colleagues to connect faith and justice.

Liberation theologies animated "political readings" of both Testaments that focused upon God's attentiveness to the poor, the prophetic insistence upon social justice, and the vocation of the church to stand in solidarity with the marginalized.[3] Most of the initial exegetical work was, however, topical, and offered mostly by theologians. Catholic and Protestant biblical scholars were slower to respond to liberation themes. Notable exceptions were Hebrew Bible scholar Norman Gottwald, whose socio-political interpretation of Israel's origins was groundbreaking in its use of sociological method and political hermeneutics, and Richard Horsley, who pioneered similar approaches to the New Testament.[4] Though initially controversial, their work eventually transformed the field.

In 1983 Gottwald and Horsley, in a collection of essays on political and social hermeneutics, identified four key "chasms" in biblical studies, between: (a) religion and the rest of life; (b) the past as "dead history" and the present as "real life"; (c) thought and practice; and (d) biblical academics and popular Bible study. "The Bible is about political-economic life inseparable from religious perspective and inspiration," they wrote, "and is full of political-economic-religious conflict and struggle." They called for biblical scholars to "recognize that their own enterprise and points of view

---

NY: Orbis, 1990); K. C. Abraham, ed., *Third World Theologies: Commonalities and Divergences* (Maryknoll, NY: Orbis, 1990); Arthur McGovern, *Liberation Theology and Its Critics* (Maryknoll, NY: Orbis, 1989).

2. See, e.g., John K. Downey, ed., *Love's Strategy: The Political Theology of Johann Baptist Metz* (Harrisburg, PA: Trinity, 1999).

3. One of the earlier attempts was George Pixley, *God's Kingdom* (Maryknoll, NY: Orbis, 1981).

4. Norman K. Gottwald, *The Tribes of Yahweh: A Sociology of the Religion of Liberated Israel* (Maryknoll, NY: Orbis, 1979); Richard A. Horsley and John S. Hanson, *Bandits, Prophets, and Messiahs: Popular Movements at the Time of Jesus* (Minneapolis: Winston, 1985).

are historically determined and parochial . . . and further recognize that certain popular readings display an affinity or analogy with certain views or struggles represented in biblical literature."[5] This represents an enduring statement of the issues addressed by socio-political readings of the Bible.

The conservative drift of culture and politics through the Reagan/Thatcher and Bush/Blair eras saw liberation theologies increasingly relegated to the activist margins of First and Third World seminaries and churches. A recent anthology of Latin American "economic readings" of Scripture shows, however, that liberation theologies continue to fertilize engaged biblical study throughout the Third World, despite less interest among First World publishers.[6] Meanwhile, a modest but steady stream of political and sociological readings of the Bible has emerged among a new generation of exegetes during this same period.[7] This field is broad enough to divide into four interrelated trajectories (the following is a selective but hopefully representative list of work in English):

a. *Thematic studies.* Driven by contemporary social concerns, these works survey biblical perspectives on specific issues such as economics,[8] violence and nonviolence,[9] and politics.[10]

---

5. Gottwald and Horsley, eds., *The Bible and Liberation: Political and Social Hermeneutics* (Maryknoll, NY: Orbis, 1993) xiv. See also Christopher Rowland and Mark Corner, *Liberating Exegesis: The Challenge of Liberation Theology to Biblical Studies* (Louisville: Westminster John Knox, 1989).

6. Ross Kinsler and Gloria Kinsler, eds., *God's Economy: Biblical Studies from Latin America* (Maryknoll, NY: Orbis, 2005).

7. For a sampling, see David Jobling et al., eds., *The Bible and the Politics of Exegesis: Essays in Honor of Norman K. Gottwald on His Sixty-fifth birthday* (Cleveland: Pilgrim, 1991).

8. See, e.g., José Porfirio Miranda, *Marx and the Bible: A Critique of the Philosophy of Oppression*, trans. J. Eagleson (1974; reprinted Eugene, OR: Wipf & Stock, 2004); Sharon Ringe, *Jesus, Liberation, and the Biblical Jubilee: Images for Ethics and Christology*, Overtures to Biblical Theology (Philadelphia: Fortress, 1985); Douglas E. Oakman, *Jesus and the Economic Questions of His Day* (Lewiston, NY: Mellen, 1986); Luise Schottroff and Wolfgang Stegemann, *Jesus and the Hope of the Poor*, trans. M. J. O'Connell (1986; reprinted, Eugene, OR: Wipf & Stock, 2009); and Richard Lowery, *Sabbath and Jubilee* (St. Louis: Chalice, 2000).

9. An early effort was George Edwards, *Jesus and the Politics of Violence* (New York: Harper & Row, 1972). More recent and sophisticated monographs are: Christopher Marshall, *Beyond Retribution: A New Testament Vision for Justice, Crime, and Punishment* (Grand Rapids: Eerdmans, 2001); J. Denny Weaver, *The Nonviolent Atonement* (Grand Rapids: Eerdmans, 2001); and Willard M. Swartley, *Covenant of Peace: The Missing Peace in New Testament Theology and Ethics* (Grand Rapids: Eerdmans, 2006).

10. From the early (and contrasting) attempt by S. G. F. Brandon, *Jesus and the Zealots* (New York: Scribners, 1967); and John Howard Yoder, *The Politics of Jesus* (Grand

Part One—Historical and Methodological Issues

b. *Liberation/social hermeneutics.* Inclusive of feminist/womanist and racial-ethnic hermeneutics, this broad rubric entails methodological approaches,[11] social-theological readings,[12] and studies of specific texts.[13]

c. *Socio-historical and sociological-anthropological studies.* Though they differ in their attitude toward historical "quests," many North Atlantic scholars have used social and anthropological theory and/or politico-historical structural analysis, in three broad trajectories:

Rapids: Eerdmans, 1972); to the influential work of Walter Wink, *Naming the Powers: The Language of Power in the New Testament* (Philadelphia: Fortress, 1984); Ze'ev Weisman, *Political Satire in the Bible*, Semeia Studies (Atlanta: Scholars, 1998); and Obery Hendricks, *The Politics of Jesus: Rediscovering the True Revolutionary Nature of Jesus' Teachings and How They Have Been Corrupted* (New York: Doubleday, 2006).

11. E.g., Michel Clevenot, *Materialist Approaches to the Bible*, trans. W. Nottingham (Maryknoll, NY: Orbis, 1985); Itumeleng Mosala, *Biblical Hermeneutics and Black Theology in South Africa* (Grand Rapids: Eerdmans, 1989); Gerald O. West, *Biblical Hermeneutics of Liberation: Modes of Reading the Bible in the South African Context* (Maryknoll, NY: Orbis, 1991); Elizabeth Schüssler Fiorenza, *In Memory of Her: A Feminist Theological Reconstruction of Christian Origins* (New York: Crossroad, 1994); Schüssler Fiorenza, *Rhetoric and Ethic: The Politics of Biblical Studies* (Minneapolis: Fortress, 1999); Schüssler Fiorenza, *Wisdom Ways: Introducing Feminist Biblical Interpretation* (Maryknoll, NY: Orbis, 2001); Cain Hope Felder, ed., *Stony the Road We Trod: African American Biblical Interpretation* (Minneapolis: Fortress, 1991); Felder, *Race, Racism, and the Biblical Narratives* (Minneapolis: Fortress, 2002); Fernando Segovia and Mary Ann Tolbert, eds., *Teaching the Bible: The Discourses and Politics of Biblical Pedagogy* (Maryknoll, NY: Orbis, 1998); Miguel De La Torre, *Reading the Bible from the Margins* (Maryknoll, NY: Orbis, 2002); Brian K. Blount, *Cultural Interpretation: Reorienting New Testament Criticism* (Minneapolis: Fortress, 1995); Bob Ekblad, *Reading the Bible with the Damned* (Louisville: Westminster John Knox, 2005); and Allen D. Callahan, *The Talking Book: African Americans and the Bible* (New Haven: Yale University Press, 2006).

12. E.g., Anthony Ceresko, *Introduction to the Old Testament: A Liberation Perspective* (Maryknoll, NY: Orbis, 1992); Walter Breuggemann, *A Social Reading of the Old Testament* (Minneapolis: Fortress, 1994); Jon Sobrino, *Christology at the Crossroads* (Maryknoll, NY: Orbis, 1978); Albert Nolan, *Jesus Before Christianity* (Maryknoll, NY: Orbis, 1978).

13. E.g., Fernando Belo, *A Materialist Reading of the Gospel of Mark*, trans. M. J. O'Connell (Maryknoll, NY: Orbis, 1981); Richard J. Cassidy, *Jesus, Politics, and Society: A Study of Luke's Gospel* (Maryknoll, NY: Orbis, 1978); Cassidy, *Society and Politics in the Acts of the Apostles* (Maryknoll, NY: Orbis, 1987); Shigeyuki Nakanose, *Josiah's Passover: Sociology and the Liberating Bible* (1993; reprinted, Eugene, OR: Wipf & Stock, 2004); Neil Elliott, *Liberating Paul: The Justice of God and the Politics of the Apostle* (1994; reprinted, Minneapolis: Fortress, 2005); Brian K. Blount, *Go Preach! Mark's Kingdom Message and the Black Church Today* (Maryknoll, NY: Orbis, 1998).

- Social history, focusing on the *sitz im leben* of the Hebrew Bible,[14] the Jesus movement,[15] and Paul;[16]
- sociological context of the NT;[17]
- readings of specific texts.[18]

d. *Socio-literary and ideological approaches.* Influenced by the Formalist challenge to historical-criticism, some are examining biblical narrative as historically specific ideological productions rather than trying to get "behind" the text. This trajectory includes:

- literary sociology/sociology of literature;[19]

---

14. E.g., Bernhard Lang, ed., *Anthropological Approaches to the Old Testament*, Issues in Religion and Theology (Philadelphia: Fortress, 1985); and Victor H. Matthews and Don C. Benjamin, *Social World of Ancient Israel, 1250–587 BCE* (Peabody, MA: Hendrickson, 1993).

15. E.g., Richard Horsley, *Sociology and the Jesus Movement* (New York: Crossroad, 1989); Ekkehard W. Stegemann and Wolfgang Stegemann, *The Jesus Movement: A Social History of Its First Century*, trans O. C. Dean (Minneapolis: Fortress, 1999).

16. E.g., Wayne Meeks, *The First Urban Christians: The Social World of the Apostle Paul* (New Haven: Yale University Press, 1983); Richard A. Horsley, ed., *Paul and Empire: Religion and Power in Roman Imperial Society* (Harrisburg, PA: Trinity, 1997); Horsley, *Paul and Politics* (Harrisburg, PA: Trinity, 2000); Steven Friesen, "Poverty in Pauline Studies: Beyond the So-called New Consensus," *Journal for the Study of the New Testament* 26 (2004) 323–61.

17. E.g., Wolfgang Stegemann et al., eds., *The Social Setting of Jesus and the Gospels* (Minneapolis: Fortress, 2002); K. C. Hanson and Douglas Oakman, *Palestine in the Time of Jesus: Social Structures and Social Conflicts*, 2nd ed. (Minneapolis: Fortress, 2008).

18. E.g., Bruce J. Malina and Richard L. Rohrbaugh, *Social-Science Commentary on the Synoptic Gospels*, 2nd ed. (Minneapolis: Fortress, 2003); Victor Matthews, *Social World of the Hebrew Prophets* (Peabody, MA: Hendrickson, 2001); John H. Elliott, *A Home for the Homeless: A Social-Scientific Criticism of I Peter, Its Situation, and Strategy* (Minneapolis: Fortress, 1990); William R. Herzog II, *Parables as Subversive Speech: Jesus as Pedagogue of the Oppressed* (Maryknoll, NY: Orbis, 1994); John J. Pilch, *Healing in the New Testament: Insights from Medical and Mediterranean Anthropology* (Minneapolis: Fortress, 2000).

19. E.g., Norman K. Gottwald, *The Hebrew Bible: A Socio-Literary Introduction* (Maryknoll, NY: Orbis, 1985); Ched Myers, *Binding the Strong Man: A Political Reading of Mark's Story of Jesus* (Maryknoll, NY: Orbis, 1988); Wes Howard-Brook, *Becoming Children of God: John's Gospel and Radical Discipleship* (Maryknoll, NY: Orbis, 1994); Wes Howard-Brook and Anthony Gwyther, *Unveiling Empire: Reading Revelation Then and Now* (Maryknoll, NY: Orbis, 1999); Warren Carter, *Matthew and the Margins: A Socio-political and Religious Reading*, JSNTSup 204 (Sheffield: Sheffield Academic, 2000); Brian J. Walsh and Sylvia C. Keesmaat, *Colossians Remixed: Subverting the Empire* (Downers Grove, IL: InterVarsity, 2004).

PART ONE—Historical and Methodological Issues

- ideological criticism, a related development that endeavors to read "against the grain," exercising suspicion about how power functions within and around the text;[20]
- post-colonial readings, a trend in literary theory recently picked up in biblical studies, that examines the legacy of imperialism, cultural hybridity and political ambiguity.[21]

It is fair to say that liberation hermeneutics disrupted whatever academic consensus may have existed in academic biblical studies prior to 1975. Kah-Jin Kuan sums up the new mood: "Biblical interpretation has begun to see shifts in paradigms since the introduction of liberation theology. As a biblical scholar, I no longer subscribe to the idea that biblical interpretation was or can ever be objective and universal."[22]

This brief survey suggests that there now exists an enormous corpus of contemporary political hermeneutics. I have two concerns about this body of literature. One is that too often these works are obtuse and/or pedantic, and thus difficult to access by non-academics who are involved in concrete struggles against oppression and for social change, and who could benefit by such critical reflection. Another is the tendency of many scholars to handle biblical material with a presumption of moral superiority. Scripture has, of course, been employed in the service of conquest and colonization through the history of Christendom since Constantine, which is why the history of interpretation must be aggressively engaged. This should not, however, obscure the "contrapuntal" fact that most of these old texts were produced by and for peoples on the margins of empire. Indeed, the biblical writers were far more countercultural than most modern postcolonial

20. E.g., George Aichele et al., eds., *The Postmodern Bible* (New Haven: Yale University Press, 1997); Gale A. Yee, ed., *Judges and Method: New Approaches in Biblical Studies* (Minneapolis: Fortress, 1995); and John J. Collins, *The Bible after Babel: Historical Criticism in a Postmodern Age* (Grand Rapids: Eerdmans, 2005). Specific readings include: Andrew Davies, *Double Standards in Isaiah: Re-Evaluating Prophetic Ethics and Divine Justice*, Biblical Interpretation Series 46 (Leiden: Brill, 2000); David Jobling, *I Samuel*, Berit Olam (Collegeville, MN: Liturgical, 1998); and Tina Pippin, *Apocalyptic Bodies: The Biblical End of the World in Text and Image* (London: Routledge, 1999).

21. E.g., R. S. Sugirtharajah, *The Bible in the Third World: Precolonial, Colonial, Postcolonial Encounters* (Cambridge: Cambridge University Press, 2001); and Sugirtharajah, *Postcolonial Reconfigurations: An Alternative Way of Reading the Bible and Doing Theology* (St. Louis: Chalice, 2003); Musa W. Dube, *Postcolonial Feminist Interpretation of the Bible* (St. Louis: Chalice, 2000).

22. Kah-Jin Jeffrey Kuan, "Reading with New Eyes: Social Location and the Bible," *Pacific School of Religion Bulletin* 82/1 (2003) 1.

scholars, who often seem far more adept at identifying "accomodation" in Scripture than in their *own* social practices. Should not the hermeneutic of suspicion go both ways?

While the field is vastly diverse and even fragmented, I believe the most significant watershed is not between competing theoretical schools. Rather it is between those who engage texts from within and on behalf of ongoing social movements for change, and those who are content with purely academic deconstructionism. A good case in point is the way in which "empire" has recently been used by many scholars as a hermeneutic key for reading the NT. This is a welcome trend, since two decades ago my own study of Mark was deemed too "politicized" for taking this approach.[23] But for some academics the analysis of imperialism stops at antiquity,[24] while for others it informs past *and* present.[25] In either case, unless historical analysis is connected to concrete engagement with, for example, the all too real rehabilitation of U.S. imperial rhetoric and policies under the second Bush regime, "empire studies" will amount to little more than another fad in biblical studies.

From a liberation perspective, the litmus test of any method will always be the degree to which it is able to animate praxis, and to which it is accountable to and involved with churches and social movements of humanization on the ground. Too many theological scholars still fall prey to the "ideology of professionalism," which generates insularity and intellectual detachment.[26] Colleagues like Lee Cormie, who are not reluctant to anchor their work in social movements, are rare. The old adage, "location, location, location," will continue to define whether our readings of the Bible are merely political in theme, or constitute a political *practice*.

---

23. See n19 above.

24. An example is Bruce J. Malina, *The Social Gospel of Jesus: The Kingdom of God in Mediterranean Perspective* (Minneapolis: Fortress, 2001).

25. E.g., Richard A. Horsley, *Jesus and Empire: The Kingdom of God and the New World Disorder* (Minneapolis: Fortress, 2003); John Dominic Crossan, *God and Empire: Jesus against Rome, Then and Now* (San Francisco: HarperSanFrancisco, 2007); Joerg Rieger, *Christ and Empire: From Paul to Postcolonial Times* (Minneapolis: Fortress, 2007); and Elizabeth Schüssler Fiorenza, *The Power of the Word: Scripture and the Rhetoric of Empire* (Minneapolis: Fortress, 2007).

26. On this, see Margali Sarfatti Larson, *The Rise of Professionalism: A Sociological Analysis* (Berkeley: University of California Press, 1977); Patrick Colm Hogan, *The Politics of Interpretation: Ideology, Professionalism, and the Study of Literature* (New York: Oxford University Press, 2006).

PART ONE—Historical and Methodological Issues

It is both my conviction and experience that the Bible comes alive precisely at the point that interpreters venture analogical comparisons to real situations of engagement with marginalized people, and with actual struggles for personal and political transformation. I proceed, then, to a reading of two biblical texts in socio-historical context, placed alongside my context of organizing and advocacy for social justice. I offer this as a suggestive example of interpretation as political practice.

Tearing Down the Walls of God's House: Third Isaiah and Ecclesial Struggles for Inclusion

> You hammer against the walls of your house.... Unfortunately, it is often a bearing wall that has to go ... Knock it out. Duck.
>
> —Annie Dillard, *The Writing Life*

We live in a world in which the social architecture of functional segregation and inequality persists. Divisions of race, class and gender have become so deep that they threaten the structural integrity of the "House," whether this is understood in terms of a church, the nation as a whole, or our entire globalized civilization. The question is whether we have the courage to take down walls that divide—even if they are bearing walls—in order to save the house.

The specter of the American House collapsing under the weight of its own contradictions has long haunted U.S. leaders. "A house divided cannot stand," warned Abraham Lincoln, appropriating the ancient verdict of Jesus (Mark 3:25) to describe the economic, social and political crisis that led to the War Between the States in the 1860s. This historical ultimatum keeps recurring in the American political unconscious:

- invoked by Martin Luther King in his famous August 1963 speech about racial justice, delivered standing in front of the Lincoln Memorial in Washington, DC;
- implied in the slogan of the 1992 Los Angeles urban uprising, the largest episode of civil unrest in the U.S. since the Civil War: "No justice, no peace!";
- confronted again as a global truth with the dramatic collapse of the World Trade Center Towers on Sept. 11, 2001.

A house constructed upon social, economic and/or ideological division will, sooner or later, either cave in because of internal structural flaws or be destroyed by those whose disenfranchisement gives them no reason to feel a stake in its maintenance.

The fact is, there have always been two Americas: not just of rich and poor, but also of inclusion and exclusion. The America of inclusion has found expression in the ideal of "liberty and justice for all," and has been embodied whenever Indian treaties were honored, Civil Rights realized, women's suffrage secured, child labor laws passed, immigrants embraced, or same-gender marriage legalized. The America of exclusion, on the other hand, was articulated in a Constitution that originally enfranchised only white landed males, and has been embodied in indigenous genocide, Jim Crow segregation, Guilded Age economic stratification, immigrant exclusion acts, restrictive housing covenants, and the Religious Right's current campaign for a Constitutional Amendment to prohibit same-gender marriage.

These two visions of America continually compete for the hearts and minds of our churches. Today Christians are once again lining up on both sides. On one side are those who understand Civil Rights logic as inevitably expansive into equal rights for all minorities, not just some—the America of Emma Lazarus' "Golden Door," Martin Luther King's "I Have a Dream," and Audre Lordes' "Sister Outsider." On the other are those who believe that justice is a limited good, and that we need to suppress pluralism and restore "purity"—the America of George Bush's imperial politics, CIA rendition flights, and James Dobson's "Focus on the Family." Where our churches locate themselves on this political and theological terrain of struggle between those who would tear down dividing walls and those who would shore them up will determine the future of faith—as it did in Nazi Germany.

A curious and troubling conversation between Jesus and his disciples in Mark's gospel toward the end of his ministry is germane. In his dramatic public action in the Temple precinct, Jesus symbolically "loots" those who have looted the poor (Mark 11:15–17). Shortly thereafter his disciples stand, intimidated and fascinated, before the imposing edifice of the Jerusalem Temple exclaiming: "Look, what magnificent structures!" (Mark 13:1). It was indeed an awesome structure, bigger than life, the architectural symbol of their nation. "Do you see these great buildings?" replies Jesus, unimpressed. "There will not be one stone left upon another" (13:2). Talk

Part One—Historical and Methodological Issues

about deconstruction! Jesus' dictum about the "divided House" turns out to be a trope for the Temple-State! Is it any wonder that the authorities wanted him dead?

"Christ has made us one, having broken down the dividing wall of hostility," wrote the author of Ephesians (Eph 2:14.). The conviction that structures of social segregation had been abolished by Jesus lay at the heart of the earliest church's message. Indeed, the apostle Paul committed his entire ministry to carrying on the related work of building a new foundation of race, class, and gender equality: "There is no longer Jew or Greek, slave or free, male and female; all of you are one in Christ" (Gal 3:28). This New Testament ethos was, of course, eventually abandoned by the church, which chose to accept Constantine's Faustian bargain. But the vision has resurfaced with every renewal movement throughout our history: among Benedictine monks and Franciscan friars, Anabaptist radicals and Methodist reformers, and in our own time through movements for Civil Rights, women's ordination, lesbian and gay inclusion, and immigrant dignity. Its roots, however, are found a half-millennium before Christ, in the proclamation of a disciple of the great Israelite prophet Isaiah.

Isaiah 56:1–8 is the opening stanza of the prophetic oracle sometimes referred to as "Third Isaiah" (Isaiah 56–66).[27] It sets a tone of radical inclusion, envisioning a time when people from all over the world, including ethnic outsiders and sexual minorities, will be welcomed as full members into God's House. This thesis is reiterated at the close of Third Isaiah: "The time has come to gather all the nations and tongues" (Isa 66:18). This is the "new heaven and new earth" that YHWH intends to bring about (66:22).

Scholars date Third Isaiah sometime in the first two generations of the Israelite exiles' return from Babylon, between the reconstruction of the Temple (515 BCE) and the time of Nehemiah (ca. 444 BCE). This was a watershed time, and two key issues faced those trying to rebuild their society. One was who was going to lead this project, the other was who was going to participate in it. Such questions always shape the political landscape, then and now.

---

27. Second (Isaiah 40–55) and Third Isaiah represent the work of prophetic successors to the eighth century Isaiah: the former during the exile to Babylon, the latter during the "reconstruction" period following the return. These writings arose most likely from prophetic "schools," evidence of which we find in the Elijah/Elisha cycles (e.g., the "company of prophets" in 2 Kgs 4:38). Here disciples carried on the work of their teachers, recontextualizing their word into another historical moment—which is, of course, what all preachers try to do every time they proclaim the Word into a given context.

Those who had been exiled to Babylon were the elites of Israelite society: priests, managers, the landed aristocracy, scribes, etc. The majority of peasants had remained in Palestine, working the land and scraping out a living, as the poor have always done under any regime. As the elites began to trickle back, they faced a dilemma: how would they reestablish their title and their privileges to land, to social status, and to political position? The returnees were a mixed bag, indeed, including land speculators and carpetbaggers trying to take economic advantage of the new settlements; priests determined to reestablish the cultic center as their power base; ultra-nationalists who saw a chance to rebuild old dreams of sovereignty; and political front men for Israel's new Persian imperial rulers who were trying to exert colonial control of the new entity in Palestine. All the elites agreed on one thing, however: they would define the reconstruction project.[28]

Such aspirations generated conflicts with the existing population over property, politics, and religion. The most dramatic example was a proposal to rebuild the Temple. When the Persians defeated the Babylonians, King Cyrus had decreed that the returning Israelite leadership could reconstruct a Temple in their homeland, but this project was opposed by the *am-ha-aretz* ("people of the land"). Cyrus' royal successor, Darius, then halted construction for political reasons, and it took concerted efforts by Israelite elites to get Cyrus' original promise honored (a drama narrated in Ezra 1–9). One need only reference the situation of Palestine since 1948 to imagine the struggles between the longtime residents on the land and ideologically motivated and politically powerful "returnees."

The strategy of the elite was to purge the peasantry by establishing new ethnic purity standards. Efforts to shore up the boundaries of nation and family stressed genealogical integrity (which advantaged the scribal class, who kept records of their lineage) and Levitical fidelity (which advantaged the priestly class). The Persian overlords were supportive of such measures: an ethnically uniform colony was easier to manage politically. This explains why the books of Ezra and Nehemiah are concerned with defining insiders and outsiders, and why the people of the land resisted their attempts to assert control.[29]

---

28. For detailed historical social analysis, see Clinton Hammock, "Isaiah 56:1–8 and the Redefining of the Restoration of Judean Community," *Biblical Theology Bulletin* 30 (2000) 46–57.

29. The chronological question of which leader came first is a notoriously thorny one, but what is clear is that Nehemiah allowed existing exogamous marriages to stand but forbade future ones, while Ezra took a more conservative position, instructing Judeans

Part One—Historical and Methodological Issues

Their "reconstructionist" position was legitimated on the basis of Deuteronomy 23:1–8, which specifically excludes "from the assembly" males who were not sexually functional, the "illegitimately" born, and foreigners. (Similar laws are found in Leviticus 21:17–21 and 22:22–24, where sexual blemishes are seen as an indication of impurity.) We might call this the social strategy of "anthropological exclusion": ruling out persons not because of anything they have done, but because of who they are in their bodies.

Third Isaiah argues vehemently against this position, taking specific issue with the view that the nation would best be protected through "ethnic cleansing" and endogamy. Instead, Isaiah 56:1–8 calls for the boundaries of the community to be preserved through ethical behavior. Whoever keeps the Sabbath, the text asserts, is entitled to full inclusion, a point underlined by the most "extreme" examples: eunuchs (heterosexually nonconforming males) and foreigners.

A dramatic opening line that crystallizes the entire argument to follow: "This is what God says: 'Maintain justice! Do what is right! Then I will vindicate you!'" This makes it clear from the outset that the issue is justice, not purity. Justice is immediately defined as obeying Torah, keeping Sabbath and turning away from evil (Isa 56:2). In appealing to Sabbath practice, the prophet is invoking the heart of the ethical tradition of Scripture. To keep Sabbath is to make sure everyone has enough and no one has too much, celebrating the gifts of the Creator by keeping both power and goods circulating rather than concentrating (Exod 16:16–19). It calls for vigilance against poverty and social marginalization and for limits to work and accumulation (Deut 15; Exod 23:10–12).[30]

But Third Isaiah goes further, addressing a part of the community that is being legally and socially excluded:

> Let not the foreigner say . . .
> Let not the eunuch say . . .
> For *this* is what God says . . . (56:3–4.)

---

who had "married out" to divorce their foreign wives. But if we are tempted to feel morally superior toward such ancient statutes, we should remember that it was not until 1967 that the U.S. Supreme Court overturned a Virginia statute barring whites from marrying nonwhites. This decision overturned similar bans in fifteen other states—but Alabama did not remove it from its constitution until 2001!

30. See my overview of this tradition in Scripture: *The Biblical Vision of Sabbath Economics* (Washington, DC: Tell the Word, 2001).

This verse un-silences the voices of those who have introjected their rejection by the dominant culture because of how they are perceived and publicly caricatured: "The LORD will surely separate me from his people," and "I am just a dry tree." Second-class citizens in our own history know all too well this self-hatred—black children trying to scrub their skin white, immigrants changing their names, women keeping silent, and gays and lesbians staying deep in a destructive closet—all to avoid the contempt of a society that barely tolerates them. Internalized self-negation and external oppression are like a constant "acid rain," one black psychologist once put it. And it is time, says Third Isaiah, for it to stop—because YHWH says differently (commentators believe the prophet's rhetoric here implies a new ruling on case law).

The eunuch who holds to the Covenant will receive, "in My house and within My walls, a monument and a name better than sons and daughters; I will give them an everlasting name that shall not be cut off" (56:5).[31] The prophet knew very well that eunuchs were, according to Levitical strictures, excluded from cultic and family life. After all, since they could not procreate they could not reap the benefits of patrimony, including land ownership. This also meant that their names would be lost to posterity, an ancient way of rendering someone socially and historically invisible. Instead, God promises an honored place in the "House," something better than patrimony, symbolized by a special "monument" and an "everlasting name." Playfully, the Hebrew word rendered as "monument" in the NRSV is *yd*,

---

31. "Will not be cut off" (*charath* in Hebrew) is a play on the Hebrew word for eunuch (*cariyc*), which comes from an unused root meaning to castrate. The verb firmly links this oracle to the "new thing" YHWH is doing at the end of Second Isaiah: "Instead of the thorn shall come up the cypress . . . it shall be a memorial to the Lord, an everlasting sign that shall not be cut off" (Isa 55:13). Eunuch occurs 42 times in OT, and is translated in the Septuagint as *eunouchos*, meaning "keeper of the bedroom," designating the role of royal eunuchs as "chamberlains." There is continuing scholarly debate about whether this term narrowly refers to those who were emasculated to serve as court retainers, or whether it is a broader term including all men who were socially emasculated because of their sexual physiology *or orientation*. Matthew 19:12 suggests that there are *eunouchoi* made by men, and eunuchs "from birth." Faris Malik has argued at length from hundreds of ancient sources that this latter designation clearly included homosexuals (www.well.com/user/aquarius/index.htm#Home%202). Frederick J. Gaiser reads the text this way in, "A New Word on Homosexuality? Isaiah 56:1–8 as Case Study," *Word & World* 14 (1994) 280–93. See also Nancy Wilson, *Our Tribe: Queer Folks, God, Jesus, and the Bible* (New York: HarperCollins, 1995); and Tom Horner, *Jonathan Loved David: Homosexuality in Biblical Times* (Philadelphia: Westminster, 1978).

usually translated as "hand" (cf. Isa. 57:8), but also as "power," "place"—or as a euphemism for "penis"!

The only social group lower in the Levitical hierarchy than eunuchs were foreigners, exactly those whom the prophet next addresses. He repeats himself: if foreigners follow, serve and love God, and observe the Sabbath and the Covenant, "I will bring them to my holy mountain, and their sacrifices will be acceptable" (56:6–7.). The House has been "remodeled" and "repurposed," in order to be "known as a place where all nations pray." This is Third Isaiah's answer to Ezra and Nehemiah's culture war on those who didn't fit the ethnic-national ideal: Don't force sexual minorities out, and let foreigners in. YHWH welcomes whosoever desires to follow the Way, regardless of who they are in their somatic identity. Third Isaiah's advocacy for faithful Sabbath-keeping over self-righteous gate-keeping is good news today, when gay and lesbian citizens are watching their civil rights erode, while gay and lesbian Christians are having their discipleship dismissed. The prophet shatters the silence that kills, and authorizes attempts to tear down the bearing walls that still divide God's House.

In Third Isaiah's view, the Jerusalem Temple was meant to be a world House, not a national shrine (as every other temple in antiquity was). But his vision did not prevail; the ethnocentric strategy of Ezra and Nehemiah carried the day. Indeed, some of those kicked out of the newly proscribed Judean body politic ended up as the despised Samaritans of Jesus' day. Chauvinism is indeed very powerful. Yet God's Word did not prove fruitless.

"Nothing From Outside Can Make You Unclean": Jesus and Ecclesial Struggles for Inclusion

> *Dichosa la casa que abriga este dia. Dichosa esta casa que nos posada.* ("Blessed is the house that today offers protection. Blessed is this house that gives us shelter.")
>
> —from the traditional Mexican litany of "Posadas"

More than four centuries after Third Isaiah, Jesus of Nazareth one day dusted off that Isaiah scroll, looked hard at his synagogue audience, and read: "The Spirit of the Lord is upon me, because God has anointed me to proclaim good news to the poor..." (Luke 4:18–19). When he was done citing Isa 61:1–2a—the heart of Third Isaiah—he added: "Today this scripture has been fulfilled in your hearing" (Luke 4:21). Jesus was announcing a renewed campaign for inclusion rooted in this prophetic tradition.

Later, in the midst of his cleansing/exorcism of the Jerusalem Temple—the dramatic culmination of his struggle with the Judean authorities—Jesus quotes directly from our text: "My House shall be called a house of prayer for all peoples" (Isa. 56:8 = Luke 19:46). It is not overstating the case to say that Jesus staked his entire ministry on the vision of Third Isaiah. Its ethos of radical inclusion animated his constant transgressions of social boundaries: eating with lepers, hanging out with women, touching the impure, teaching the excluded. If Third Isaiah was so formative for Jesus, then, perhaps it ought to guide us also through the well-mined battlefields of our current culture wars.

To strengthen our resolve, we should note that in the often overlooked parabolic teaching of Mark 7:14–23, Jesus spins an argument that is remarkably similar to Third Isaiah's. The literary context finds Jesus having to defend his disciples' practice of sharing table fellowship with "unclean" outsiders (Mark 7:1–5). The set up of the scene contrasts Jesus' proximity to the marginalized poor with that of the Pharisees by comparing their relationship to the town square:

> And wherever he went into villages or cities or the countryside, they laid the sick in the marketplaces (Gk: *en tais agorais*) and begged Jesus that they might touch even the fringe of his cloak; and all who touched it were healed. (6:56)

> For the Pharisees . . . do not eat unless they wash their hands diligently . . . and when they return from the marketplace (Gk *ap' agorās*) do not eat anything unless they ritually purify themselves [or it]. (7:3–4)

The emphasis on public space, table fellowship and the "politics of touch" makes it clear that this represents yet another prophetic skirmish with the Purity Code. This is a three-part episode:

> 7:1–5: Pharisees' challenge to Jesus' disciples; explanation of the Purity issues involved;
>
> 7:6–13: Jesus' counter-attacks on Pharisaic authority;
>
> 7:14–23: Jesus returns to the original issue of meal-sharing, offering a "parable."

Part One—Historical and Methodological Issues

The question here is whether the table will be a place where in-group boundaries are maintained or where the social "outsider" may be embraced.

Jesus' disciples are apparently following his example of ignoring certain purification rites at table (7:2). Washing hands, produce, and utensils had nothing to do with hygiene, but with the symbolic removal of impurity (7:3–4). These conventions, together with kosher dietary rules, functioned politically (defining ethnic identity) and socially (who one ate with and what one ate reflected one's status in the class hierarchy). The fact that Mark sets this debate in relation to the "marketplace" also suggests an economic dimension in the background. Pharisaic regulators were concerned that marketplace food had been rendered unclean at some stage (i.e., seed sown on the Sabbath or fruits harvested without properly separating out tithes), and sought to control such "contamination." Many Galilean peasants resented these Pharisaic "middlemen" in the processes of production, distribution, and consumption of produce.[32]

The Pharisees are accusing the disciples of group disloyalty and defending their own social and economic status as economic and cultural brokers. Moreover, they charge that Jesus' community is ignoring the "tradition of the elders" (7:5). This was a body of legal interpretation that the Pharisees claimed had been handed down orally alongside the written Torah. Jesus refuses to recognize the authority of this "human tradition," contrasting it with the "commandment of God" (7:8–13). Not surprisingly, he then appeals to Isaiah to underline his point (Mark 7:6–7 = Isa 29:13). The allusion is germane: Isaiah's oracle denounces false prophets (Isa 29:10) and people who "cannot read" (29:12), and promises that "the wisdom of their wise shall perish" (29:14)!

In a deft bit of casuistry, Jesus moves from defendant to prosecutor by invoking a bit of "case law" (Mark 7:9). He argues in 7:10 that Torah enjoins a responsibility to provide economic support for one's aging parents (see Exod 20:12) and conversely condemns those who would try to escape this obligation by pronouncing a curse (see Exod 21:17). He accuses the Pharisees of circumventing this obligation by allowing (presumably wealthy) people to will their estates to the Temple, declaring them *korban* (Mark 7:11). Such vows of dedication froze a family's assets until at death they were released to the Temple treasury, for which they represented an important source of revenue. But because this practice leaves the dependent elderly financially ostracized, the putatively pious "vow" to the Temple

---

32. See my discussion of this in *Binding the Strong Man*, 47–53, 157–61, 217–23.

becomes in fact an economic "curse" upon the elderly (7:12), and thus "nullifies the command of God" (7:13).

The principle here is the same we see in earlier Markan conflict stories: putting those who are vulnerable before the demands of institutions or the sophistry of the privileged (see especially the sequences in 1:40-3:6 and 5:1-43). Mark is again trying to show that when religion legitimates socio-cultural inequities, it subverts justice. Economic critique lies at the core of these interventions: Mark, who began our episode by linking the Pharisees with the Jerusalem scribes (7:1), later indicts the scribal class and the Temple treasury in systemic exploitation of the poor (12:38-44).[33]

Mark concludes with a signal to the reader to pay careful attention: "Listen to me all of you, and understand" (7:14). Jesus' teaching, characterized in the next verse as a parable, is concise and to the point: "There is nothing which goes into a person that can defile; only that which comes out of a person defiles" (7:15). This mysterious trope is immediately decoded for the Twelve in the following household scene (7:17). Using the physical body as a metaphor for the body politic (employed also by Paul in 1 Cor 12:12-30), Jesus contends that social boundaries constructed by the Purity Code are powerless to protect the integrity of the community: "contamination" can only arise from within.

Mark interprets this to mean that Jesus "declared all foods clean" (7:19). Not only does this re-enfranchise marginalized Jews; a kosher diet must no longer function to proscribe table fellowship with non-Jews either! Mark agrees with both Luke (see Acts 10:9-16) and Paul (see Rom 14) that obstacles to building community with ethnic outsiders must be removed—no matter how fundamental to the culture! This extraordinary call is underlined by the ensuing episodes in Mark. First, Jesus sacrifices his own Jewish male honor in order to welcome a female foreigner "to the table" (Mark 7:24-37). Then the circle of enfranchisement is expanded by the feeding of Gentile multitudes (8:1-9). Mark concludes this narrative sequence with Jesus' warning to his disciples to "Beware of the leaven of the Pharisees and of the Herodians" (8:15). Social and political exclusivity jeopardizes the "one loaf" around which the church is called to gather (8:16-21).[34]

Taking a page from Third Isaiah's book, Jesus' teaching concludes that the true "site of purity" is not the body but the heart, the moral center of

33. Ibid., 320-23, 431-34.
34. Ibid., 203-10, 217-23.

Part One—Historical and Methodological Issues

a person in Hebrew anthropology (7:18–20). A vice-list follows, alluding in part to the prophet Hosea's denunciation of public crime in Israel: theft, adultery, and murder (7:21 = Hos. 4:2). Jesus thus re-draws the lines of group identity: the ethnocentricity of the Purity code is replaced by the rigor of collective, ethical self-scrutiny.

All groups establish boundaries to determine who is in and who is out. These can be moral, such as when they help protect weaker people from domination by stronger people. But while this "defensive" function is usually cited as justification for borders and walls, more often the actual relations of power are the opposite: they function to protect the strong from the weak, defending privilege and maintaining inequality. In what may be at once his most radical and most widely ignored teaching, Jesus rejects all culturally proprietary boundaries that allege to protect one's own community from perceived external threats. Scapegoating or excluding outsiders cannot protect us—only our own ethical behavior can do that. We should not underestimate how radical Jesus' proposition was for a first century Jew. An analogy for modern North Americans might be re-defining U.S. citizenship not by one's papers, but by one's genuine commitment to the Bill of Rights: an ideology of "open borders"!

Each Advent since 1994, a small group of Christians make a pre-Christmas pilgrimage to the barren landscape of the U.S.-Mexico border at San Ysidro/Tijuana. It is a celebration of *posadas*, the traditional liturgy celebrated by Mexican Catholics throughout the American Southwest during the last nine days of Advent. Marchers accompany statues of the Holy Family from house to house around the *barrio*, waiting to be recognized and allowed in so that the Christ-child may be born. But this *"posada sin fronteras"* (shelter without borders) is public, political theater at a door that is closed and heavily guarded: we converge on the menacing border fence, a ten-foot high metal wall donated to the U.S. Border Patrol by the Pentagon after Desert Storm—one war's surplus bolstering another war's front lines. It is organized by immigrants' rights groups on both sides of the border to protest anti-immigrant legislation and popular prejudice.

The traditional litany is recited back and forth across the fence, the role of the Holy Family seeking refuge sung by the Mexican group, while we Californians recite the lines of the hard-hearted innkeeper: *Yo no puedo abrir; no sea algun tunante* ("I cannot open, for you may be bad people"). The no-man's-land of the border is bathed by floodlights and thick with Border Patrol vehicles and helicopters, "innkeepers" who spend millions of taxpayer dollars in an effort to reduce illegal entries across this, the world's most heavily used border crossing. Their mission is to keep out the very ones who a century earlier were expressly invited to the U.S. by the extraordinary verse of the immigrant poet Emma Lazarus that is inscribed on the Statue of Liberty: "Give me your tired, your poor, your huddled masses yearning to breathe free. . . . Send those, the homeless, tempest-tossed to me; I lift my lamp beside the golden door." *No seas inhumano; tenos caridad* ("Don't be inhuman; have mercy on us"), sings the Mexican "Joseph." We hear but cannot see one another. "*Ya se pueden ir, y no molestar,*" threatens the Innkeeper. *Porque si me enojo les voy a pegar* ("Better go on, don't bother us. For if I become angry, I shall beat you up.") We use the occasion to talk about the human rights abuses at this border, and to commemorate the hundreds of undocumented immigrants who have died from Border Patrol violence or the harshness of the crossing. When the litany finishes, doves are released on both sides of the fence and fly off, unrestrained by the metal fence, the new global economic order's Berlin Wall. It is an amazing public liturgy in the only place where First and Third World stand adjacent, a free-fire zone in the war against the poor. Here we celebrate hope along a wall that runs right through the heart of this little congregation—and through our church and nation.

For U.S. citizens, these are issues of national identity, to choose which America to embrace. Israel's ethic of compassion toward outsiders was shaped by its own history of pain: "You shall not wrong or oppress a resident alien, for you were aliens in the land of Egypt" (Exod 22:21). The U.S., too, is a nation of immigrants. And for Christians it is a matter of "hearing" Jesus' teaching afresh (Mark 7:14), and that of Third Isaiah before him. If we refuse to take sides with today's outsiders, we too are "without understanding" (Mark 7:18a).[35]

Conclusion: Interpreting the Bible as Political Practice

Third Isaiah's vision focuses on ethics, not anthropology, and so does Jesus in Mark 7:1–23. As Martin Luther King Jr., famously put it, the issue is "the content of one's character, not the color of one's skin." It's not about sexual

---

35. For more on this see Ched Myers and Matthew Colwell, *Our God Is Undocumented: Biblical Faith and Immigrant Rights* (Maryknoll, NY: Orbis, 2012).

PART ONE—Historical and Methodological Issues

orientation but social practice, not about what's between your legs but what's in your heart. The current conversation in our churches concerning whether or not sexual minorities are welcome as full participants in discipleship, and whether Christians should offer sanctuary of undocumented immigrants,[36] must surely stand under this Word of God.

Unfortunately our denominations prefer to approach these issues through studied ambivalence, interminable commissions, "don't ask/don't tell" avoidance, and repressive politeness. And some so-called Christians engage in mean-spirited gay and immigrant bashing. The Christian Right has turned the war on terror abroad into a war of terror at home against those who don't fit the national ideal, as it lobbies hard to preserve the heterosexual monopoly on marriage and to militarize our national borders.

There are many sound ethical and political reasons why democratic citizens should support gays and lesbians in their struggle for full inclusion into both church and society. And issues related to the involuntary migration of peoples, and to the geopolitical definition of human communities, are complex in the modern world, and deserve our careful reflection and deliberation. But these are finally theological and pastoral issues for Christians. Our responsibility is to encounter immigrants and refugees not as statistics, but as human beings who endure extraordinary hardship and trauma in their struggle to survive; to come to know persons of different sexual orientation as folks who struggle with intimacy, love, and commitment—just as heterosexual people do.

The power of Bible study as political practice can help. This is perhaps best illustrated in the well-known and surprisingly successful case of the Jubilee 2000 campaign. We took the Levitical exhortation that Israel should periodically redistribute wealth and land and applied it to ecumenical organizing on behalf of the world's most highly indebted nations. Other examples of biblical interpretation in conversation with social movements I have recently worked with (both in publication and popular education) include:

1. Considering the prophetic critique of ancient imperial clear-cutting of the Cedars of Lebanon in light of specific struggles to save old growth forests in Canada and Brazil;[37]

---

36. See www.newsanctuarymovement.org.

37. "'The Cedar has fallen!' The Prophetic Word vs. Imperial Clear-cutting," in *Earth and Word: Classic Sermons on Saving the Planet*, ed. David Rhoads (New York: Continuum, 2007) 211–23.

2. Reading Eph 2–3 as "Paul's Letter from a Birmingham Jail," correlating the apostle's strategy of resistance to social codes of race to those of Dr. Martin Luther King, Jr., as part of anti-racism work in churches;[38]

3. Applying Isaiah 3's indictment of the "spoil of the poor" in the houses of the wealthy to a capacity-building effort to promote "social investing" in poor neighborhoods in the U.S. among middle class Christians and Jews;

4. Reading Mark 13's warning to disciples not to be deceived by the propaganda of wartime, during the first months of the second Gulf War in 2003, and correlating it to Dr. King's prescient "Beyond Vietnam" speech of 1967;[39]

5. Interpreting Jesus' wilderness temptations in Luke 4 as a "vision quest," in the context of a 2002 Aboriginal "justice walkabout" in Australia;[40]

6. Reading Luke's Emmaus Road story through the lens of M. L. King's assassination in Memphis in 1968;[41]

7. Reappropriating the obscure exhortation to self-amputation in Mark 9 with the help of the modern addiction/recovery movement as a struggle for individual and community liberation;[42]

8. Examining Paul's invitation to become "ambassadors of reconciliation" (2 Cor 5–6) in conversation with the Greensboro, North Carolina Truth and Community Reconciliation Project, 2002–2006;[43]

---

38. See Ched Myers and Elaine Enns, *Ambassadors of Reconciliation, Vol I: New Testament Reflections on Restorative Justice and Peacemaking* (Maryknoll, NY: Orbis, 2009) chap. 4.

39. "Mark 13 in a Different Imperial Context," in *Mark, Gospel of Action: Personal and Community Responses,* ed. John Vincent (London: SPCK, 2006) 164–75.

40. Based upon work published earlier: "The Wilderness Temptations and the American Journey," in *Richard Rohr: Illuminations of His Life and Work,* eds. A. Ebert and P. Brockman (New York: Crossroad, 1993) 143–57.

41. "Easter Faith and Empire: Recovering the Prophetic Tradition on the Emmaus Road," in *Getting on Message: Challenging the Christian Right form the Heart of the Gospel,* ed. Peter Laarman (Boston: Beacon, 2006) 51–67.

42. "Beyond the 'Addict's Excuse': Public Addiction and Ecclesial Recovery," in *The Other Side of Sin,* eds. Susan Nelson and Andrew Sung Park (Albany: SUNY Press, 2001) 87–108.

43. See ibid, chap. 1; and ibid, Vol II, chapter seven.

9. Looking at the story of Huldah (2 Kings 22) in light of the work of a Catholic feminist to critique and reclaim her tradition;[44]

10. Reading Jesus' ministry around Capernaum in Mark 1–3 synoptically with M. L. King's nonviolent Civil Rights campaigns.[45]

This kind of Bible study is not just possible but necessary if we are to recover the church as a popular movement for humanization, compassion and justice. It can and should be practiced in the spaces between the seminary, the sanctuary, and the streets, where colleagues like Lee Cormie have done their best work.[46]

Third Isaiah and Jesus both call us to become a House of radical hospitality that reserves a special place for the otherwise excluded. As John's gospel puts it: "In my Father's house there is lots of room" (John 14:2). Our communities of faith must be about discipleship, not disenfranchisement; communion, not exclusion. Regardless of what we do, however, the God of justice will continue to welcome the outsider who wishes to follow, and to warn erstwhile insiders that using God's name will never protect a "den of thieves" from judgment. There is no divided house that can stand, which is why Jesus invites us to dismantle every dividing wall—even if they seem to be bearing walls. May the churches follow Jesus, who followed Isaiah, who followed Yahweh, into a House for all peoples.

---

44. Foreword to Joanna Manning, *Is the Pope Catholic? A Woman Confronts Her Church* (New York: Crossroad, 1999).

45. "Was Jesus a Practitioner of Nonviolence? Reading Mark 1:21—3:19 through Martin Luther King," *The Bible in TransMission* (2005) 3–5.

46. See my reflections on this pedagogic task: "Between the Seminary, the Sanctuary and the Streets: Reflections on Alternative Education," *Ministerial Formation* (Geneva: WCC, July 2001) 49–52. See also the work of the Center and Library for the Bible and Social Justice (http://clbsj.org), founded in 2011 by pioneering biblical scholars Norman K. Gottwald and John H. Elliott.

2

Christian Ethics, Social Sciences, and Moral Imagination[1]

MARILYN J. LEGGE

MOTIVATED BY HIS ROBUST, conscientized Catholic faith, Lee Cormie belongs to radical faith-and-justice traditions. Building on this legacy he has been tenaciously and tenderly thinking, acting, and advocating for radical change.[2] He knows in his bones that relationship is the medium of Christian faith and has long embraced the theo-ethical task to analyze and imagine what thwarts and destroys eco-social and personal well-being, acting against oppression in the matrix of communities and networks where we devote our lives. For example, I found in my files his 1979 class handout on "Liberation Hermeneutics," which helps us imagine what is at stake: "The deepest challenge, then, to every reading of the Bible and of the God revealed there, concerns its capacity to inspire concrete action in solidarity with all the oppressed, including the earth, and the redefinition of our identities, communities, organizations, and priorities in terms of this orientation."

---

1. I thank Jeff Nowers and Néstor Medina for inviting me to write about "Christian Ethics and Social Sciences." Liz Bounds, Pamela Brubaker, and Michael Bourgeois immeasurably helped me as did the editorial and library assistance of Simon Watson.

2. In 1979 I was a theological student in Cormie's class on Latin American liberation theology at the Toronto School of Theology; we have been hearty colleagues at this institution since 1998.

Part One—Historical and Methodological Issues

This vocation is sustained by a passion for justice or right relation. Lee Cormie's work is animated by critical social sciences, eco-social movements, liberative readings of the Bible, and newer voices in theology with their thirst for new life in an eco-social order increasingly burdened by neoliberal political economics. Sensitized to global crises—ecocide, greed-amassed wealth, and luxury alongside exponential poverty, war, and violence—Cormie engages polyvocal theo-ethical "irruptions" sprung from the seismic historical shifts that absorb his intellectual life. For example, the theological voices of women, of those from the global south and from minority communities in the global north have been producing eccentric theological knowledge of "the signs of the times." Consequently, Cormie constructs accounts of the state of the world on the basepoints of solidarity and accountability, informed by biblical and critical social-scientific analyses, while imagining subversive alternatives and vigilant action arcing toward horizons of abundant life. He is an intrepid, intercultural, and critical moral theologian who "mediates between the academy and social-justice networks."[3]

In making this tribute to Lee Cormie, I welcome the hearty notion of Christian ethics as a performative "art-science" that relies thoroughly on imagination.[4] Imagination evokes a "passion for the possible" where passion is "the basis of our noninstrumental relations for others, and it takes us beyond fixed character, social roles, and institutional arrangements."[5] In this essay, imagination refers to the power to sort, shape, and integrate disparate elements of varied social worlds using images, symbols, stories, theories, and rituals. This capacity can be used for good and evil. For example, slavery, the conquest and colonization of indigenous peoples, and the demonization of Islam by Christian imperialists are hegemonic social imaginaries which imperial powers use to shape and sustain perceptions and material relations based on control and subordination of groups and territories. However, since "another world is possible" as the World Social Forum declares, imagination also functions as the creative capacity neces-

---

3. Gregory Baum, "Critical Theology Replies to Ray Morrow," in *Critical Theology in North America* (Kansas City: Sheed & Ward, 1994) 5. The Roman Catholic tradition is more likely to use the term moral theology to discuss what Protestants have traditionally referred to as Christian ethics. I use the terms interchangeably.

4. See Daniel C. Maguire, "Ethics: How to Do It," in *Death by Choice* (New York: Schocken, 1975) 77–114.

5. Mark Johnson, *Moral Imagination: Implications of Cognitive Science for Ethics* (Chicago: University of Chicago Press, 1993) 200.

sary for the inherent practical, interdisciplinary, and evaluative character of Christian ethics—it is the "meta-" habit of mind by which we think and learn how to live.[6]

The moral life can be understood, in part, as a search for images whereby we try to interpret our own sufferings, problems, and joys in relation to the experiences of concrete others and their social worlds. Biblical metaphors give sustenance and guidance, for example, of dry bones dancing, of manna in the wilderness, and of unlikely friendships and agents bearing divine clues. Imagination allows us to follow hunches, desires, and suspicions, to breakdown, recreate, communicate, and animate different possibilities and practices. Imagination, then, is vital for doing Christian ethics—it is the faculty by which we connect the often fragmented and disparate personal, political, praxiological, and ecclesial relations.[7]

My task here is to explore the role of social sciences (read as critical social theory) in a disruptive and liberative agenda; to identify how these tools are connected with the alchemic power of imagination; and, finally, to consider briefly how critical social science and moral imagination act as yeast in the bread of the current intercultural church initiative of the United Church of Canada. At its thirty-ninth Triennial General Council in 2006, the United Church officially and publicly committed itself to become an intercultural and racially just church.[8] By approving the document, "A Transformative Vision," a range of policies, strategies, and budgets was initiated to become an intercultural church. One key to this project is to imagine and practice deeper self-criticism or reflexivity. According to Michael Quinn Patton, reflexivity is

---

6. For elaboration of aspects of this process and content of imagination, see Laurent A. Parks Daloz et al., *Common Fire: Leading Lives of Commitment in a Complex World* (Boston: Beacon, 1996) 133–35.

7. I am grateful to Greer-Anne Wenh-In Ng for this heuristic device: see "Salmon and Carp, Bannock and Rice: Solidarity between Asian Canadian Women and Aboriginal Women," in *Off the Menu: Asian and Asian North American Women's Religion and Theology*, ed. Rita Nakashima Brock et al. (Louisville: Westminster John Knox, 2007) 198.

8. Renamed from Ethnic Ministries, the current Intercultural and Diverse Communities in Ministry Unit, in partnership with the Aboriginal and Francophone ministries, continues to lead The United Church of Canada in its efforts to become an intercultural church, by "act[ing] justly within its own structures, courts, policies, and practice" (Section 3 of The United Church of Canada Anti-Racism Policy from the 37th General Council 2003); www.united-church.ca/beliefs/policies/2000/t314.

> a way of emphasizing the importance of self-awareness, political/cultural consciousness, and ownership of one's perspective. Being reflexive involves self-questioning and self-understanding. . . . To be reflexive is . . . is to understand an ongoing examination of *what I know* and *how I know it*.[9]

This intercultural church project also has implications for Christian social teaching. It invites co-religionists, whatever their identifications, to live interculturally and to act institutionally with accountability and moral imagination toward right relations in a deeply pluralist and often violent world. I support this initiative and its vision to form both different sensibilities of being alert Christians and churches *with* sturdier participation in various publics where others are not motivated by similar or even Christian convictions. With these premises in mind, I turn to the role of social science in a liberative theo-social ethics.

Christian Ethics and Social Sciences

Why do social sciences matter to moral theology? Christian ethics investigates and evaluates the material conditions of life, the practices and teachings of persons, communities, and multiple publics with respect to their narratives of identifications, responsibility, values, and moral vision.[10] Social sciences, such as anthropology, ethnography, sociology, political economy, and critical race, whiteness, class, and postcolonial studies, are sources that analyze the "what is." They provide analyses of social problems that identify and examine social facts and values that matter for those groups of people who try to build a more just society.

In this pragmatic view, Elizabeth Bounds understands such theory "as a reflexive hermeneutical tool enabling exploration of experience, in which we are constantly reconstructing the theory in light of practice, watchful for the ways our own theoretical assumptions and social locations preselect what we see and how we understand."[11] In short, the social sciences contrib-

---

9. Michael Quinn Patton, *Qualitative Research and Evaluation Methods*, 3rd ed. (Thousand Oaks, CA: Sage, 2002) 64–65, cited in, "A Guide For Evaluating Theological Learning," *Association of Theological Schools,* Handbook of Accreditation, sec. 8; www.ats.edu/Deleted%20Files/HandbookSection8.pdf.

10. For example, see Traci West, *Disruptive Christian Ethics: When Racism and Women's Lives Matter* (Louisville: Westminster John Knox, 2006) 41–49.

11. Elizabeth M. Bounds, "Gaps and Flashpoints: Untangling Race and Class," in

ute knowledge of social relations and their historical mediations required for doing ethics. As Cormie puts it, the social sciences are "indispensable in our efforts to develop a more adequate theological anthropology and understanding of theological method, and in general to interpret the meaning of Christian faith and life today."[12] Cormie's enduring commitment, then, has been to ponder, probe, and wonder about the connections between politics, social sciences, and moral theology.[13]

Theological ethics critically appropriates social sciences and their accounts of social life. However, because social sciences are imbued with particular worldviews and images of the social order, there are consequences, depending on which social science accounts are used, in terms of method and ethical stance. Therefore, criteria or principles are crucial to adjudicate which theories are valid and how they are appropriated in constructing any theo-ethic. For example, Jesuit moral theologian John Coleman supplies these four criteria: (1) the images of the human (and images of their one earth home, I must add); (2) the sufficiency of the social science account of the primary evil to be addressed; (3) the account of what is going forward in history; and (4) the moral agents who will move or carry social transformation.[14] These general criteria help sort out why we need theory; however, they do not tell us how the social science used is to be evaluated for its adequacy. Therefore, I embrace the moral principle of justice-love to put flesh on those critical bones and to entice moral imagination.

Disrupting White Supremacy from Within: White People on What We Need to Do, ed. Jennifer Harvey et al. (Cleveland: Pilgrim, 2004) 129.

12. Lee Cormie, "Society, History, Meaning: Perspectives from the Social Sciences," in *Catholic Theological Society of America: Proceedings of the 34th Annual Convention, Atlanta, Georgia, June 13–16, 1979*, ed. Luke Salm (New York: Catholic Theological Society of America, 1980) 47.

13. On the various ways of relating social science under what he calls the theological tent, see Michael H. Barnes, "Introduction," in *Theology and the Social Sciences*, ed. Michael H. Barnes (Maryknoll, NY: Orbis, 2001).

14. John A. Coleman, SJ, "Every Theology Implies a Sociology and Vice Versa," in *Theology and the Social Sciences*, ed. Barnes, 25–28. See also Beverly Wildung Harrison's comparison of theological realism, historical sociology, and neo-classical economic theory in "The Role of Social Theory in Religious Social Ethics," in *Making the Connections: Essays in Feminist Social Ethics*, ed. Carol S. Robb (Boston: Beacon, 1985) 74–80.

PART ONE—Historical and Methodological Issues

CHRISTIAN ETHICS AND MORAL IMAGINATION

> We know what God requires of us: to do justice, love kindness, and walk in God's way. (Micah 6:8)

In liberative theo-ethics, justice-love as moral norm is pivotal to grapple with the unjust sufferings of oppression and violation as well as to accompany and live with accountability to those who near the burdens of distorted relations of power. Following Marvin Ellison, justice-love refers to our longing for psycho-spiritual and bodily well-being, to imagine right-relatedness with others. Justice-love requires "mutual respect and care and a fair sharing of power."[15] This explicit intersection of the personal and public, the body and mind, the intimate and social connects the work of the social sciences with that of moral imagination.

John Paul Lederach assures us that imagination is the most creative—and humbling—resource for transformation. Harvesting the fruit of his work from decades in global peacebuilding efforts, he considers the moral imagination to be "the capacity to imagine something rooted in the challenges of the real world yet capable of giving birth to that which does not yet exist."[16] We enjoin the work of imagination with critical social analysis and action to stay open to and in touch with God who is the power of justice-love to better understand the position one is in and to do what is possible to make a difference.

Moral images are metaphors that shape and organize our moral lives.[17] "Sisterhood and brotherhood," "the world as God's body," "Christian base community," and "intercultural church" are moral images.[18] Therefore, while imagination does participate in reason, sensing, judgement, understanding, and conscience,[19] its role is to seek and create spaces beyond the

---

15. See Marvin M. Ellison, *Same-Sex Marriage? A Christian Ethical Analysis* (Cleveland: Pilgrim, 2004) 142–43. On basepoints or conjunctions for adequate feminist methodologies, see also Elizabeth Bounds et al., "Introduction," in *Welfare Policy [feminist critiques]*, ed. Elizabeth Bounds et al. (Cleveland: Pilgrim, 1999) 12–17.

16. John Paul Lederach, *Moral Imagination: The Art and Soul of Peace Building* (Oxford: Oxford University Press, 2005) ix, 29, 182.

17. I draw on Johnson, *Moral Imagination*, 65, and his citation of Hilary Putnam, *The Many Faces of Realism* (La Salle, IL: Open Court, 1987) 52.

18. See, for example, Sallie McFague, *Metaphorical Theology: Models of God in Religious Language* (Philadelphia: Fortress, 1982); McFague, *The Body of God: An Ecological Theology* (Minneapolis: Fortress, 1993).

19. See Parks Daloz et al., *Common Fire*, 132, with reference to Samuel Taylor

places that exist. Not confined by what is, or what is known, imagination is the art of creating what does not exist.[20]

Whereas dominant moral theologies appeal to our rational faculties and to dogmatic formulations, liberative theological ethics place importance not only on discursive communication, but also on the function of images, myths, and rituals in the continuing process of "conversion to the Other" and seeking a shared mutual humanity.[21] For example, the primary feminist protest against the underlying dualism of the mind/body split in the Western theological tradition is to be found in its challenge to the notion that the basic category of theological envisagement is "the concept." As Beverly Harrison puts it, "Concepts function to explain reality. Theological language evokes reality . . . the primal and irreplaceable mode of theological discourse is the image and relatedly, the metaphor, . . . those fundamental images that put us in touch with life through vision."[22] Imagine what it would be like to release thwarted power, mobilize and share resources, and to inspire creativity.

In *Common Fire: Lives of Commitment in a Complex World*, the process of imagination is depicted as happening around the edges of current understanding, where we work to move beyond current knowledge and give form to our emerging experience. For descriptive purposes, this process may be subdivided into five phases, each flowing into the next.[23] The instigating feature is the awareness of contradiction between what is and what should be. We become curious or troubled or devasted by dissonance such as experiencing or witnessing injustice. Becoming *conscious of contradiction and conflict* interrupts familiar ways of being and can turn what we know best into "something strange and puzzling." If we take time to *pause*, for example, in sleep, contemplation, solitude, or play, to do something outside the apparent fixed and stable arrangements we are used to, we might discover a new *image-insight* to name and convey the truth of the experience. Unless one finds a connection between the new insight and lived-world

---

Coleridge, *The Friend*, vol. 1, ed. B. Rooke (Princeton: Princeton University Press, 1969) 177.

20. Lederach, *Moral Imagination*, 28.

21. See, for example, Kwok Pui-Lan on the sacred status of women's stories of struggles for personhood in "Discovering the Bible in the Non-Biblical World," *Semeia* 47 (1989) 36.

22. Beverly W. Harrison, "Restoring the Tapestry of Life: A Vocation of Feminist Theology," *The Drew Gateway* 54 (1984) 42–43.

23. See Parks Daloz et al., *Common Fire*, 133–4.

experience, the insight will languish. It is crucial, therefore, to move into a process of *repatterning and reframing* so that the image-symbol becomes a key to recomposing the usual pattern of meaning and understanding; and if the new insight about how to live in the world is valid and embraced, it needs to be articulated and acted upon in the midst of an interested public.

It is precisely where our habits are ill-adapted to our commitments (e.g., to justice-love) and to hitherto unforeseen problems, newly emerging purposes, and evolving technologies that we need moral imagination. The process of imagination outlined above provides one way to read the intercultural church project in connection with the work of social sciences in theological ethics. How is the creative process, with its experimentation, discovery, provisionality, and imagination, being encouraged and nourished? New moral mapping becomes effective when practiced.

Why Christian Ethics Needs Moral Imagination and Critical Social Theory: The Case of the Intercultural Church Project

> In the company of God and one another, our community [of the United Church of Canada] can be transformative . . . and live out its commitment to racial justice as an intercultural church where there is mutually respectful diversity and full and equitable participation of all Aboriginal, francophone, ethnic minority, and ethnic majority constituencies in the total life, mission, and practices of the whole church.[24]
>
> Faith has many different cultural expressions, and God's loving presence is in each one. The living faith that sustains and supports ethnic minority communities is no less vital than the faith that lives in any other congregation. The Ethnic Ministries Council was inaugurated in 1996 [and the subsequent intercultural church initiative in 2006], not to create more racial ethnic hierarchy in the United Church but to find new ways of empowering the voices of ethnic minorities, to value their faith and faith communities in the church, and to hear their stories with hurting hearts. The Council

---

24. Executive of the General Council, Permanent Committee Programs for Mission and Ministry, Ethnic Ministries Re-visioning Task Group, "A Transformative Vision," The United Church of Canada, 39th General Council 2006, 13–19 August 2006, 137–38; www.united-church.ca/files/organization/gc39/workbook1_commissions.pdf.

> also invites the majority church to come close enough to these stories to share their own. We can all choose to "stick together," in the broadest possible sense, if those we choose to stick together with are as diverse as the people of the church are.[25]

For a dis-spirited and dwindling post-Christendom institution like the United Church of Canada, the intercultural church project can be understood as an act of survival and revitalization. Rebecca Chopp defines imagination as "the ability to think the new" because it is "an act of survival."[26] But survival has many meanings. The intercultural church project is born to renew a Christian mandate—in this time and place it is to encourage different images and strategies of being justly intercultural. The vision depends on what it has taken to survive, whether as aboriginal, francophone, or another racial or minority people, or as white mainstream culture people. Transformation, therefore, has different challenges for different communities. If the church is to grow in faith, hope, and love, becoming reflexive—self-aware, politically/culturally conscious, and owning one's perspective—is key for being justly and interculturally related.

In the language of ethics, conscience is the ethical compass that tunes reflexivity. To be a person of reflexive character is to be a moral agent. This formal category denotes the human capacity to name and make sense of oneself as a creature who acts "morally" in a world of contingency and ambiguity. It also implies that we can be held accountable for our choices and actions. "Agency" then encompasses both character and conduct, both our moral "being" and our moral "doing."[27] Imagination, like reflexivity, is a crucial faculty of agency. Imagination is ethical in its capacity to understand and relate through what Mark Johnson calls "our imaginative rationality."[28] That is, we must not only feel for or rationally calculate the

---

25. Kim Uyede-Kai, "Ethnic Ministries: The Sound of a Church," online: http://www.united-church.ca/files/intercultural/sound.pdf. Since this essay was written, new work has been done on living into this transformation. See The United Church of Canada's "Intercultural Ministries: Living into Transformation," March 24–26, 2012, Executive of the General Council of the United Church of Canada, online: www.gc41.ca/sites/default/files/intercultural-ministries.pdf.

26. Rebecca Chopp, "A Rhetorical Paradigm For Pedagogy," in *Teaching the Bible: The Discourses and Politics of Biblical Pedagogy*, ed. Fernando Segovia and Mary Tolbert (Maryknoll, NY: Orbis, 1998) 307.

27. Bruce C. Birch and Larry L. Rasmussen, *Bible and Ethics in Christian Life*, rev. ed. (Minneapolis: Fortress, 1989) 40.

28. See Johnson, *Moral Imagination*, 77, 187. He argues that moral concepts are infused with image and metaphor which require us to understand the imaginative, metaphorical structures of meaning.

well-being of others; we must also go out toward them, move our bodies into their worlds where we can then relate in imagination, feeling, and expression. I believe that morally sensitive people are capable of touching and learning from the reality of others with whom they are interacting or to whom their actions might affect. One response to the moral challenge of living interculturally with justice is "empathetic imagination," the capacity to sensitively "take up the part of others," and the ability to envision responsible constructive action.[29] Moral agents are being called to act their way into being as intercultural Christians with integrity. Integrity, according to Margaret Urban Walker, is "a kind of reliability" where others can count on us to take responsibility for our lives in relation.[30]

I find that critical race, feminist, class, and postcolonial social theories are especially helpful for ethical reflection on the intercultural praxes of faith, politics, church, and moral agency. The categories of reflection that arise from the use of these theories (e.g., difference, transformation, agency, social subject position) will become concrete with reference to the case of the intercultural church initiative. Emilie Townes' discussion of liberation in spiritual and personal/social dimensions clarifies theo-ethical grounds for a justice-seeking, spiritually-nurturing intercultural church:

> The aim of liberation is to restore a sense of self as a free person and as a spiritual being. [It] concentrates on the acquisition of power that enables each person to be who she or he is. . . . [It] fosters the security to give that self to others in a love that requires no response in kind. . . . Social liberation is participation in the world. It is a concern for others as we bring ourselves together to witness to our faith. . . . Liberation is a process. . . . It is the hope of freedom that drives liberation. . . . Liberation is God's work of salvation in Jesus.[31]

Townes' theo-ethical imagination for transformation dovetails beautifully with the hope of becoming an intercultural church.

---

29. See Johnson, *Moral Imagination*, 106, 189–99.

30. Margaret Urban Walker, *Moral Understandings: A Feminist Study in Ethics* (New York: Routledge, 1998) 115.

31. Emilie M. Townes, "Ethics as an Art of Doing the Work Our Souls Must Have," in *The Arts of Ministry: Feminist-Womanist Approaches*, ed. Christie Cozad Neuger (Louisville: Westminster John Knox, 1996) 148.

IMAGINING SOCIAL RELATIONS AS SEEKING TO BE JUSTLY INTERCULTURAL

The image of "sticking together" relies on imagining a theo-ethical accountability to diversity. Janet Jakobsen uses a critical social theory of diversity as the ongoing production "of differentiation that creates social categories which form the matrix of social life into which each individual is born and within which each lives."[32] With attention to difference, complex social identities are formed as we become who we are as socially positioned, other-regarding, moral agents. Intercultural relations also challenge reigning theories of moral agency based on notions of the supposedly abstract, universal, disembodied subject. An important task, then, for taking up the challenge of becoming a transformative intercultural church is to re-imagine one's moral agency in terms of complex social identities, especially as shaped by and in relation to diasporic communities and their global movement.[33]

Recent demographics from Statistics Canada estimate that by the year 2017 people who are "visible minorities" will be more than half of the population of Toronto (and one-fifth of the nation).[34] As cited above, the intercultural church project has been envisioned as a negotiation among diverse, plural, and interactive voices, viewpoints, and theologies—that is, "racial justice."[35] An intercultural, racially just church will be aided by a Christian ethics based in social theories shaped by "the energy and vision that come from those who are less comfortable in any society."[36] Robert Young's scenario gets us into the challenge of transforming reality:

32. Janet R. Jakobsen, *Working Alliances and the Politics of Difference: Diversity and Feminist Ethics* (Bloomington: Indiana University Press, 1998) 5.

33. See also Kwok Pui-Lan, *Postcolonial Imagination and Feminist Theology* (Louisville: Westminster John Knox, 2005) 49. Majority refers here to the culture with power to establish and enforce norms in a context; in Canada even where white elites are numerically a minority, the norms which govern are set and enforced by their codes.

34. A. Bélanger, É. Caron Malenfant et al., *Population projections of visible minority groups, Canada, provinces and regions*, 2001–2017, Demography Division, Statistics Canada, Ottawa, March 2005, 26, iii; www.statcan.ca/english/freepub/91-541-XIE/91-541-XIE2005001.pdf.

35. See, for example, *That All May Be One: A Resource for Educating Toward Racial Justice*, ed. Wenh-In Ng (Toronto: Justice, Global and Ecumenical Relations of The United Church of Canada, 2004).

36. Charles Lemert, "Social Theory: Its Uses and Pleasures," in *Social Theory: The Multicultural and Classic Readings*, ed. Charles Lemert, 3rd ed., (Boulder: Westview, 2004) 12.

PART ONE—Historical and Methodological Issues

> Have you ever been the only person of your own colour or ethnicity in a large group or gathering? It has been said that there are two kinds of white people: those who have never found themselves in a situation where the majority of people around them are not white, and those who have been the only white person in the room. At that moment, for the first time perhaps, they discover what it is really like for the other people in their society, and metaphorically, for the rest of the world outside the west: to be from a minority, to live as a person who is always in the margins, to be the person who never qualifies as the norm, the person who is not authorized to speak.[37]

It should not be a surprise that intercultural relations can be anxious and contested spaces.[38] The intercultural ecclesial project is shaping a space to exercise moral agency at the interstices of interdependent, intercultural interaction fraught by racism and other forms of oppression.[39]

Critical race, class, diversity, and whiteness studies as well as engaged postcolonial theories stress how one's identifications in terms of subject position shift from one geographic and cultural setting to another. For example, theories of hybridity arise to imagine how social identities are constituted at the interstices of cultures. They emphasize the cultural graftings that occur in geographical migration, in those intercultural spaces produced by migration, immigration, exile, or existence in "borderlands" or "crossroads."[40] We just have to think about those who live between conflicting and often competing cultures and how they may identify with one culture emotionally and be curious about another intellectually.

Some find comfortable ways to name their interstitial belonging, such as Choice Okoru, born into the Urhobo ethnic group of Nigeria, who proudly explains that "being an African makes me a spiritually and emotionally healthier Canadian."[41] Others explore a social world of dissonant

---

37. Robert J. C. Young, *Postcolonialism: A Very Short Introduction* (Oxford: Oxford University Press, 2003) 1.

38. See Susan Stanford Friedman, *Mappings: Feminism and the Cultural Geographies of Encounter* (Princeton: Princeton University Press, 1998).

39. See, for example, Emilie M. Townes, *Womanist Ethics and the Cultural Production of Evil* (New York : Palgrave Macmillan, 2006).

40. Useful introductions include Ania Loomba, *Colonialism/Postcolonialism*, 2nd ed. (New York: Routledge, 2005); and Reina Lewis and Sara Mills, eds., *Feminist Postcolonial Theory* (New York: Routledge, 2003).

41. Choice Okoro, "Being and Becoming Black"; www.united-church.ca/intercultural/becoming/black.

differences of the hybrid, multi-marginated worlds. But out of this deep conflict, moral imagination is born, which Rita Nakashima Brock marks as "interstitial integrity": "This refusal to rest in one place, to reject a narrowing of who we are by either/or decisions, or to be placed always on the periphery, is interstitial integrity [which] opens ways of speaking about the construction of complex cross-cultural identities that include subordination, but destabilize and contest it." As an intercultural moral agent, Brock exercises moral discrimination and self-evaluation and seeks to engage in solidarity with others who also live in the interstices.[42]

The Sound of a Church Responding: Drumming and Accountability

> The drums . . . were only able to sound because the drum skins had been tightly drawn; they had a tension great enough to sound a call when struck. In the same way, ethnic minorities in the Church have been challenged to take the tensions of their marginalization, to use them to call to one another, and to resonate in the hearts of others.[43]

I believe that the historical project of growth and transformation toward being an intercultural church will need particular strategies to confront and resist white racism by those of us who benefit from white skin privilege. No longer will the liberal Protestant tradition of including "others"—in this case, those of non-dominant cultures—into the set of dominant social relations already established, be adequate. Sherene Razack's critical race theory is well reflected in the intercultural church initiative traced in the proviso that transformation will only occur if we learn how each of us is implicated in systems of domination, subordination, and privilege, which profoundly shape our understanding of each other. A key challenge for the United Church will be to reduce the tendency of securing "innocence, a determined non-involvement in the social relations being analyzed."[44] I think

---

42. Rita Nakashima Brock, "Interstitial Integrity: Reflections toward an Asian American Woman's Theology," in *Introduction to Christian Theology*, ed. Roger A. Badham (Louisville: Westminster John Knox, 1998) 187, 191.

43. Uyede-Kai, "Ethnic Ministries."

44. Sherene Razack, *Looking White People in the Eye: Gender, Race, and Culture in Courtrooms and Classrooms* (Toronto: University of Toronto Press, 1998) 170.

PART ONE—Historical and Methodological Issues

Razack's politics of accountability—as opposed to a politics of inclusion—is an excellent strategy fitting the vision.[45]

For most of us in the United Church, an ethics of accountability will need to be guided by a search for the ways in which we are complicit in the subordination of others. It requires attention to inter-related complex social identities. For example, those of us who are white, caucasian, middle-class women benefit from those economic and political processes which produce immigrant and refugee women from the global south, and we come to know and perform ourselves in ways that reproduce such social hierarchies. And those who do not recognize the norm they benefit from because they match the "culturally and experientially specificity," hold on to the norm as a universal and neutral ideal of humanity in which all can readily participate without regard to discursive social relations inscribed along axes such as race, gender, religion, nation class, or sexuality.[46] Tracing our complicity in these shifting social relations will mean thinking and accepting that differences are pre-given, knowable, and do not exist in a social and historical vacuum.

Therefore, to become interculturally just and justly intercultural, requires exploring the histories, social relations, and conditions of power that position persons and structure social worlds and groups unequally in relation to one another. Then we will be able to give reasons for what can be known, thought, and said. Note well that this work is not reducible to a statement such as, "since I can never know what it feels like to be Korean or indigenous/First Nation or African, I need not think about race." Instead, to keep us growing as an intercultural space, let us ask: "Who is describing and assessing the intercultural realities and how do we hear these descriptions and what relations do they secure?"[47] This hermeneutics of suspicion aims to build our capacity and reliability as intercultural moral agents. Then we can take responsibility for our lives in the complex and disturbing relations we are called to transform—and others can count on us.

To think practically and to imagine what is involved in sustaining the intercultural church project, I recommend John Paul Lederach's *The Moral Imagination*. He writes about a process that is "forged by the capacity to

---

45. Ibid., 159.

46 Iris Marion Young, *Justice and the Politics of Difference* (Princeton: Princeton University Press, 1990) 164.

47. Razack, *Looking White People in the Eye*, 170.

generate, mobilize, and build the moral imagination." From long experience, he culls four practices which develop moral imagination:

1. the capacity to imagine ourselves in a web of relationships that includes our enemies;
2. the ability to sustain curiosity that embraces complexity without reliance on dualistic polarity;
3. the fundamental belief in and pursuit of the creative act;
4. the acceptance of the inherent risk of stepping into the mystery of the unknown that lies beyond the too familiar landscape of violence.[48]

These cues are consistent with a moral imagination of intercultural metaphors such as ecclesial drumming. The role of cultural and artistic resources cannot be overstated for seeking "right relations." The creative process animates the art-science of theological ethics; it is not tangential and should be cultivated to resist and transform destructive geographies and realities of injustice such as racism and its violence. The wellsprings feeding personal and social change are the artists' ways—experimentation, discovery, provisionality, and imagination. When applied to everyday life and to building networks and communities of intercultural interaction and justice-seeking, violence is healed through creative processes and acts.

The moral imagination emerging from protracted struggles for abundant life is specific, metaphoric, breathable, intimate, serendipitous, public, playful, and passionate. Another process for intercultural engagement, "world traveling," has been articulated by Maria Lugones. Given the constraints on who we are becoming and how we live in socially constituted and contingent circumstances, the intercultural church project will depend on the grace of flexibility. This flexibility, this traveling between worlds, is a skilful, creative, rich, enriching and, given certain circumstances, a loving way of being and living.[49] Traveling to different worlds can develop virtues of empathy, openness to that which we are not, and a deep commitment to relationships with those who are different. However, like any concept, world-traveling is ambiguous. Problematized ethnic prejudice and racism can produce a double-standard in which a majority group is absolved

---

48. Ibid., 5.

49. See María Lugones, "Playfulness, 'World'-Travelling, and Loving Perception," in *Making Face, Making Soul—Haciendo Caras*, ed. Gloria Anzaldúa (San Francisco: Aunt Lute, 1990) 394–96.

from any responsibility to engage in the minority group's world, though the minority group has no choice but to live in the majority's world. The lack of knowledge about and appreciation of marginalized cultures makes this world-traveling mostly a one-way affair. By taking the ambiguity and situatedness of our own lives seriously, we are enabled to exercise intercultural moral agency, travelling to the world of others, and being mutually encouraged to world-travel together.

To guide world-travelling as an imaginative and moral exploration, we need criteria. Criteria for this praxis-based moral theology would include: What are our primary communities of accountabilities? What vision informs our being in the world? Does this moral practice help us understand our own personal experience and shed light on global happenings? Does this moral practice help guide and energize faithful and responsible action against injustice and ecocide? How is the creative process, with its experimentation, discovery, provisionality, and imagination being encouraged and nourished? Does this Christian ethic encourage living accountably and with passion for justice-love in personal/public/ecclesial/cosmic life?

As Lee Cormie well appreciates, ambiguity will continue to be part of the ethos. Ambiguity does not mean, however, that we are confused or indecisive; rather, to embrace ambiguity is to walk more humbly, aware of the mystery of human and cosmic life. Embracing ambiguity does not mean we will think less clearly or stop struggling to be cogent and effective articulators of "passion for the possible" and for things to be "otherwise." Rather, ambiguity confronts us with the inadequacy of our concepts and practices which then returns us to the complexity and wonder of knowledge and life. Living with ambiguity means that our best laid plans may never work out. It does not mean, however, that we can give up on Christian ethics as an art-science with passion for abundant life as its pulse. The work of moral imagination is risky, creative and experimental "wherein one can expect the occasional if not regular foot in mouth. That is the nature of innovation. It is the nature of pursuing change."[50] Expect no less of liberative social theo-ethics and its theoretically engaged and imaginative praxis.

---

50. Lederach, *Moral Imagination*, 5.

3

The Social Gospel and the Social Sciences

Robert C. Fennell

While the development, nature, and legacies of the Social Gospel movement in the U.S. and Canada have been well documented, the ways in which this movement made specific use of social-scientific description and analysis are less frequently investigated. This chapter outlines briefly a perspective on the Social Gospel as not merely a religious phenomenon but also a network of movements that sought to engage social-scientific tools in service to the goal of societal amelioration. Political theory, economic theory, and sociology are three such tools that were employed. This paper argues that the application of these tools within Social Gospel discourse (roughly between 1880–1920) formed imprecise and idiosyncratic amalgams with the religious impulses of some exemplars of the movement: Walter Rauschenbusch, A. E. Smith, Nellie McClung, and J. S. Woodsworth. These social-scientific tools served to inform, expand, and illustrate the theological dimensions of their thought. The analysis that follows suffers the disadvantages of generalizing about both the U.S. and Canadian contexts and subcontexts, but these limitations will perhaps be balanced by the heuristic value of regarding the movement as a binational phenomenon. While commonalities within the Social Gospel in both the U.S. and Canada will be identified, Canadian emphases will be evident.

Part One—Historical and Methodological Issues

The Social Gospel

Many thorough accounts of the "Social Gospel movement" have already appeared in print.[1] My purpose here is simply to sketch the broad outlines of this movement (really a loosely related series of movements) in order to foreground that which follows: namely, illustrative cases of the use of political theory, economic theory, and sociology as essential correlates of the theological dimensions of the Social Gospel. Less will be said in this paper about the distinctively theological concerns of the movement, though of course a grasp of such concerns is essential to a full understanding.

The Social Gospel was principally a Protestant impetus that combined religious conviction with social, political, and economic analysis and programs designed to alleviate poverty and other social ills. In the United Kingdom it was associated with persons such as Robert Owen, F. D. Maurice, and J. M. F. Ludlow (and later William Temple); with Walter Rauschenbusch, Washington Gladden, and Shailer Mathews in the United States; and with Salem Bland, J. S. Woodsworth, and Nellie McClung in Canada. Beginning with insightful observations of living and working conditions (especially in cities), and combining deeply held (often evangelical) faith convictions with tendencies toward theological liberalism, these social reformers were active in church and society, in academic settings and political forums. They sought in every way possible to ameliorate the suffering they saw so clearly around them. From soup kitchens to standing for political office, from practical support for striking workers to innovations in public education, health, and housing, the Social Gospel program had a wide-angle lens as it sought truly to transform the world. Community services emerged within church buildings on weekdays as individuals, whole congregations, and denominations became deeply invested in social action and service to the society around them.

At the end of the nineteenth century, there was a mighty convergence of political, economic, religious, cultural, and social forces in the U.S. and Canada. Politically and economically, it was a time of socialist labor movements rising amidst the predominance of capitalism; industrialization was

---

1. See, among others, Richard Allen, *The Social Passion: Religion and Social Reform in Canada, 1914–28* (Toronto: University of Toronto Press, 1971); and Susan Curtis, *A Consuming Faith: The Social Gospel and Modern American Culture* (Columbia: University of Missouri Press, 2001). Another recent collection of essays on the Social Gospel and its continuing impact in the present era is Christopher H. Evans, ed., *The Social Gospel Today* (Louisville: Westminster John Knox, 2001).

met with an interest in collectivism; and influence was felt from both English socialism and Karl Marx's theories. Both a general economic depression and the consolidation of industry and industrial power were significant factors.[2] Socially, a new individualism and varying degrees of community fragmentation were endemic. Non-Anglo-Saxon, non-Protestant immigration was rapidly increasing the urban population, eroding the perception of security and social homogeneity among many with Anglo-Saxon ancestry. Mass social problems were documented and analyzed for the first time, bringing to light crises in housing, unemployment, overcrowding, "chaotic urban development,"[3] illiteracy, low wages, and addictions.[4] Concurrently, social Darwinists and some wealthy citizens criticized the impoverished for their sloth and immorality. Why hadn't such people simply adopted and benefited from the great progressivism and positive outlook—"the robust optimism, activism, and pragmatic temper of America"[5]—that the middle and upper classes enjoyed? Thus the Social Gospel movement emerged in North America within a convergence of a number of factors, some of which, when considered side by side, seem somewhat contradictory today: liberal Christian theology; evangelistic fervor; "higher criticism" in biblical studies; revivalism; increasing dissatisfaction with social conditions such as mass urban poverty and its suspected link with industrialization; the temperance movement; women's suffrage; the hegemony of capitalism; Darwinian theory (applied not only biologically but also socio-politically); and the rise of socialist sentiment that intersected with the political disenfranchisement of non-Anglo-Saxon immigrants.

The theological background of the Social Gospel was likewise multifaceted. The theological liberalism of the nineteenth century pursued critiques of traditional doctrines, and boldly held up forms of biblical criticism that were newly suspicious of scriptural inerrancy and authority. Liberalism's rejection of the orthodoxy of "the Fathers" gave rise to the "New Theology." In North America, the New Theology was the heir of

2. Richard Allen, "The Background of the Social Gospel in Canada," in *The Social Gospel in Canada: Papers of the Interdisciplinary Conference on the Social Gospel in Canada, March 21–24, 1973, at the University of Regina*, ed. Richard Allen (Ottawa: National Museums of Canada, 1975) 9.

3. Curtis, *A Consuming Faith*, 3.

4. See, especially, J. S. Woodsworth, *My Neighbour: A Study of Social Conditions, A Plea for Social Service* (Toronto: University of Toronto Press, 1972).

5. Richard Cauthen, *The Impact of American Religious Liberalism*, 2nd ed. (Lanham, MD: University Press of America, 1983) 86.

Part One—Historical and Methodological Issues

the German liberalism and idealism of Schleiermacher, Kant, Hegel, and Ritschl; yet it was also influenced by progressivism and evangelical revivalism.[6] A somewhat unlikely combination of philosophical skepticism with trust in religious experience and social progress prevailed. One advocate explained,

> We accept the Christian faith because of the *reasonableness* of its entire substance, and not because we have somehow become persuaded that a [divine] revelation has been made.[7]

There was a confidence in rationality and impartial analysis, coupled with the valorization of personal piety and devotion to an understanding of a powerful, compelling, transformative Jesus Christ. Traditional orthodoxy, in contrast, was perceived as too authoritarian, fideistic, unreflective, and unresponsive to the great forces of the day: Darwinian theory, the new biblical criticism, and "the problems of a rapidly industrializing social order."[8] Instead, a great shift to "practical" and "relevant" religion was favored: "the social gospel . . . is modern and is out for realities."[9] Context became a leading consideration in theological work.

Within the theological framework of the Social Gospel itself, emphasis was placed on particular themes. The first was the coming Kingdom of God as a goal to be pursued in the present, not something to be longed for in an infinitely distant future. Secondly, there was an interest in the incarnational and immanentist aspects of Christianity—the presence of God among people here and now—and a shift away from focus on the atonement. Finally, and perhaps most distinctively, the Social Gospel urged upon Christians the view that salvation was a collective affair: the righteousness and redemption of the whole of society were prior and more urgent concerns than private conversion or sanctification.[10] This collective or "social salvation" was to be enacted through specific forms of societal ameliora-

6. Allen, "The Background of the Social Gospel in Canada," 12.

7. Theodore Munger, cited in Curtis, *Consuming Faith*, 294 (emphasis added).

8. Gary Dorrien, *The Making of American Liberal Theology: Imagining Progressive Religion, 1805–1900* (Louisville: Westminster John Knox, 2001) xvii.

9. Walter Rauschenbusch, *A Theology for the Social Gospel* (1918; reprinted, Eugene, OR: Wipf & Stock, 1996) 148.

10. The prevailing view among Social Gospel advocates was that "Christians were responsible for their brothers' and sisters' redemption as much as their own" (Curtis, *Consuming Faith*, 5). For more on this distinctive notion of social salvation, see William R. Hutchison, *The Modernist Impulse in American Protestantism*, 2nd ed. (Oxford: Oxford University Press, 1982).

tion: a new deal for the poor; the reordering of economic systems, including, perhaps, the redistribution of capital; a renewed, fairer political system; popular education; affordable, adequate housing for all; and so on. Such social programs, championed explicitly by individual Christians, Christian leaders, and some Christian congregations and denominations, were, of course, meant to be outward expressions of the first theological theme: the coming Kingdom of God. The *present* realization of the Kingdom of God was thus the goal: a realm of justice, equity, freedom, and bread for all persons, without distinction of class, age, nationality, race, or gender—here and now. There was perhaps a naïve optimism about the inevitability of this Kingdom's manifestation, indeed its natural evolution, within the near term of history. Thus there was, within the early Social Gospel, a distinct shift away from a distant eschatological horizon toward a *realized* eschatological vision: "[r]ather than dwelling on future promises of celestial bliss," Social Gospel proponents "occupied themselves with the evils of poverty, depravity, and injustice in this world" and sought to address them directly.[11]

Toward these goals of the Social Gospel, its proponents vigourously spoke (in both sermons and public addresses) and wrote (in the press and in tracts, articles, and books). They became active in political processes, and sought to reform, direct, and participate in the mission agendas and projects of their denominations. Some became leaders in the wider society and in political parties. Direct intervention in the political and socio-economic conditions of society, they believed, would bring about the Kingdom of God ever more speedily: a *realized* kingdom on earth, in which the poor would be fed and clothed, the sick healed, and the great inequities of society eradicated. In this great adventure, it was believed that religion and science would happily co-operate.

The unusual combination of theological ferment and close attention to contextual realities gave the Social Gospel unique power. The Social Gospel platform—in the Church and beyond it—was informed by religious convictions, to be sure. However, engagement with the social sciences, sometimes in their nascent form, was also constitutive of the Social Gospel approach. It is to this latter question—the application of the social sciences—that the balance of this paper will give attention. Specifically, it is political theory, economic theory, and sociology that we shall consider, and we shall see each though the lens of their application by specific Social Gospel advocates of the late nineteenth and early twentieth centuries.

11. Curtis, *A Consuming Faith*, 6.

Part One—Historical and Methodological Issues

Political Theory

The political orders of the U.S. and Canada in the late nineteenth century were far from monochrome, but they were highly stable. Movements and parties and policies shifted and developed, but the macrostructures of political organization were fundamentally established. U.S. bicameral republican government was by then well-ensconced, more than a century after the revolutionary break from England and a few decades after the resolution of the Civil War. In Canada, the years following the 1867 Confederation were heady and enthusiastic, and loyalty to Britain remained very strong (at least among majority English-speakers) within the constitutional monarchy that bound together the Dominion. The Red River and Northwest Rebellions, while dramatic, were relatively short-lived and quickly suppressed. New Canadian provinces were created and welcomed into Confederation (Manitoba, British Columbia, and Prince Edward Island in the early 1870s, and Saskatchewan and Alberta in 1905).[12]

Against this backdrop of two somewhat different expressions of democratic federalism, the rise of socialist political ideology and the slow but steady accommodation of socialist values in Canada (in contrast to the U.S., where socialism tended to be less warmly embraced), were each related to patterns of immigration in the nineteenth and early twentieth century. In particular, the influx of skilled and socialist-minded workers into Canada from the United Kingdom meant the importation of "a trade-union consciousness from a country where the labor movement was already highly developed."[13] Socialist commitments were already well-developed among migrants from Eastern Europe also. Ivan Avakumovic has argued that those "from the British Isles displayed a propensity to join socialist protest movements in the Prairies"—notably through existing democratic forms.[14] Indeed, British trade unionists preferred to work within existing democratic structures: many trade unionists' organizations simply assimilated into

---

12. In both the U.S. and Canada, only male citizens could vote. Women won the vote in Canada in 1916 provincially (first in Manitoba) and 1918 federally, and in the U.S. in 1920.

13. Norman Penner, *The Canadian Left: A Critical Analysis* (Toronto: Prentice-Hall, 1977), 1.

14. Ivan Avakumovic, *Socialism in Canada: A Study of the CCF-NDP in Federal and Provincial Politics* (Toronto: McClelland & Stewart, 1978) 247.

existing parties.[15] Central and Eastern Europeans, however, often favored more revolutionary reform within fringe movements.

Many churchgoers who organized under the banner of labor interests made a simple equivalence between Christianity and socialism: "Christ was the first socialist" became a common refrain.[16] This socialist political impulse profoundly impacted the Social Gospel movement. The movement, indeed, found a welcome home amidst the linkages between organized labor and pro-labor Christians. This also coincided with a rise in popular participation in political processes on both sides of the border. Political action seemed natural to Social Gospel advocates, for it was within the political sphere that they believed the greatest impact could be made upon society. Through direct participation in government, policy could be shaped that would enact the "Kingdom values" so deeply cherished by Social Gospel advocates.

One such value was the right and duty of ordinary workers—that is, labor—to share in the governance of the state and to contribute to its policy. In Canada, a variety of parties consequently emerged that gave voice to the political interests of labor. Diverse configurations of a Labour, Workers', or Farmers' Party appeared in all provinces except Newfoundland and Prince Edward Island, as did a Communist Party.[17] Common to most of these parties, as diverse as they were, was the goal of a "square deal" for ordinary workers, farmers, the rural population, the urban poor, and immigrants. Anti-capitalist sentiment ran high. By actively shaping the new political parties' policies, Social Gospel advocates explicitly sought to transform society in congruity with their theological convictions. In particular, government intervention was itself seen as a form of collective salvation that improved conditions and hastened the coming of the Kingdom: "if the kingdom of heaven ever comes to your city, it will come in and through the City Hall," declared Washington Gladden.[18] In opposition to the preferred economic policy of most North American governments (laissez-faire capitalism), a

---

15. Colin Campbell and William Christian, *Parties, Leaders and Ideologies in Canada* (Toronto: McGraw-Hill Ryerson, 1996) 140–41.

16. As noted in ibid., 142.

17. F. C. Engelman and M. A. Schwartz, *Political Parties and the Canadian Social Structure* (Toronto: Prentice-Hall, 1967) 35.

18. Washington Gladden, cited in Curtis, *A Consuming Faith*, 130.

new drive toward "cooperation, social responsibility for justice, and an interventionist welfare state" emerged.[19]

One exemplar of the close integration between the labor movement, the churches, and political engagement was A. E. Smith (1871-1947). Smith, a Methodist minister, eventually broke with his denomination and sought more direct political involvement in conjunction with his leadership of a local, populist, non-denominational "People's Church" in Brandon, Manitoba. The Methodist root resulted in the fruit of political activism and political office for Smith, as he took a seat in the Manitoba legislature in 1920. In Smith's view, service to others was a higher goal than personal salvation; the overturning of unjust systems of domination by the rich and powerful was essential; and the exploitation of workers in the profit-driven capitalist economic order must be denounced. Smith, *apropos* of the present paper, in fact advocated a de-emphasis on religious dogma in favor of a church that would embrace "the study of sociology, economics, and 'class problems.'"[20] To these ends, Smith argued initially for a democratic process of gradual but steady change, for "the first step in transforming society was to challenge the capitalist control of the public schools, churches, and the press." [21] Through his career and public life, Smith became increasingly radical and ultimately joined the Communist Party of Canada, and favored more revolutionary forms of political change.

Nellie McClung (1873-1951) represents a related but different sort of engagement with the Social Gospel through the political arena.[22] A novelist, essayist, political activist, Church Unionist, and one of Canada's most famous proponents of the Social Gospel, McClung combined a passion for the emancipation and full political participation of women with a passion for social amelioration. All of these concerns cohered, for McClung, in a commitment to faith in action, and to the social salvation that the incarnate God desires.[23] This early liberationist believed that through Christian par-

19. Curtis, *A Consuming Faith,* 3.

20. Tom Mitchell, "From the Social Gospel to 'the Plain Bread of Leninism': A. E. Smith's Journey to the Left in the Epoch of Reaction after World War 1," *Labour/Le Travail* 33 (1993) 130.

21. Mitchell, "From the Social Gospel," 133. For more on Smith, see also Allen, *The Social Passion.*

22. For much more thorough accounts of McClung's contributions, see Randi Warne, *Literature as Pulpit: The Christian Social Activism of Nellie L. McClung* (Waterloo, ON: Wilfred Laurier University Press, 1993); and Carol L. Hancock, *No Small Legacy: Canada's Nellie McClung: Blazing a Trail for Faith and Justice* (Winfield, BC: Wood Lake, 1986).

23. Hancock, *No Small Legacy,* 73.

ticipation in a democratic political process, God's desire for the flourishing of humanity could and should be accomplished:

> There is enough for everyone, if we could get at it. There is food and raiment, a chance to live, and love and labor—for everyone; ... [but] some others have reached out and taken more than their share, and try to excuse their "hoggishness" by declaring that God did not intend all to travel on the same terms, but you and I know God better than that.[24]

Indeed, McClung argued, the "creator of us all ... is not willing that any should perish, but that all should live and live abundantly."[25] The reform of the political order—immediately if not sooner—was essential to that "abundant life" for all.

Accordingly, McClung often presented politically-charged interpretations of the Bible that ran counter to conventionally pious approaches, especially with respect to the "proper place" of women. Perceptive in her observations of the social and economic realties of ordinary people, McClung was sharply aware of gender inequities such as unequal rates of pay. In Jesus she saw a champion of equality between men and women. Reflecting upon social ills such as liquor traffic, the political disenfranchisement of women, and prostitution, McClung used the parable of the Good Samaritan to point out that society needs not only Samaritans to help the wounded, but also someone "to go out and clean up the road!"[26] As was true of many persons in the Social Gospel movement, McClung read Scripture and expressed her theological convictions through the lens of social amelioration and political transformation, including the elevation of the status of women. Indeed, the successes of the suffrage movement are the expressions of public life for which she is best known today. But McClung was also astute in her analysis of Russian Communism and the better alternatives that democratic, co-operative socialism presented in the Canadian context.[27] Her involvement with the Social Gospel was intricately linked with involvement in politics, including her election to the Alberta legislature in 1921.

Unlike Smith and McClung, however, most persons involved in the Social Gospel movement sought (and expected) gradual, progressive,

24. Nellie L. McClung, *In Times Like These* (Toronto: McLeod, 1919) 8.
25. Ibid., 176.
26. Ibid., 125–27.
27. See Nellie L. McClung, *More Leaves from Lantern Lane* (Toronto: Allen, 1937) 51–52.

incremental change within the political order. For many, this was seen to be simply the inevitable evolution—within history—of a just socialist society. The sense of inevitability was linked both to the conviction that God's hand was active within the events of history, and to the era's confidence in the Darwinian account of natural phenomena—here translated to the political arena. Human society would simply and naturally *evolve* toward greater enlightenment, greater justice and compassion, greater fairness and the sharing of resources. It was the Social Gospel advocates' task to announce and herald and hasten that evolution. Yet most, by far, rejected the revolutionary insurgency that the Bolsheviks had chosen in Russia.[28] The notion of progressive, inevitable social evolution was linked to a particular reading of the testimony of Jesus, and especially to an organic, progressive understanding of the Kingdom of God indicated in such parables as the growing seed (Mark 4:26-29) and the mustard seed (Mark 4:30-32). With this interpretive eye cast upon the Bible, all of Jesus' teachings were seen to support the Social Gospel view that the Kingdom of God was growing, maturing, and ripening, and would inevitably and quickly come to fulfillment in and through the political order.

Economic Theory

The diverse economic understandings among Social Gospel proponents came from mixed sources. The application of such understandings was present in their many efforts, but was often indirect. Economics, as a discrete discipline, was in many ways in its infancy. Marx, of course, had been active in the period just preceding the Social Gospel movement, and was certainly influential in the emerging economic understandings of the religious reformers of the day. However, he was usually seen to be too radical. Marxism was rarely specifically conjured, especially after the Bolshevik Revolution of 1917: there was deep fear throughout North America of such extremist options.[29]

Among economists contemporary with the Social Gospel movement, Thorstein Veblen (1857–1929) provided a socialist analysis for the North American context. Veblen challenged the prevailing classical economic

---

28. Hence the widespread antagonism, for example, to the 1919 Winnipeg General Strike.

29. In fact, the "anti-Red" sentiment among the general public contributed, I would argue, to the eventual decline of the Social Gospel's popularity.

theory (drawn from Adam Smith and John Stuart Mill) that both Canadian and U.S. policy makers typically privileged. The prevailing theory espoused a form of capitalism that was largely an expression of late mercantilism. Veblen was critical of such "'parasitic' lines of business" that invariably placed private profit ahead of community interests.[30] Like many Social Gospel advocates, Veblen applied principles from Darwinian thought: in his case, however, the application was to economic theory. He was first to coin the term "conspicuous consumption" to describe and excoriate the wastefulness of many wealthy persons.[31] Similarly, he critiqued traditional economic theory for its naïve acceptance of hedonism and self-interest as necessary and good phenomena, preferring instead to point out the truly collectivist nature of economic forces. Like Marx, however, Veblen held to the principle of inevitable conflict within economic structures, especially capitalism: "internal contradictions within capitalism would [naturally] lead to its overthrow."[32] Like Social Gospel proponents, Veblen lifted up the importance and power of *labor*—not only capital—in shaping society and the structure of economies. While Veblen was not, within the bounds of this paper's investigation, necessarily engaged by any specific Social Gospel proponent,[33] the nature of his critique of traditional capitalist economics illustrates the shifting landscape of North American socio-economic thought in the late nineteenth century. There was no unassailable, monolithic economic theory in the ascendancy. Thus the application of economic analysis to the religious interests of the Social Gospel took place within an increasingly plural culture of economic thought.

By way of illustration, then, we can now glimpse how socialist and collectivist economic theory was operative in the thought of a leading Social Gospel advocate, Walter Rauschenbusch (1861–1918). Rauschenbusch wrote freely and assertively, combining economic, political, social, and theological reflections without distinguishing them clearly. His

---

30. Roger E. Backhouse, *The Ordinary Business of Life: A History of Economics from the Ancient World to the Twenty-First Century* (Princeton: Princeton University Press, 2002) 196.

31. See Thorstein Veblen, *The Theory of the Leisure Class*, ed. Martha Banta (Oxford: Oxford University Press, 2007).

32. Backhouse, *Ordinary Business*, 197.

33. It would be most fruitful to consider, in another study, the possible interaction and mutual influence between Veblen and figures such as Graham Taylor, who began teaching at Chicago Theological Seminary in 1892, the same year that Veblen came to teach at the University of Chicago.

interpretation of the Bible routinely attended to economic realities, such as the nature and impact of tax collection by Jews within Roman-occupied Palestine.[34] His analysis also reviewed the history of European and American microeconomics, as well as the then-current state of American macroeconomics. Rauschenbusch studied closely the effects of taxation and the relative value of wage increases over several decades. He described the shift from cottage industries to factories, from independent owner-operators to whole-industry monopolies. Within the development of widespread industrialization, Rauschenbusch also saw the development of widespread poverty.[35] The "line-up of two antagonistic classes"—embodied in unending conflicts between capitalism and co-operation, or capital and labor, or masters (corporations) and slaves (workers)—was a dualistic reality that Rauschenbusch frequently assessed in his writings.[36] In such analyses, Marx's economic theories must almost certainly have been influential for Rauschenbusch (for instance, his language about "controlling the means of production"). Contact with Veblen's views may also have been entirely possible, since they were contemporaries.

Despite the prosperity that capitalism had brought to Western countries, Rauschenbusch saw that prosperity was also responsible for "the production of human wreckage . . . exploitation and oppression . . . [and] a materialistic spirit."[37] Furthermore, he regarded the inevitable outcomes of unbridled capitalism to be antidemocratic. This, for Rauschenbusch, was enormously grievous and a fatal flaw of any proposed economic system. But this dualism between capitalism and oppression in modern American life was also repugnant to him for religious reasons:

> In all the operations of capitalistic industry and commerce the aim that controls and directs is not the purpose to supply human needs, but to make a profit for those who direct industry. This in itself is an irrational and unchristian adjustment to the social order, for it sets money up as the prime aim, and human life as something secondary, or as a means to secure money. This supremacy

---

34. For example, see Rauschenbusch, *The Social Principles of Jesus* (1920; reprinted, Eugene, OR: Wipf & Stock, 2003) 68.

35. For this and similar analyses, see Rauschenbusch's chapter titled, "The Present Crisis," in his *Christianity and the Social Crisis* (1907; reprinted, Eugene, OR: Wipf & Stock, 2003) 211–86.

36. Rauschenbusch, *Christianizing the Social Order* (1912; reprinted, Eugene, OR: Wipf & Stock, 2011) 312, passim.

37. Rauschenbusch, *A Theology for the Social Gospel*, 111.

of Profit in Capitalism stamps it as a mammonistic organization with which Christianity can never be content.[38]

Finally, in this brief review of Rauschenbusch, we see that he applied his survey knowledge of the history of economics to a realized eschatology: "the Kingdom of God must also be the commonwealth of co-operative labor."[39] The coming Kingdom must be not only spiritually complete, but also economically just. An "outlook toward the future in which the 'spiritual life' is saved and the economic life is left unsaved is both unchristian and stupid" for the "common possession of the economic resources of society" was a *sine qua non* of God's plan for humanity.[40] Rauschenbusch drew freely on the tools of economic inquiry—although formal economics as a discipline was only just emerging—and combined it with his keen historical awareness. Together, economic and historical inquiry served his progressivist and ameliorist goals. It was his theological acuity that won him the greatest fame, but in order to illuminate his religious insight, Rauschenbusch accessed, as a matter of course, a social-scientific frame of reference for data, analysis, and more complete understanding.

Sociology

Sociology is the final dimension of social-scientific analysis within Social Gospel thought that we shall consider. Sociological tools—including demographic studies, the use of statistics, empirical descriptions of social behavior, and so forth—were in the early stages of formal development in the nineteenth century within the work of such figures as Emile Durkheim, Max Weber, and Auguste Comte. Sociology as a discipline of the universities took root in North America between 1890–1920.[41] As an emerging discipline, many of sociology's concerns were very close to those of the Social Gospel movement: amelioration of living conditions, especially in urban areas; understanding and responding to collective needs; and the creation of public policy that would serve the disenfranchised. Like the Social Gos-

---

38. Rauschenbusch, *Christianizing the Social Order*, 312–13.
39. Rauschenbusch, *A Theology for the Social Gospel*, 55.
40. Ibid., 224.
41. Douglas F. Campbell, *Beginnings: Essays on the History of Canadian Sociology* (Port Credit, ON: Scribblers', 1983) 1. Campbell's chapter on sociology and the Social Gospel warrants special mention as a far more adequate treatment of the subject than is possible in the present essay.

PART ONE—Historical and Methodological Issues

pel itself, sociology was an interdisciplinary task. These linkages were not lost upon church leaders, who set up a number of special commissions and committees to study "sociological questions" in concert with their religious agendas.[42]

Among the best exemplars of Social Gospel proponents who made use of sociological tools was J. S. Woodsworth (1874–1942).[43] While Woodsworth is better known in Canadian history as a politician and the founder of the Co-operative Commonwealth Federation (which, in turn, is the forerunner of the New Democratic Party), his sociological perspectives, especially as expressed in the early part of his career, are instructive within the present study.

Woodsworth began his professional life in the pattern of his father, as a Methodist student minister in Manitoba. Academic study and observations of life in Toronto and Oxford exposed him to a variety of socialist and reformist ideas that influenced his political and spiritual understandings. These he brought with him upon his return to Western Canada. Although he was ordained within the Canadian Methodist Church, Woodsworth had significant doctrinal differences with orthodox Christianity, and he eventually left active parish work and resigned from the Church. His writings were less "purely" theological in nature than some other Social Gospel thinkers, as he became increasingly involved in social action and political life. Such direct involvement included his support of the controversial 1919 Winnipeg General Strike, which resulted in his brief imprisonment. In prior years, these social and political emphases had not always been entirely pleasing to his pro-establishment Methodist congregants, one of whom suggested that Woodsworth ought to preach "less ill-digested sociology and more simple gospel preaching."[44]

42. Campbell, *Beginnings*, 21.

43. There were, of course, many others who engaged sociological tools in service to the Social Gospel. Salem Bland was a well-known and influential social theorist of "The New Christianity"—which was also the title of his 1920 book (Toronto: McClelland & Stewart). See also Charles A. Ellwood, who composed a variety of definitions and empirical formulas for such notions as "social justice" and sought to apply them to social analysis. One such formula proposed that "the satisfactoriness of each individual life is directly proportionate to the sum of justice in human society"; see Charles A. Ellwood, *Christianity and Social Science: A Challenge to the Church* (New York: Macmillan, 1923) 91.

44. An anonymous lawyer, cited in Kenneth McNaught, *A Prophet in Politics: A Biography of J. S. Woodsworth* (Toronto: University of Toronto Press, 1959) 24. It is also noteworthy that Woodsworth and his contemporary, Salem Bland (*inter alios*), were also

Woodsworth was appalled at the poverty, overcrowding, disease, and degradation within Canada's urban immigrant districts, especially after having witnessed slum conditions in London and Edinburgh as a student. He felt compelled both to study the causes of such troubles, and to seek to address them via the transformation of social, economic, and political policies and processes. The beginning of such transformation, he believed, was a careful study of the actual lived conditions of ordinary people. In the midst of his pastoral work in inner-city Winnipeg, Woodsworth began to compile photographs of, graphs about, and statistical information on immigrants and their lives.[45] The population of the Prairie provinces had nearly doubled between 1901–1906, and much of this growth arose through non-Anglo-Saxon immigration.[46] Woodsworth carefully described the various ethnic groupings that accounted for this population surge, providing detailed statistics.

Next, Woodsworth recounted many of the specific yet common experiences of immigrants: poverty, separation from loved ones, illness, language barriers, bewilderment, relief and regret, hard labor, substandard housing, inadequate sanitation, segregation, and prejudice. Such descriptions were forms of social analysis that eventually prompted in Woodsworth his larger claims that political policy must address, and address justly and compassionately, the challenges presented by the surging population. Urban life, in particular, pressed upon the Canadian scene the realities of interdependent living, in which business, culture, religion, education, politics, and daily life were thoroughly intertwined. For Woodsworth, this urbanization was an

---

treated with great suspicion and even hostility by many within the Methodist Church in Canada. On this, see Oscar L. Cole-Arnal, "The Prairie Labour Churches: The Methodist Input," *Studies in Religion/Science Religieuses* 34 (2005) 3–26.

45. J. S. Woodsworth, *Strangers Within Our Gates, or Coming Canadians* (Toronto: University of Toronto Press, 1972); first published in 1909. See also Woodsworth's *My Neighbour*. Originally published in 1911, the latter book presented new data but made very similar arguments about the need for interventionist policies. Kenneth McNaught's *A Prophet in Politics* provides a very thorough account of the contexts and development of Woodsworth's thought. For the approach and analysis he was undertaking in *Strangers* and elsewhere, Woodsworth gave credit to similar work done by Josiah Strong in the U.S. See Strong, *Our Country: Its Possible Future and Its Present Crisis* (New York: Baker & Taylor, 1885). My thanks to Phyllis Airhart of Emmanuel College, University of Toronto, for noting this connection.

46. Woodsworth, *Strangers Within Our Gates*, 16.

ambiguous development, however: "the city may become a menace to our whole civilization."[47]

Nevertheless, Woodsworth accepted the fact that city life was increasingly the norm for Canadians. The question was how to address the social problems and inequities inherent in this norm. City planning, public health schemes, housing and wage reforms, public ownership of utilities, the development of playgrounds and other sports facilities, crime prevention, child welfare—all these and more fell under Woodsworth's critical and discerning eye. In this analysis he concurred with J. H. T. Falk, then General Secretary of the Associated Charities of Winnipeg, who argued that "without the examination and remedying of social and economic causes little advance will be made in the campaign against misery, want, disease and death."[48] Government social services, in tandem with the churches' ministries, were the way in which such issues had to be addressed, and Woodworth proposed a number of schemes for doing so.

Like other Social Gospel advocates, Woodsworth believed that the Hebrew prophetic tradition urged upon the Church (and society at large) a concern that was clearly reflected throughout the Biblical record: namely, that social salvation and mutual responsibility were imperatives of God's purposes for humanity. The then-current realities and problems of immigration and urbanization were simply the peculiar nexus in which such mutual service ought to be expressed:

> The churches to whom has been granted a vision of the Kingdom of God cannot ignore the presence of such large numbers of foreigners. "Difficult to reach them?" Of course it is, but this is *the problem* of the church in Canada.[49]

The careful enumeration, tabulation and other forms of analyses of all the data he collected, especially among immigrant populations, indicates Woodworth's confidence in the tools of sociology in service of the religious goals he brought with him as a minister, Social Gospel thinker, and politician. Sociological description became for Woodsworth an essential way of "narrating the needs," as it were:

> If it is right to help the sick it is right to do away with filth and overcrowding and to provide sunlight and good air and good food.

47. Woodsworth, *My Neighbour*, 23.
48. Falk, cited in ibid. 184.
49. Ibid., 240 (emphasis in original).

We have tried to provide *for the poor*. Yet, have we tried to alter the social conditions that lead to poverty?[50]

By providing detailed statistics, but also by reflecting on the human dimensions of suffering and the interconnected needs faced by urban dwellers, Woodsworth was able to bolster his claims about the Social Gospel's call to the Church and the nation to respond in concrete, programmatic ways to the neighbor. The political vision that developed and integrated his socialist commitments in later years was nurtured within these early sociological studies.

Conclusion

In a fashion too brief to be quite adequate, we have surveyed three forms of social-scientific inquiry that informed and influenced the Social Gospel: political theory, economic theory, and sociology. The use and impact of these three were so significant, in fact, that it would be quite erroneous to suggest that the Social Gospel movement was in any sense exclusively a theological phenomenon. It was indeed an idiosyncratic, interconnected web of concurrent movements that even today escape sharp definition. The often imprecise or allusive nature of the appeals to social-scientific forms of inquiry is certainly related to the ways in which these fields were not themselves sharply defined and distinguished as disciplines in the late nineteenth and early twentieth centuries. Moreover, the theological discourse of the Social Gospel was constituted, in large measure, precisely *in and through* the social-scientific tools of the day. Dogmatic theology, on its own, was not seen to be adequate to the task of fulsome social description and societal transformation. The deeply-felt religious calling of many Social Gospel advocates, indeed their evangelical enthusiasm, impelled them to transcend and supplement the very theological foundations from which they had begun.

---

50. J. S. Woodworth, undated sermon, cited in McNaught, 26.

4

Washing His Hands of the Enlightenment

A Critique of John Milbank[1]

Christopher Craig Brittain

It has unfortunately become commonplace in contemporary theology to adopt a dismissive attitude towards the intellectual ideals of the Enlightenment. If Immanuel Kant's famous essay is taken as a manifesto for the tradition, the Enlightenment can be characterized as an emergence out of self-imposed "immaturity" through a willingness to think for oneself, supported by sufficient intellectual freedom and courage to engage in the independent questioning of inherited tradition.[2] Ethical and political im-

---

1. This discussion of Milbank's political theology is offered in a spirit similar to that I experienced in a conversation with Lee Cormie many years ago. During a course on Latin American liberation theology, much to Professor Cormie's amusement, I expressed my bafflement over Michael Novak's claim (in his *Will It Liberate?* [New York: Paulist, 1986] 134–48) that the problems in Latin America were due, not to limitations in capitalism or the oppression of the poor by its structures, but were the result of limitations on "economic liberty" and the oppression of "economic activists" in Latin America. Some elements of the discussion have appeared previously in chapter 3 of Christopher Craig Brittain, *The Weight of Objectivity* (Saarbrücken: Lampert, 2010); they appear here with permission.

2. Immanuel Kant, "An Answer to the Question: What is Enlightenment?" in *Perpetual Peace and Other Essays*, ed. and trans. Ted Humphrey (Indianapolis: Hackett, 1983) 33–48.

plications were developed out of this emerging worldview, including the dignity of the individual subject, which became encoded in law through concepts such as legal "rights."[3] For theologians like Stanley Hauerwas, however, modern liberal Christianity has been far too accepting of these ideals of enlightened modernity. He criticises Christians who mistakenly assume that these values are the logical consequence of objective rational thought, rather than recognising the "tradition-dependent character" upon which any account of reality depends.

Hauerwas points to the liberation theology of Gustavo Gutiérrez as a case in point. He suggests that Gutiérrez's concern that theology recognize human beings as "artisans of our own destiny," and support liberation movements which seek to free human beings "from all servitude," has the problematic "ring of the Enlightenment." Why is this of concern? Because, according to Hauerwas, "the salvation promised in the good news is not a life free from suffering, free from servitude, but rather a life that freely suffers, freely serves."[4] For Hauerwas, the adoption of Enlightenment ideals by Christian theology undermines the "distinctive witness of the church" and reduces liberation theology to a political movement shaped by the values and assumptions of secular modernity. Modern individual subjects, according to Hauerwas, take their own self-interests and desires far too seriously, to the detriment of obedience to divine authority, as witnessed to by the Christian tradition.

Such a rejection of the Enlightenment, and of Latin American liberation theology in particular, is developed by John Milbank into a wideranging critique of modern theology. He vividly illustrates his position by likening the traditions of the Enlightenment to the figure of Pontius Pilate. In the account found in the Gospel of John, Milbank suggests that Pilate can be taken as representative of the Enlightenment, "since he both rules and inquires after truth." He summarizes the scene in which Jesus of Nazareth is presented before Pilate in the following manner:

> "What is truth?" he asks, as if to ask "What is enlightenment?" But notoriously, he only jests, and will not stay for an answer. If he had

---

3. For accounts of this development, see Louis Dupré, *The Enlightenment and the Intellectual Foundations of Modern Culture* (New Haven: Yale University Press, 2004); Peter Gay, *The Enlightenment: The Science of Freedom* (New York: Norton, 1969).

4. Stanley Hauerwas, *After Christendom* (Nashville: Abingdon, 1991) 53.

Part One—Historical and Methodological Issues

stayed, of course, he would actually have *seen* the truth, enthroned before him as a suffering body.[5]

By turning his back on Christ's broken body, Milbank suggests that Pilate thereby separates "the inquiry after truth from sensory vision." The "rational gaze" is here figuratively separated from "revelation," and thus from the only source—in Milbank's opinion—of truth. This is to say that the Enlightenment, just like Pilate, is unable to recognise the truth about reality because it restricts knowledge about the world to what is immediately evident and seemingly obvious to the human eye.

One could turn this illustration against Milbank, however, and assert that just as Pilate in this scene washes his hands of responsibility for Jesus' execution, Milbank's political theology washes its hands of the political and philosophical traditions of the Enlightenment and everything they represent: democratic institutions that mediate between political and cultural difference; argumentative procedures with which to negotiate differences of opinion; systems of analysis and self-criticism which are not exclusively bound to tradition and community consensus. This chapter examines Milbank's position from the perspective of liberation theology, and argues that he encourages an a-historical acceptance of ecclesiastical authority based on the arbitrary elevation of the Christian narrative above all other discourses in society. The implications of Milbank's critique of liberation theology leave Christian thought with few resources for conceiving how modern pluralistic society might function, other than to advocate suspicion and encourage conversion. The limitations of such a view support the conclusion that a responsible theological position would do well to develop a more nuanced critique of the Enlightenment as it seeks to meet the challenges presented by a modern secular society. Milbank's washing his hands of the resources of the Enlightenment simply repeats Pilate's failure to perceive the reality that presents itself in front of him. Such abandonment of the resources that other traditions offer to theology is neither responsible, nor faithful to the church's calling. The chapter analyses this issue by focusing particularly on the weaknesses of Milbank's account of subjectivity.

---

5. Milbank, "Knowledge: The Theological Critique of Philosophy in Hamann and Jacobi," in *Radical Orthodoxy*, ed. John Milbank et al. (London: Routledge, 1999) 25.

Milbank's Critique of Social Theory

The initial manifesto of Milbank's "Radical Orthodoxy" is outlined in his book, *Theology and Social Theory*. The thesis of the monograph is that modern Christian theology has become overly humble and acquiescent before the authority of contemporary science and social theory. Such theology is faulted for surrendering its truth claims by permitting the sciences to describe the "facts" about material reality. Milbank argues that theology has mistakenly accepted secular reason's assumption that society can be conceived of as an autonomous sphere that can be grasped objectively. But this is to ignore, he continues, the fact that all descriptions of reality are based on an ungrounded metanarrative, or *mythos*, upon which supposedly scientific "stories" about the world are developed. According to Milbank, social science's perspective on human society is no more objective than that offered by Christian theology, so that "social theories are in themselves theologies or anti-theologies in disguise."[6]

Sociological explanations of Christianity are thus considered illegitimate by Milbank. He rejects the secularization thesis often offered as an account of modernity, in which the world is desacralized by a "metaphor of the removal of the superfluous and additional to leave a residue of the human."[7] Such a worldview, Milbank continues, is neither historically accurate nor scientific, but is merely an interpretation based on a "pagan" *mythos*—the worship of power. The rise of modernity, with its individualism and autonomy, was the result of a corruption of Christian doctrine, of "pagan" mythologies, which forced the retreat of religion out of public society, leaving the "secular" realm to be managed by competing forces of power.[8] Milbank claims that only a return to a unified Christian theological worldview, and to a unified Christian practice, will enable society to escape from an endless cycle of violence and the worship of power.

Epistemological Implications

Leaving aside the question of whether Milbank's account of the social sciences is accurate, there are considerable implications here for how one

---

6. Milbank, *Theology and Social Theory* (Oxford: Blackwell, 1990) 3.
7. Ibid., 9.
8. Ibid., 129.

evaluates the nature of human knowledge that require careful scrutiny (although these can only be briefly mentioned here).[9] Milbank argues that "a claim to know truly, a claim to know at all, as Plato argued, only makes sense within the framework of *meathexis* (participation)."[10] This suggests that only "insiders" can grasp reality "as it really is," for only they have been taught to see it through the proper lens of the Christian tradition. On this basis, he makes the following assertion:

> [T]heology, in the face of secular attack, is only on secure ground if it adopts the most extreme mode of counterattack: namely that unless other disciplines are (at least implicitly) ordered by theology . . . they are objectively and demonstrably null and void, altogether lacking in truth.[11]

Milbank states that "Radical Orthodoxy, re-invoking pre-modern positions . . . does not consider there to be any secure reason without reference to our remote and uncertain vision of the divine." Thus, until one accepts the Christian metanarrative (as Milbank understands it), one is chained to the wall of Plato's cave, as Milbank echoes the "Platonic view that reason, to be reason, in some sense knows before it knows." Only those initiated into the true order of reality hidden behind sense experience might leave the shadows of the cave and enter into the sunlight of reality: "to reason truly one must be already illumined by God."[12]

This position is clearly set up in direct opposition to the Kantian slogan of the Enlightenment: *Sapere Aude*! ["Have courage to use your own understanding"]. But while one cannot deny that there are substantial intellectual and political limitations among the assumptions of the Enlightenment tradition,[13] the way in which Milbank (and Hauerwas) essentially imply a foreclosure on independent thought and any external criticism of tradition

---

9. See my "Against Eschatological Over-Determination: Can Social Science Contribute to Theology?" in *Theology, University, Humanities*, ed. Christopher Craig Brittain and Francesca Aran Murphy (Eugene, OR: Cascade Books, 2011) 150–72.

10. Milbank, "The Conflict of the Faculties: Theology and the Economy of the Sciences," in *Faithfulness and Fortitude: In Conversation with the Theological Ethics of Stanley Hauerwas*, ed. Mark Thiessen Nation and Samuel Wells (Edinburgh: T. & T. Clark, 2000) 43.

11. Ibid., 45.

12. Milbank, "Knowledge," 24.

13. For a theological critique of the political agenda of enlightened liberalism, which links it to the rise of the nation state, see William T. Cavanaugh, *The Myth of Religious Violence* (Oxford: Oxford University Press, 2009).

is a medicine that kills the patient it intends to cure. For to scold Gutiérrez and other liberation theologians for adopting concepts like "freedom" and the "rights of the individual" as rhetorical tools with which to challenge the economic and political oppression of the poor, is to deny the significance that such resources have for supporting the voices of those who have been absented from society and church. Gutiérrez raised this concern at the very outset of the emergence of liberation theology in Latin America: "By 'absent' [human beings] I mean: of little or no importance, and without the opportunity to give expression themselves to their sufferings, their comraderies, their plans, their hopes."[14] The implications of Milbank's sweeping theological critique of the Enlightenment, constructed in the name of a Christian metanarrative whose authority ought not to be questioned by individual subjects, threaten to render silent once again those human beings that Gutiérrez sought to include within Christian theology, and whom Lee Cormie has called upon the church to recognize as seeking "to affirm their own dignity, to speak for themselves concerning their sufferings, joys and visions of society."[15]

The Impoverished Subject

From the perspective of liberation theology, therefore, the primary issue with Milbank's political theology is not his epistemological assumptions, but rather the political implications that his "Radical Orthodoxy" has for those human beings marginalized by existing societal conditions. Rather than seeking to enable human beings to acknowledge and develop their own agency and power, Milbank warns that this image of the human being is simply shaped and manipulated by the needs of the secular nation state: "the modern soul and the modern state are self-legible."[16] An analysis of his alternative understanding of human subjectivity, however, demonstrates how impoverished a conception it is.

---

14. Gustavo Gutiérrez, *A Theology of Liberation: History, Politics, and Salvation*, rev. ed., trans. Sr. C. Inda and J. Eagleson (Maryknoll, NY: Orbis, 1988) xx.

15. Lee Cormie, "Movements of the Spirit in History," in *Talitha Cum! The Grace of Solidarity in a Globalized World*, ed. Mario DeGiglio-Bellemare and Gabriela Miranda García (Geneva: WSCF, 2004) 243.

16. Milbank, "The End of Enlightenment: Post-Modern or Post-Secular?" *Concilium* 6 (1992) 39.

Part One—Historical and Methodological Issues

In a genealogical narrative of the emergence of the modern concept of the individual subject, Milbank draws upon Friedrich Nietzsche and Michel Foucault to assist in a deconstruction of the Enlightenment's "story" of its development. This is undertaken to demonstrate how a variety of different fictions about subjectivity have been articulated throughout history. Milbank argues that the modern preference for originality and freedom presupposed by the Enlightenment story is merely "a matter of taste." Nietzsche and his followers, he continues, treat this preference as objectively true when they consider cultures closer to realizing these ideals as "more natural" or superior (Nietzsche on Homer, etc.).[17]

Milbank contends that the preference for originality, freedom, and creative will represents the adoption of yet another *mythos*. He argues that a "differential ontology," which demonstrates that "discourses of truth are so many incommensurable language games," need not suggest that "the ultimate, over-arching game is the play of force, fate, and chance."[18] Such a conclusion represents an "ontology of violence." So, while Nietzsche is to be commended for demonstrating that "the western quest for truth . . . discovered that the untruth of truth is power," Milbank asserts that "this power-reality must be refused, and the Platonic quest must be taken up again, yet this time as a wager of faith that there is 'another world' not dominated by power."[19]

Milbank's narrative becomes rather contradictory at this point. Affirming the conclusions that Nietzsche and Foucault suggest about Western thought and history, he simply asserts that their diagnosis of the nature of power is alterable. He suggests that one can decide to escape to another realm where violence and power are no more. While all politics are revealed to be founded on myth, one can refute Nietzsche's celebration of the strong, only not by rational argument, law, or democratic politics. Instead, "it is possible for the weak to refuse the necessity of this strength by telling a different story."[20]

With his "selective attitude to the postmodern critique,"[21] Milbank employs certain elements of deconstruction, without accepting the implications that these same elements are often thought to demand. The portrait of

---

17. Milbank, *Theology and Social Theory*, 281–82.
18. Ibid., 279.
19. Ibid., 319.
20. Ibid., 283.
21. Ibid., 295.

local narratives engaged in endless competition or conflict with each other can be challenged, he argues, by an ontology of the peaceful co-existence of differences. This "selective attitude" does not, however, allow for a coherent argument: one must acknowledge the equality of all differences, but one must also affirm that one form of difference is superior.

One can summarize this position as stating that one must be able to reject all forms of reliable knowledge about the world, but at the same time be able to claim reliable knowledge about ultimate reality. As Milbank puts it, "the Platonic impulse to enthrone the good is 'saved,' yet in terms which refuse the Platonic cult of the untainted 'original' along with the Platonic idea of truth."[22] One would think the resolution of such an antinomy would require a tremendous amount of mental gymnastics, but the crux of Milbank's argument is simply to present the Trinity as peaceful co-existence of difference. Despite the fact that the world's reality appears fragmented and conflictual, the problem is merely one's perception of it. If one understood reality "as it really is," then, Milbank suggest that all of society's conflicts would come to an end.

Further insights into Milbank's understanding of subjectivity and the shifts of meaning within narratives appear in fragments throughout *Theology and Social Theory*. He states that positions within narrative communities are altered and modified, not as the result of dialectical examination or out of responses to criticism, but simply out of "the poetic ability to innovate."[23] This position is developed in particular through an engagement with Maurice Blondel's concept of action. For Milbank, Blondel's "self-dispossessing action" points the way "to a postmodern social theology."[24] It helps, he claims, to avoid the mistakes of Karl Rahner's version of integralism, which he believes discards the idea of a state of pure nature at the price of naturalizing the supernatural. In Rahner's theology, Milbank contends, the social becomes an autonomous sphere which does not need to turn to theology for its self-understanding. By locating the supernatural existential within the *a priori* structure of the human spirit, he argues that Rahner makes supernatural grace merely a part of human nature. Social process becomes conceptualized as transcendence, and salvation is collapsed into finite and fallible acts of human liberation. Milbank argues that this is articulated most clearly in Latin American liberation theology, which he portrays as

22. Ibid., 296.
23. Ibid., 345.
24. Ibid., 209.

merely imposing a gloss of religious terminology to what is, in effect, secular political activity.[25]

Blondel's concept of action avoids such pitfalls, Milbank suggests; for he, "more than anyone else, points us beyond secular reason."[26] According to Blondel, the human will is never equal to itself, and it demands a completion that transcends its own resources. An action is permanently in excess of the finite, for it "is always richer by an infinity than what precedes it."[27] Milbank argues that Blondel demonstrates that the subject does not have control of even its own actions. To act or to think "may be to create, to assert oneself, but it is equally to lose oneself, to place what is most ours . . . at a total risk."[28] Milbank states that such logic of action requires recognition of the supernatural. It demands that philosophy acknowledge its own inadequacy, and admit that all thought is participation in divine creative action, "the force of origination," involving simultaneously a "kenosis, a self-emptying mediation." The transcendent dimension is present in all human action, so that in every action is found an implicit hope which is also a sacrifice: "our offering of ourselves to others so that the action constitutes a 'bond' between us."[29]

Charles Davis is much less enthusiastic about Blondel's work and Milbank's interpretation of it. Davis maintains that Blondel's attempt to escape from a secular framework to an overtly supernatural context amounts to a return to "pre-modern modes of thought."[30] Blondel overcomes the opposition between autonomy and heteronomy simply by invoking this supernatural. By surrendering themselves to God, or, as Milbank phrases it, by associating "all action with self-immolation and sacrifice," human beings achieve their autonomy. [31] This can imply, however, a position that advocates that human beings ought to accept their fate, and submit to the divine order of the world. Davis concludes, therefore, that in Blondel's theology,

---

25. Ibid., ch. 8, especially 206–8 and 221–24.
26. Ibid., 219.
27. Ibid., 210–11.
28. Ibid., 214.
29. Ibid.
30. Charles Davis, *Religion and the Making of Society: Essay in Social Theology*, Cambridge Studies in Ideology and Religion (Cambridge: Cambridge University Press, 1994) 6.
31. Milbank, *Theology and Social Theory*, 214.

as well as in that of Milbank, "we are unable to move of ourselves towards our own destiny."[32]

Milbank's understanding of practice, intended to open up an alternative form of action that respects difference, results in a conservative social theory that risks validating the *status quo*. The limitations of this interpretation of Blondel are heightened when Milbank insists that the logic of action only truly comes to the fore when combined with allegiance to a particular series of acts—those which belong to Christianity.[33] The subjectivity Milbank describes is one that is restrictive and confining. His understanding of narrative as a "form of life" forecloses on self-critique, as it treats the Christian tradition as a monolithic entity with clear and precise boundaries, which ought not to be called into question by individuals who have failed to be properly "trained" through immersion in the tradition.

It is noteworthy that the recurring themes of Milbank's description of subjectivity are sacrifice and self-emptying. To act is to renounce living for oneself, for self-assertion and preservation, he suggests, are the roots of secular reason and violence. Against the idea of an autonomous, self-critical subject, Milbank maintains that "every identity is repetition."[34] While he employs Blondel's work to emphasize the results of the subject's action, here Milbank offers a Kierkegaardian reading of the origins of this action. The shift from rest to motion, from possibility to act, does not result from logical deliberation or consistent self-assertion. Instead, such shifts "have the character of positive 'leaps' which display no logic outside of their own occurrence." One attempts "to *repeat* precisely, but in different circumstances, and so not *identically*, the things we have performed in the past."[35] The "ruination of reason" that results from "Cartesian/Kantian" thought and from the Greek polytheistic *mythos*, is transformed by Christianity through a repetition of a different *logos*, expressed in the identity of Christ.[36]

According to Milbank, Kierkegaard's concept of inwardness shows that "the subject itself is not the locus of interiority, but is rather 'within' a perpetual transition that it can never survey in a theoretical manner from without."[37] Subjectivity and truth, therefore, are only resolved by

32. Davis, *Religion and the Making of Society*, 7–9.
33. Milbank, *Theology and Social Theory*, 216.
34. Milbank, "The Sublime in Kierkegaard," in *Post-Secular Philosophy*, ed. Phillip Blond (London: Routledge, 1998) 132.
35. Milbank, *Theology and Social Theory*, 211.
36. Milbank, "The Sublime in Kierkegaard," 139.
37. Ibid., 136.

Part One—Historical and Methodological Issues

"an unfounded decision." This aspect of Milbank's argument continues to problematize his notion of subjectivity. Theodor Adorno's conclusions about Kierkegaard's understanding of subjectivity can be said to apply here to Milbank: while seeking to make consciousness "purify itself of the guilt it acquired in having supposed itself autonomous," subjectivity is effectively sacrificed.[38] Adorno argues that in Kierkegaard's thought, the external world is "neither part of the subject nor independent of it. Rather, this world is omitted. It supplies the subject with the mere 'occasion' for the deed, with mere resistance to the act of faith."[39] The specific content of any historical moment is, in the final analysis, insignificant to Milbank. What matters is that one "leap" into the fold of the proper narrative, which itself will steer the subject through the proper course of actions. Milbank undermines the concreteness he seeks by transforming human action and subjectivity into abstract categories.

The following remarks by Jürgen Habermas, referring to the thought of Giambattista Vico, could be taken as a criticism of Milbank's conception of practice and subjectivity:

> Humanity is recognized as the author of history, yet it lacks the qualities which would make it history's subject: it is not all-powerful and provident; men [sic] make their history, yet they do not make it with consciousness.[40]

It is noteworthy that in his two-volume study, *The Religious Dimension in the Thought of Giambattista Vico*, Milbank portrays Vico as a philosopher whose thought inaugurated the kind of "counter-modernity" he seeks.[41] Vico's principle "*verum et factum convertuntum*," Milbank argues, is another example of the realization that knowledge is "of the made," involving unplanned social outcomes. Motive, will and plan are not prior to action, and, therefore, it is not individual choice, but a general social narrative, which forms identity and structures society.[42] Vico wrote:

> But in the night of thick darkness enveloping the earliest antiquity, so remote from ourselves, there shines the eternal and never

38. Theodor W. Adorno, *Kierkegaard: Construction of the Aesthetic*, trans. Robert Hullot-Kentor (Minneapolis: University of Minnesota Press, 1989) 107.

39. Ibid., 29.

40. Jürgen Habermas, *Theory and Practice*, trans. John Viertel (London: Heinemann, 1974) 244.

41. Milbank, *Theology and Social Theory*, 4.

42. Ibid., 41.

failing light of a truth beyond all question: that the world of civil society has certainly been made by men, and that its principles are therefore to be found within the modifications of our own human mind.[43]

For Milbank, this vision implies that action "always goes beyond philosophy." It anticipates a "sociology of the supernatural," in which the presence of grace is recognized in the historical process, and thus can be interpreted "without the need to transcend the bounds of mere narration." Rather than taking Vico's *factum* (the made) back into the rational subject (which, says Milbank, is what Hegel does), one must remain with what is in excess of the human product.[44] By retaining this "poetic dimension" of existence—which Milbank claims is precisely what Cartesian foundationalism rejects—both scepticism and dogmatism are avoided, as is a world subordinated to human control. Like Blondel, Vico restores "the transcendality of *factum*."[45]

Vico's understanding of *verum et factum* has had considerable influence on the traditions of social theory that influenced the development of liberation theology. Karl Marx's footnote in volume one of *Capital*[46] has led many scholars to speculate on Vico's influence on the Marxist tradition.[47] There is at least some validity to the claim that Vico anticipated the notion of reification which became central to Georg Lukács' philosophy.[48] Later Marxian critics like Max Horkheimer, however, developed misgivings that the *verum-factum* principle could apply to the present and future, as well as to analyses of the past. Some scholars had assumed that a new science of history would emerge once the social world was constituted through human rational action, and they translated Vico's vision of a divine provi-

---

43. Giambattista Vico, *The New Science of Giambattista Vico*, 3rd ed. [1744], trans. Thomas Goddard Bergin and Max Harold Fisch (Ithaca, NY: Cornell University Press, 1968), 96.

44. Milbank, *Theology and Social Theory*, 225.

45. John Milbank, *The Religious Dimension in the Thought of Giambattista Vico*, vol. 1 (Lewiston, NY: Mellen, 1991) 327–28.

46. Karl Marx, *Capital*, vol. 1, trans. Ben Fowkes (London: Penguin, 1976) 493. The relevant passage of the footnote reads, "as Vico says, human history differs from natural history in that we have made the former, but not the latter."

47. See Giorgio Tagliacozzo, ed., *Vico and Marx: Affinities and Contrasts* (Atlantic Highlands, NJ: Humanities, 1983).

48. Martin Jay, "Vico and Western Marxism," in *Vico: Past and Present*, ed. Giorgio Tagliacozzo (Atlantic Highlands, NJ: Humanities, 1981) 199–200.

dence working behind human action into scientific laws and predictions of the future course of history.[49]

Horkheimer's colleague Adorno argues forcefully against this tendency, insisting that no collective subject (Lukács' proletariat) exists to forge history in this way: "To this day history lacks any total subject, however construable. Its substrate is the functional connection of real individual subjects." He continues by quoting from Marx's *The Holy Family*: "it is not 'history' that uses man as a means to pursue its ends, as if it were a person apart. History is nothing but the activity of man [sic] pursuing his ends."[50] As for deriving meaning through creative action, whose results are then recognized and made sense of, Adorno maintains, "the concept of sense involves an objectivity beyond all 'making': a sense that is 'made' is already fictitious. It duplicates the subject, however collective, and defrauds it of what it seemingly granted."[51] In other words, the failure to distinguish clearly between intended and unintended results of human action, which is blurred by Milbank's idea of the "poetic-historical dimension" of practice,[52] results in a vague theological doctrine of providence, while undermining the agency of the human subject.

This problem recalls the quotation from Habermas cited above. Habermas highlights Adorno's concern by accusing Vico of stretching "providence as though it were a net under the trapeze of history."[53] Milbank's interpretation intends to avoid such a charge, insisting that providence in Vico's work does not function in history like an "immanentist guarantee."[54] He interprets Vico's concept of providence through an idea of the universal and transcendental status of language. The "hand of providence" refers to the constraints of the "linguistic products" which bind human beings together. He suggests that this immanent process also requires a metaphysical grounding, as it involves a teleological pressure that pushes "towards the

---

49. Ibid., 203–4. For an example of Horkheimer's early enthusiasm for Vico's thought, see his "Beginnings of the Bourgeois Philosophy of History," in *Between Philosophy and Social Science*, trans. G. Frederic Hunter et al. (Cambridge, MA: MIT Press, 1995) 313–88.

50. Theodor W. Adorno, *Negative Dialectics*, trans. E. B. Ashton (New York: Continuum, 1973) 304.

51. Ibid., 376.

52. Milbank, *The Religious Dimension*, 1:328.

53. Habermas, *Theory and Practice*, 244.

54. Milbank, *The Religious Dimension*, 1:332–33.

true, good and beautiful."[55] The inclusion of human projection and activity into this conception, Milbank argues, avoids the charge that human subjectivity is defrauded.

This discussion of Vico's idea of providence helps illuminate Milbank's understanding of narrative and how he conceives of the way in which it structures human thought and action. Human society, he argues, is constrained and influenced by social processes, which encourage unconscious and regular patterns of behavior. "The real question," he continues, "is that of the *quality* of the 'unconscious' processes."[56] The importance of practice for Milbank, then, is not the Western Marxist concept of the unity of theory and practice, nor is it liberation theology's idea that *praxis* on behalf of the poor reveals the truth. "Supernatural practice," he argues, is founded in "theological theory." There is "no priority of practice, but instead a single, seamless, theory/practice which has one privileged canonical moment." Theology as "metanarrative realism" legislates how one is to act.[57] Here is the "net" Habermas identifies in Vico's thought. Obey the Christian narrative, Milbank proclaims, and its truth shall make you free.

Not only does this vision de-emphasize the agency of human subjects by dubbing the "orthodox" Christian narrative (which remains undefined by Milbank) as the source of true action, but it also contradicts the very line of argument Milbank has employed up to this point in order to claim the primacy of narrative and the folly of social theory. Having completed a "deconstruction" of secular reason by using postmodern theory to assert the supremacy of "local narratives," Milbank then turns on the postmodern theorists and insists that one particular local narrative is superior to all others. The practical effect of this theoretical move is significant: having challenged an understanding of human subjectivity which values individual expression and self-assertion, Milbank argues for the superiority of one specific tradition—his own understanding of Christianity—and treats those formed by traditions other than this as inferior.

---

55. Ibid., 2:253–54.
56. Milbank, *Theology and Social Theory*, 272.
57. Ibid., 251.

Part One—Historical and Methodological Issues

The End of Enlightenment Yields the End of Dialogue

Milbank argues throughout *Theology and Social Theory* that, while Christianity might be described as an unfounded mythological narrative, "all other myths, or narrative traditions, affirm or barely conceal an original primordial violence."[58] From Plato onwards, he suggests, anything non-Christian in Western culture is based on an ontology of violence. Christianity, he argues, appears "even objectively—as not just different, but as *the* difference from all other cultural systems."[59] The unique pattern of Christian action, in which virtue becomes "charity," is such that he believes he can say, "*only* Christianity, once it has arrived, really appears ethical at all."[60] Such a claim is not an "appendage" to the faith; it belongs "to its very essence." Thus, Christian theology may confidently maintain that "other religions and social groupings, however virtuous-seeming, were finally on the path of damnation."[61]

The tone of such an assertion in a modern pluralistic context is startling. Milbank quickly discards his "postmodern" rhetoric once he begins to speak directly about Christianity; now it is objectively superior to other local narratives. Dialogue between religions, Milbank argues, or any appreciation of religious pluralism, are inherently corrupt. He accuses pluralism of being disrespectful of the difference of other traditions because it assumes a commonly recognized subject—"religion" as a genus—which obscures the "truth of difference."[62] He professes that a position which is truly respectful of difference and otherness, and also of peace and justice, "can only, in fact, be a Christian" position.[63] At this point, the thrust of Milbank's theology becomes explicit. His assertion that "theology need only embrace as absolute its own narrative,"[64] along with a disdain for dialogue with other traditions that challenge or criticize the authority of this absoluteness, does

---

58. Ibid., 262.
59. Ibid., 381 (emphasis original).
60. Ibid., 362 (emphasis original).
61. Ibid., 389–90.
62. Milbank, "The End of Dialogue," in *Christian Uniqueness Reconsidered: The Myth of a Pluralistic Theology of Religions*, ed. Gavin D'Costa, Faith Meets Faith Series (Maryknoll, NY: Orbis, 1990) 175–77.
63. Ibid., 176.
64. Milbank, *Theology and Social Theory*, 268.

not merely represent a "half-turn back to pre-modernity;"[65] Milbank is intending to shift modern theology into full reverse.

This adoption of a pre-modern position includes the elevation of the Church as an absolute authority. Only the Church, with its unique social perspective, provides the "key to all human performance."[66] Milbank describes membership in the *ecclesia* in the following manner:

> To be a part of the Church [insofar as it really *is* the Church] is to have the moral luck to belong to the society which overcomes moral luck. For the Church exists as a "practice of perfection," as the working of charity, which ceaselessly tries to remove the obstacles in the way of people becoming perfect.[67]

It is a revealing passage. The brackets attempt to mask an enormous problem with Milbank's ecclesiology. He admits that churches often fail to function like they should, so he is forced to parachute the *real* "Church" into his argument from outside history. This "post-political theology" is, therefore, based on an idealist a-historical ecclesiology. In Milbank's deployment, the eschatological nature of the theological distinction between the "invisible" and the "visible" church is eroded, as his ecclesiology proceeds as if the church's fullness is currently actualised. But in Augustine's great work, the *Civitas Dei*, which Milbank describes as a "nomad city,"[68] is really no city at all. Neither does Augustine equate the "City of God" with the boundaries of the historical church. Gillian Rose suggests that Milbank offers "Christian New Jerusalem for old Athens." He effectively destroys the idea of a city because "its task of salvation deprives it of site; while its inclusive appeal deprives it of limit or boundary."[69] Milbank presents an abstract vision of an opposition between two false alternatives: a pure heavenly Church that abides in the peaceful co-existence of difference found within the Trinity, or the chaotic violence and nihilism of everything outside of the Christian metanarrative.

A further problem raised by the above passage has to do with what one is to make of the statement concerning the possession of the "moral luck" to be part of Christian culture. Through the cracks of Milbank's

65. Milbank, "Postmodern Critical Augustinianism," *Modern Theology* 7 (1991) 225.
66. Milbank, *Theology and Social Theory*, 230.
67. Ibid., 231 (emphasis added).
68. Ibid., 392.
69. Gillian Rose, *The Broken Middle: Out of Our Ancient Society* (Oxford: Blackwell, 1992) 281.

PART ONE—Historical and Methodological Issues

argument one can glimpse an admission that those not born into a Christian environment might find it difficult to accept its claim to absoluteness. He argues that "only because one first experiences the 'shape' of incarnation, of atonement," can one perceive society and absolute reality correctly.[70] Furthermore, "God has first to teach us, just as ethics must first be learned from the virtuous."[71] Such rhetoric is all too familiar to those aboriginal children in Canada who were interned in church-run "residential schools" for "their own good."[72]

Despite maintaining that Christianity denies the necessity of sovereign rule and violence, Milbank's tone is consistently paternalistic towards those outside the boundaries of his vision of the Church. Speaking against liberation theology's desire to listen to the voices of the oppressed, he suggests:

> Dialogue . . . is not relevant to the poor and dispossessed, because justice toward them is not primarily a matter of listening to them, but constructing *for them* and with them the circumstances in which they can join in many conversations.[73]

In such view, what is important is not valuing the freedom of others, nor is it respecting their difference and self-determination. What Milbank's post-political theology stresses is conforming to *the* correct belief system and *the* authentic mode of practice. Those already in the Church may then construct for others the correct model of living, and tell them the correct

---

70. Milbank, *Theology and Social Theory*, 217.

71. Ibid., 362.

72. From 1920 until the early 1970s, "residential schools" were set up in Canada by the Department of Indian Affairs to force indigenous children to leave their families and abandon their traditional language and culture. The intent of these measures, states a 1920 summary, "is to continue until there is not a single Indian in Canada that has not been absorbed into the body politic, and there is no Indian question"; see Geoffrey York, *The Dispossessed: Life and Death in Native Canada* (Toronto: Little, Brown, 1989) 23. Milbank might mourn the violence such acts involved, but his position towards non-Christians is not far removed from such rhetoric. In an essay that discusses Milbank, Stanley Hauerwas concludes that "Christians should try to convert Native Americans, but since I am not living among Native Americans, *I have little idea what that means.* . . . What I do, of course, challenge is the assumption that conversion has primarily to do with an individual's self-understanding rather than his *being put in the context* of a different community with a different set of practices," Hauerwas, *Wilderness Wanderings* (Boulder, CO: Westview, 1997) 194 (emphasis added). It is regrettable that someone who holds such a view does so without concerning himself with what conversion might mean to a "Native American."

73. Milbank, "The End of Dialogue," 183 (emphasis added).

stories to narrate. Thus, although forced conversion is not advocated, the tone and implications of Milbank's position are themselves violent. Rather than engage in dialogue, Christians should "subvert other discourses" and regard the other with "suspicion." At least in this article his intention is blunt and direct: "I do not pretend that this proposal means anything other than continuing the work of conversion."[74]

The basis of Milbank's claim that "Christianity denies ontological necessity to sovereign rule" is simply the idea that if everyone submitted'to "orthodox" Christian doctrine, problems of social cohesion and conflicts between worldviews would be eliminated.[75] This simplistic, not to mention unrealistic, idea is also a-historical; it fails to mention the historical splits between various churches, along with the violent behavior of many of their members. The social order Milbank describes is, as Gillian Rose argues, one without any institutions, which would "represent the middle, broken between morality and legality, autonomy and heteronomy, cognition and norm, activity and passivity."[76] The "harmony" and "charity" of his "holy city" are invoked, without offering any place for conflicts to be mediated and resolved. If there can be no mediation, or dialectical movement, one is left helpless in the face of the totalizing domination of the absolute authority of the Church.[77] This, says Rose, "is to encounter not pure freedom but pure power and to become its perfect victim."[78]

During the course of his harsh criticism of liberation theology, Milbank offers an intriguing aside: "Not without distress do I realize that some of my conclusions here coincide with those of reactionaries in the Vatican."[79] One wishes that this distress resulted in deeper reflection on the challenges facing particular human beings in Latin America at that time. One also wonders what specifically it was about his own position's resemblance to the Vatican's persecution of liberation theologians that distressed him so. Perhaps Milbank's attempt to wash his hands of the Enlightenment has not

---

74. Ibid., 190.

75. Milbank, *Theology and Social Theory*, 416–17.

76. Rose, *The Broken Middle*, 284–85.

77. For another critique of the political implications Milbank's position, from the perspective of liberal democracy, see Christopher J. Insole, "Against Radical Orthodoxy: The Dangers of Overcoming Political Liberalism," *Modern Theology* 20 (2004) 213–41.

78. Milbank, *Theology and Social Theory*, 287.

79. Ibid., 208.

been as thoroughly successful as his rhetoric implies? Might this brief admission be his version of Lady Macbeth's "Out damned spot"?

For all of the emphasis in contemporary theology on the "tradition-based" nature of human reasoning, one of the primary insights of liberation theology remains as valid now as it was when Gutiérrez first published *Theology of Liberation* in the 1960s. This is the recognition that how one understands a slogan such as that advocated by Hauerwas—Christianity is "a life that freely suffers"—depends greatly upon the social context in which it is uttered and interpreted. Likewise is it the case with Milbank's declaration that "theology need only embrace as absolute its own narrative." Rather than adopt the self-enclosed defense strategies that these theologians advocate, there are clear grounds to conclude that contemporary theology's attempt to defend itself against corruption by human arrogance and misunderstanding is bolstered, not hindered, by a healthy respect for the intellectual and political traditions of the Enlightenment, which Milbank is too readily prepared to jettison. The argument here is not that the traditions of the Enlightenment offer something "essential" that Christianity inherently lacks; rather, the point is simply to highlight the fact that the very attitude that Christians lack nothing—and can thus learn nothing from those outside of their own comfortable worldview—is a sign of neither orthodoxy or faithfulness. Too many tragic examples of the consequences of such arrogance abound in the history of the Christian churches. Rather than wash their hands of the Enlightenment, then, may Christians find more faithful orientation in the call to wash the feet of the poor and downtrodden in our midst.

5

Discerning Movements of the Spirit

The World Social Forum and the Work of Theology

JANET CONWAY

IN CONSIDERING "THEOLOGY AND the crisis of engagement," I want to pick up a central thread woven throughout Lee Cormie's scholarship, that of emancipatory social movements and, more recently, their astonishing convergence in the anti-globalization movement and the World Social Forum. In a series of essays on globalization, ethics, history, and christology, the World Social Forum has featured as a prominent reference for reading the signs of the times and for theological reflection. In this chapter, I explore Cormie's claims about the World Social Forum and what they imply about the crisis of engagement and ways forward for critically engaged theology that is, in his own words, "beyond liberation."

Cormie's recent work, I contend, is less an argument about engagement with the social sciences than it is about grappling with a rapidly changing social world and, in fact, myriad crises in the paradigm of scientific knowledge both to apprehend what is underway and to provide critical leverage with which to act ethically. As human beings face unprecedented threats to survival, knowledge of the social world has never been more important. Yet modern science is also the source of human beings' vastly expanded capacities to act on the world, to increasingly alter the very nature of the created order, and to usher in disasters on a wholly new scale—as he puts it: "epochal transitions associated with developments in science, modes of knowledge production and new technologies."[1] In this context, the challenge to theology is to engage, not abstractly with the social sciences, but foremost with social movements struggling for another possible world, and secondly, with modes of social-scientific knowing that can help theology discern the presence and meaning of these movements of the spirit in the current historical moment. Ultimately however, he argues, that in the midst of these epochal transitions, "our responses involve leaps of faith which contribute to tipping the balance among divergent possible futures."[2]

I am a scholar of social movements, indebted to the Christian tradition for my own ethical and political formation but writing more in social-scientific than theological modes. I share with Cormie his sense of the centrality of social movements in struggles over the future and his appreciation of the significance of the World Social Forum as a world-historic development which merits the attention of theologians and social scientists alike. With him, I have been tracking developments there with keen interest.

In what follows, drawing on several of his recent essays, I situate the World Social Forum in Cormie's work on "movements of the spirit." I want to argue further that the World Social Forum is a profoundly faith-filled undertaking in which the "new voices" are everywhere apparent and their specifically Brazilian ecclesial and theological expressions have been and continue to be deeply influential. However, Cormie's work troubles the liberationist discourses that prevail at and about the World Social Forum. He raises profound questions about the apocalyptic character of the present, consideration of which has remained largely outside the liberationist traditions, both theological and political. I explore his work for implications of this critique and return to consider the World Social Forum through one of the theological pathways he proposes.

---

1. Lee Cormie, "Movements of the Spirit in History," in *Talitha Cum! The Grace of Solidarity in a Globalized World*, ed. Mario Di Giglio-Bellemare and Gabriella Miranda Garcia (Geneva: World Student Christian Federation, 2004) 238–39.

2. Lee Cormie, "Another History Is Possible: Christologies from Below," *Toronto Journal of Theology* Supplement 1 (2008) 73.

The "New Voices": Social Movements and the World Social Forum

For decades, Cormie has been preoccupied with the "new voices" of the social movements of the 1960s and 70s: those for Third World liberation, feminism, civil rights, and black power, indigenous rights, peace, and ecology, and with chronicling the ever-expanding eruptions of "newer" ones: for sexual diversity and for rights of people with disabilities, for example. His work has been marked by an insistence on the centrality of recognizing "social movements as primary actors/forces in shaping the social world, and as primary sites of our encounters with the Divine in history."[3] In the churches, an array of liberation and contextual theologies testified to the presence of these new voices within the Christian tradition and theological recognition of their importance more generally.[4] He has argued consistently that, for the churches, enacting the hermeneutical privilege of the marginalized means paying scholarly and political attention to the movements that, however imperfectly or problematically, testify to injustice and express the perspectives and aspirations of those who are suffering.

Despite their great and expanding diversity in terms of the injustices to which they pointed, the life experiences and world regions from which they sprung, liberation theologies have been characterized by their attention to suffering, marginalized, and voiceless populations and their insistence on the preferential option for the poor and oppressed as at the heart of biblical faith. In Cormie's work, the new voices are "movements of the Spirit" and in the present conjuncture, one of the signs of the times is their growing convergence and solidarity as seen in processes like the anti-globalization movement and the World Social Forum. The World Social Forum represents one of the major poles in debates about "globalization," he argues, and therefore should be a central point of reference for churches in their own grappling with what is underway in the world today.[5]

The World Social Forum was initiated by a coalition of Brazilian organizations to convene groups and movements opposed to neoliberal globalization from around the world at the height of the anti-globalization mobilizations. The idea was to create a gathering, an open space, in which

---

3. Cormie, "Movements of the Spirit in History," 238.
4. Cormie, "Another History Is Possible," 74–75.
5. Lee Cormie, "Ethics of Globalization," paper presented at the Society of Christian Ethics annual meeting, Pittsburgh, 2003.

these groups would self-organize, mounting activities for one another in order to communicate their struggles, to make visible alternatives to neoliberalism already emergent in their practices and ways of life, and to build broad political convergence across difference. Since its origins in 2001 in Porto Alegre, Brazil, the World Social Forum has grown exponentially so that it now regularly attracts over 100,000 people in its world-scale gatherings and many more tens of thousands through regional and local fora taking place on every continent around the world.

After three years in Porto Alegre, Brazil, the World Social Forum moved to Mumbai, India in 2004 and in 2007, to Nairobi, Kenya. Brazil remains the homeplace of the World Social Forum, but there is a widespread commitment to moving the world event geographically to other sites in the global South. This is a strategy for expanding and deepening the Forum's inter-continental and cross-cultural character. Each World Social Forum event/process is "placed" but transnational, localized but characterized by an expanding globality. The civil society entities present at the World Social Forum vary considerably depending on the location of the events but are in every case amazingly diverse in their demographic make-up, organizational forms, cultural expressions, geographic roots, and reach, strategies, tactics, and discourses.

There are antecedents to the World Social Forum—in the UN conferences and parallel NGO fora of the 1990s, in the *encuentros* of the Zapatistas of the late 1990s, in the mass anti-globalization demonstrations—but the expanding array of forces now regularly convened in one space by the World Social Forum is unprecedented. This is true in terms of the diversity of groups, movements, modes, issues, and constituencies represented, the expanding geographic and cross-cultural reach, the sheer numbers of participants, and in the accessibility of the Forum and the program to any group anywhere who can mobilize the resources to participate. Its newness furthermore lies in the expanding scope of its globality, its multi-scale character in incorporating activists from the most localized to the transnational, and its highly participatory, horizontalist, and autonomist culture of organizing.

Although its innovativeness is widely recognized, there are multiple origin stories about the World Social Forum that claim various historical legacies. Some posit the continuity of the anti-globalization movement with 500 years of indigenous resistance to colonialism in the Americas.[6] Oth-

---

6. Robin Broad, and Zahara Heckscher, "Before Seattle: The Historical Roots of the

ers point to the more than two centuries of struggle by popular movements for democracy against absolutism and almost that long against capitalism for socialism. Arising in Europe, diffusing world-wide, these "anti-systemic movements" appeared in the rise of the new left in the 1960s and 70s before their most recent expression in the anti-globalization eruptions at the end of the last century.[7] The political centrality of the "global South" within the World Social Forum testifies to continuity with the tradition of Bandung and the last century's anti-colonial movements for national liberation in Asia, Africa and the middle East, and aspirations for third world socialism.[8]

In the context of Latin America, the lineages of the World Social Forum include decades of struggle against military dictatorship and U.S. intervention, both overt and covert, in the region. In Brazil specifically, as the birth place of the World Social Forum, founders cut their teeth in these struggles and related ones for human rights, labor, and land rights, and the rights of the poor in one of the most economically polarized societies on the planet. Also, significantly, key leaders like Joao Pedro Stedile of the Movimento Sem Terra (the Landless Movement) and Francisco Whitaker, founder and *eminence grise* of the World Social Forum, its chief apologist and political philosopher, testify to their political formation in the progressive Catholic church as early as the 1950s, its pastoral initiatives, lay organizations, and later in what came to be known as liberation theology.[9]

This is especially apparent in the writings of Francisco Whitaker. Whitaker represents the CBJP, *Comissão Brasileira de Justiça e Paz* or Brazilian Commission for Justice and Peace, a lay organization linked to the National Conference of Brazilian Bishops. It has extensive links to church-based popular movements and human rights groups throughout Brazil and brought its progressive Christian international connections and its

---

Current Movement against Corporate-Led Globalisation," *Third World Quarterly* 24 (2003) 713–28.

7. Immanuel Wallerstein, "The Dilemmas of Open Space: The Future of the WSF," *International Social Science Journal* 182 (2004) 629–37.

8. Bret Benjamin, *Invested Interests: Capital, Culture and the World Bank* (Minneapolis: University of Minnesota Press, 2007).

9. Joao Pedro Stedile, "Landless Battalions: The Sem Terra Movement of Brazil," *New Left Review* 15 (2002) 77–104; Chico Whitaker, "From Vatican II to the World Social Forum," *ACMICA: Australian Catholic Movement for Intellectual and Cultural Affairs*, May 2005; www.acmica.org/pub_gigacz-chico.html. See also Sonia E. Alvarez, "Globalized Localisms: The Travels and Translations of the World Social Forum Process," paper presented at the Cultural Difference and Democracy Interdisciplinary Worksop, Ohio State University, 2007.

liberation theology roots to the founding of the WSF.[10] For him, the World Social Forum signals the return of utopia. In the wake of the collapse of socialism and triumphalist claims of the "end of history" and "there is no alternative" to neoliberal capitalist globalization, the success of the Forum attests to a widespread hope and faith that another world is possible. "The World Social Forum has set in motion a process of thinking about what another world would be like if it were centered on human needs and not on the logic of money."[11]

The World Social Forum is open to any group anywhere in the world who professes opposition to neoliberalism, who is not a political party, and who is not engaged in armed struggle. The World Social Forum is an autonomous space in that it is non-governmental, non-party, and non-confessional. The Forum is a space to unlearn the practices of the twentieth-century left, its hierarchies, violence and authoritarianism, and to learn how to resolve conflicts non-violently, to dialogue with difference, to learn how to live with diversity, and to recognize multiple paths for changing the world. Closely related to this commitment is the World Social Forum's embrace of pluralism and diversity and its stated opposition to *pensamientos unicos*, that is, forms of thought which are totalizing and which suppress other possible ways of thinking, of which neoliberalism is the paradigmatic example.

These discourses of the World Social Forum, the centrality of non-violence and the embrace of pluralism, are deeply rooted both in the struggles against dictatorship and in a critique of the Latin American left, and a resulting profound commitment to democracy and participation—not primarily in the putatively representative institutions of the liberal nation state, but rather in the groups and movements of globalizing civil society. The Forum, like the anti-globalization movement, is expressive of the crisis of representative democracy, a loss of faith in the state and in political parties. In both is a concomitant affirmation of the horizontalism of network politics, a recuperation of the autonomist and anti-authoritarian strands of the new left, and a belief in prefigurative politics, or an insistence on the consistent relation between means and ends. Furthermore, in Whitaker's writings and reflective of a deep-seated ethic in the anti-globalization movement especially among youth, there is an emphasis on personal

---

10. Alvarez, "Globalized Localisms," 7.

11. Chico Whitaker, *A New Way of Changing the World* (Nairobi: World Council of Churches, 2007) 169.

commitment, ethical consistency, and the need to enact in practice the relations one wishes to see prevail in the world.[12]

> [O]ver and beyond simply contesting and resisting and taking power, changing the world requires a range of diversified political action. . . . [S]uch action must develop in societies from the inside outwards and from the bottom up, with the participation and creativity of all their members on the basis of their concrete needs; such changes are already underway, and there is no need to wait for complete, ideal models of society to be proposed or imposed form the top down; and no change will be lasting unless it is accompanied by internal change, from the inside out, in each member of society.[13]

Central to the functioning of the World Social Forum to date has been the understanding that it is not a deliberative process. The World Social Forum is not conceived of as a unitary entity; no one can therefore "represent" or "speak for" the Forum. This is continually contentious within the World Social Forum but it has continued to be central to its character and functioning. The International Council deliberates over operationalizing the World Social Forum, and the participating groups and organizations use the occasion of Forum events to deliberate about their campaigns; the World Social Forum as a whole, however, does not deliberate, make decisions, or embark on common actions.[14]

The Brazilian architects of the World Social Forum vigorously defend the Forum as a non-deliberative space for free association over against those who want to turn the Forum into a more unified organization for specific political ends.[15] They argue that the horizontal networking of the

12. For discussion of this ethic in the anti-globalization youth movements, see Janet Conway and Daniel Morrison, "A New Political Generation? New Forms of Youth Engagement in Canada and Beyond," in *Power and Resistance: Critical Thinking About Canadian Social Issues*, ed. Wayne Antony and Les Samuelson; Halifax: Fernwood, 2007) 243–64. See especially Whitaker, *A New Way of Changing the World*, 186–93.

13. Whitaker, *A New Way of Changing the World*, 17.

14. It is critical to maintain a distinction between the World Social Forum and its governing and organizing bodies, the key ones being its International Council (IC) and International Secretariat. While IC deliberations are an important pole in shaping the world-scale World Social Forum process, the proliferation, dynamism, geographic dispersion and multiculturalism of Forum processes continually overwhelm the IC and any occasional attempts to control and or represent the World Social Forum.

15. For two sides of this space vs. movement debate, see Chico Whitaker, "The WSF as Open Space," in *World Social Forum: Challenging Empires*, ed. Jai Sen et al. (New Dehli:

World Social Forum is helping foster a new political culture premised on mutual recognition, learning, co-responsibility, and co-operation across difference. They see the praxis of the Forum as fostering the emergence of a new political actor, that of "planetary civil society," imbued with a new political culture. It is society that will change the world, not the Forum itself, but the Forum is singular in the functions it has assumed.[16] The most contentious and enduring debate about the World Social Forum, including among its proponents, has to do with this assertion that it is a "space" to serve, incubate, and advance progressive movements, but is not itself a movement.

Whitaker and other Brazilian founders also insist that the World Social Forum is not a space of power, but one of consensual association, self-management and horizontal exchange. The fact that the Forum is not an entity in itself, does not issue statements, take positions, or embark on actions, protects it and its participants from being consumed by internal struggles for hegemony. Its non-deliberative character frees its participating groups to encounter one another, to listen and to learn, and to be transformed in ways they could not be otherwise. In this view, the Forum's central function is one of cultural transformation of the movements and groups of civil society that respond to its summons.

In my view, the World Social Forum, as a political form and organizing methodology, has generated unprecedented creativity and collaboration among disparate actors in major world regions. The limits of this undertaking are not yet in sight and it is a grand experiment which needs to be respected, nurtured, and safeguarded. In Whitaker's words, the World Social Forum has issued a powerfully compelling summons to which hundreds of thousands of people and thousands of organizations have responded. The Forum's embrace of pluralism and diversity is, in my view, *post-liberal* in its clear condemnation of neoliberal capitalism and the inequalities and oppression it has entrenched. In placing a premium on practice, in opposing the hegemony of "any single way of thinking," in cultivating an ethic of solidarity among suffering and struggling people, their organizations and movements, and in asserting its critical positionality in the Global South, the World Social Forum's praxis of pluralism is something new, both post-Marxist and post-liberal, the broader implications of which have hardly

---

Viveka Foundation, 2004) 111–21; and Teivo Teivainen, "The WSF: Arena or Actor," in *World Social Forum: Challenging Empires*, 122–29.

16. Whitaker, *A New Way of Changing the World*, 17–18.

been hinted at. In its anti-neoliberal positionality and its central concern for the victims of the Washington Consensus, the World Social Forum also embodies a thorough-going, if unstated, preferential option for the poor.

To return to a claim made above, the World Social Forum is a deeply faith-filled undertaking, profoundly influenced by the legacies of Latin American liberation theology on the emancipatory movements of the region. It is also a site where the changing contours and plural futures of liberation theologies are being mapped and debated, especially through the World Forum on Theology and Liberation, which has regularly used the occasion of the World Social Forum to meet.[17] Less explicitly confessional but, in my view, permeated by liberationist Christianity, Whitaker's writings testify to the leap of faith taken by the organizers and to which all who participate in the World Social Forum are invited. Whatever their religious or political traditions, all involved in the process are invited to believe in the power of ordinary people acting as political subjects in civil society, in their capacities for self-management and for non-oppressive social relations, in their affirmation of diversity, in their desire to organize democratically, in their embrace of non-violence, and their shared conviction that "another world is not only possible, she is on her way. And, on a quiet day, [we] can hear her breathing."[18]

END TIMES AND NEW BEGINNINGS

For Lee Cormie and for many others, the World Social Forum represents "the good news of convergence among popular movements"[19] at a time of epochal transition in human history. He, along with Whitaker, posits the appearance of an emergent planetary civilization, made possible for the first time through revolutions in communication and transportation. Sharing a deep critique of neoliberalism and neoimperialism alongside an abiding hope and joy in the World Social Forum and its potentialities, Cormie

---

17. Jim Hodgson, "Fifth World Social Forum Convenes: WSF Continues to Stimulate Theological Thinking and International Solidarity," *Catholic New Times*, 6 (2005), http://findarticles.com/p/articles/mi_moMKY/is_4_29/ai_n13628938/print; Stefan Silber, "Complex and Alive: Recent Developments in the Theology of Liberation," *Herder-Korrespondenz*, October 2006, www.con-spiration.de/texte/english/2006/liberation-e.html.

18. Arundhati Roy, Speech at the Closing of the 2003 World Social Forum, Porto Alegre, Brazil.

19. Cormie, "Movements of the Spirit in History," 239.

however, is more haunted by the apocalyptic character of the present than most discourses of the World Social Forum allow. This is as true of the liberationist theological discourses as of the emancipatory discourses of modernity that prevail there.[20]

Cormie is especially acutely aware of the ambiguous power of modern science and the creation of new powers for both good and evil that remain outside the purview, indeed beyond the range of vision, of most critical political theories and practices of the present. These threats growing alongside the burgeoning movements for global justice create an "inescapable dialectic of fear and hope."[21] In this context, the potential contributions of biblical studies, theology, christology, and ethics has never been greater. He writes: "the alternative (to the marginalization of theology and ethics in public discourse), increasingly evident in liberationist and post-colonial biblical studies, is to probe the bible and Christian traditions for insights into how our forebears in faith responded in analogous contexts."[22]

In his own work, he has pointed in two directions: one is a call for theology to be more fully incarnational, by which he means more thoroughly historical, attentive to context, conflict, and agency, and debates over their meaning in the past and the present; the second is to become more fully trinitarian in developing a fuller appreciation of Spirit, that is, being open to the "ongoing primordial creativity . . . and the requirement of theological creativity at the heart of the tradition."[23]

In grappling with the apocalyptic scenarios that are increasingly plausible visions of the future, one avenue of theological exploration has been that of Pentecost, and with it, the fear, loss, and confusion felt by the early Christians following Jesus' execution, the impending disaster of the Roman destruction of the Temple, and the annihilation of the forms of religious faith and political life associated with it for the Jewish (and Jewish-Christian) people. The Pentecost story grapples with both the absence and the mysterious and changing character of the presence of Jesus. Cormie writes:

20. Of the thousands of groups and activities that instantiate any particular World Social Forum, one can certainly find examples of attention to the issues of extreme crises: genocides, pandemics, nuclear threats, nanotechnologies, collapse of food and water sources, and the like. My point is that serious confrontation with the questions of human survival, that is, more generalized apocalyptic scenarios that these suggest is seriously lacking in the dominant discourses at and about the World Social Forum.

21. Cormie, "Ethics of Globalization," 7.

22. Ibid., 17.

23. Cormie, "Movements of the Spirit in History," 249.

"The early Christian finally articulated these experiences theologically in terms of the Spirit who inspires the coming together of diverse peoples of the empire in the *ekkelsia*, the assemblies of the people of God; together that continue the incarnate presence of the Divine in history witnessing to the coming new *basileia* (kingdom or reign)."[24]

He goes on to argue that there are many analogies between the world of the early Christians and our own, including the omnipresence of empire, its incredible powers for both creativity and violence, and the encounters with cultural and religious diversity that it, in part, enables. In this context, the World Social Forum is both a sign of the times and a sign of hope for the future, especially as it points to broader solidarities and the possibility of communicability across difference. The primacy of diversity, pluralism, and participation in the politics of the new social movements is in opposition to the neoliberal and neo-imperial project that is systematically suppressing difference, even the *possibility* of difference, through its monocultures.

In promoting the "convergence of difference," the World Social Forum recognizes diversity and pluralism, not as problems to be overcome but as conditions to be embraced, valued, promoted, and protected. Recognition of diversity and the promotion of pluralism are fundamental to the World Social Forum and to its deep-seated resistance to the hegemony of "any one way of thinking." Diversity will simply always be. New differences—new identities, ways of life, belief systems—will always will be emerging. No one politics will ever adequately incorporate this irreducible reality. At the same time, the World Social Forum is actively and successfully promoting the *convergence* of difference and increasingly, *dialogue* across difference.

In important ways, this is a "post-liberal" politics in that it is situated within a shared, indeed non-negotiable, opposition to neoliberal globalization and grounded in acts of practical, cross-movement solidarity that transcend seemingly incommensurable differences. Commitment to dialogue and a foundational recognition of pluralism does not imply the absence of firmly-held values or political commitment, but it does require an epistemology embracing partial, situated, positional knowing as the basis for open, provisional, but "reliable-enough" knowledge for politics. Movements' need to act and the diverse discourses and practices constantly emergent will always outstrip the best available theories.

The belief in and demonstrated capacity to act on provisional knowing, and to act together with others who think, live, and dream differently,

---

24. Ibid., 255.

Part One—Historical and Methodological Issues

relies on a culture and politics of social learning and capacity building, and a shared willingness to confront the exclusions of one's own movement. It suggests notions of democracy, revolution, and utopia as open-ended projects-in-process, worked out in practice, open to question and to new "others," and always needing renovation. The architects of the World Social Forum embody this in particularly powerful ways when they insist that the Forum is not a unitary entity or agent, but rather a "pedagogical and political space."[25]

This new democratic imaginary places a premium on practice. A new world is coming into being in and through the practices of progressive social movements. In this roiling politics of seemingly limitless diversity and pluralism, one recognizes one's allies through their concrete practices of solidarity. It is also through practice that the movements are producing the knowledges they need in the making of another world with the space for many worlds within it. Through countless concrete initiatives, experiments, and projects, and reflection on their successes and limits, the movements learn, teach, change, and try again.

The World Social Forum has been central to the convergence of both anti-globalization and anti-war movements. Its processes and methods are promoting extraordinary levels of self-organizing world-wide and sowing new transnationalisms. The Social Forum is successfully fostering *convergence* among movements world-wide through the promotion of *pluralism*. It is this extraordinary paradox, that embracing diversity is producing unprecedented co-ordinated action on global and other scales, that is key to the generative power of the Social Forum and suggestive of a new democratic politics on a world scale. This is not to say that the outcomes are certain but, with Cormie, to affirm:

> [T]hese are experiences of Pentecost in our time, powerful new experiences of the Spirit, poured out across the differences, gaps and barriers which have traditionally divided peoples, in the different tongues, accents and dialects of the peoples of many places, cultures and languages, religions and politics, calling for repentance and conversion, inspiring us to broader solidarities and more inclusive identities, and pointing the way forward in this

---

25. William F. Fisher and Thomas Ponniah, "Introduction: The World Social Forum and the Re-Invention of Democracy," in *Another World is Possible: Popular Alternatives to Globalization at the World Social Forum*, ed. William F. Fisher and Thomas Ponniah (London: Zed, 2003) 6.

time when the whole creation is groaning in the labor of new birth (Rom 8:22).[26]

This, it seems to me, is the work of theology in our time.

---

[26] Cormie, "Movements of the Spirit in History," 257.

Part Two

Contextual and Constructive Proposals

6

ORiginAL Voices

Eradicating the "Fearful Asymmetry" or Power Imbalance between indigenous and Western Thought in History and Theology

CARMEN LANSDOWNE

I AM A FIRST Nations theologian, and this chapter is an attempt to answer Linda Tuhiwai Smith's call to create indigenous theories which respond to our unique (and non-Western) epistemologies. I find neither "oral tradition" nor "oral history" appropriate for moving indigenous academic scholarship forward in a way that cultivates a culturally "safe space."[1] I will show, from an indigenous point of view, how accounting for the orality of indigenous epistemologies is a theological, pedagogical, and political undertaking; I will also make an argument for why mainstream academia must answer the call to justice by using both the disciplines of history and theology to "make space" for the unique gift of what I call ORiginAL voices. By reviewing the current definitions of "oral traditions" and "oral history," as they are used in anthropological and historical disciplines, I will make an argument for ORiginALity as a methodology that recognizes the spatiality of indigenous epistemology as inherently valid and a worthy interlocutor in academic discourse.

1. Linda Tuhiwai Smith, *Decolonizing Methodologies: Research and Indigenous Peoples* (London: Zed, 1999) 184.

Part Two—Contextual and Constructive Proposals

Introducing "ORiginALity"

In the spring of 2007, I attended the Talking Stick Festival at the Roundhouse Community Arts and Recreation Center in Vancouver. The festival included a showcase of First Nations writers, specifically novelists and poets, in a celebration of what was called *ORiginAL Voices*. I appreciated the visual signification in the capitalized letters emphasizing the orality of Native cultures. In this chapter I appropriate the same visual signification to demonstrate that conceiving of indigenous epistemological difference as ORiginAL is a more appropriate way forward than what the typically Western categories of oral tradition and oral history can contribute.

Anthropologist Jan Vansina defines "oral tradition" as "both a process and its products . . . The process is the transmission of such messages by word of mouth over time until the disappearance of the message."[2] "Oral history" on the other hand, has been defined as "the recording of personal testimony delivered in oral form,"[3] a sort of "record of perceptions, rather than a re-creation of historical events."[4] More appropriately, it has been defined as "the genre of discourse which orality and writing have developed jointly in order to speak to each other about the past."[5] Perhaps this is why there is a temptation to conflate the "oral traditions" of Canada's First Nations with the disciplinary methodologies of "oral history." There is a failure to distinguish between "oral tradition" and "oral history" and, worse still, a dismissal of oral traditions as academically inappropriate even by oral history's standards.

As an undergraduate studying history, I was taught to believe that oral history methodologies were best suited to the history of societies with oral traditions. Moreover, I was taught to conform to the standard methodological frameworks established by historical positivism in the academy, including the citation and documentation of "authentic" oral accounts as defined by Western academic "oral historians." In graduate school, however, I became intensely dissatisfied with what I perceived to be systemic

---

2. Jan Vansina, *Oral Tradition As History* (Madison: University of Wisconsin Press, 1985) 3.

3. Valerie Raleigh Yow, *Recording Oral History: A Guide for the Humanities and Social Sciences*, 2nd Edition (Walnut Creek, CA: Altamira, 2005) 3.

4. Tamara Haraven, "The Search For Generational Memory," in *Oral History: An Interdisciplinary Anthology* (Walnut Creek, CA: Altamira, 1996) 248.

5. Alessandro Portelli, "Oral History as Genre," in *Narrative and Genre*, ed. Mary Chamberlain and Paul Thompson (New York: Routledge, 1998) 23.

problems in historiography, most notably the failure of the academy to produce histories that articulated an adequate sense of connection to the present realities of the communities that they sought to represent. Indeed, some of my own writing was a direct reaction to how I perceived these systemic problems as intellectual imperialism in a center of Western learning that continued to devalue indigenous voices. As Angela Cavender Wilson has argued, this justification of indigenous worldviews against perceived (and real) attack by non-Natives is a common occurrence. She writes, "We realize that it is not just our individual academic freedom or right to an opinion that is at stake. We know that in our home communities our people are continuing to die at exceptionally early ages and that our lands and rights as indigenous peoples are under constant threat."[6]

"No one in oral societies," writes Vansina, "doubts that memories can be faithful repositories which contain the sum total of past human experience and explain the how and why of present day conditions."[7] This statement attends in part to the reality of most indigenous peoples globally. While his own scholarly work has focused on the oral traditions of African societies, his analyses and deconstructions of oral traditions are in many ways applicable to many of the indigenous societies in the Americas, and therefore also applicable to the First Nations in what is now divided into Canada and the United States. "Among the various kinds of historical sources," he argues, "[oral] traditions occupy a special place. They are messages, but unwritten; their preservation entrusted to the memories of successive generations of people."[8] According to Vansina, only in the last fifty years has the problem of methodology became concerned with how to treat oral tradition in historical discourse.[9] The problem remains precisely how to value what has traditionally been unvalued. It is not simply a matter of properly recording and transcribing oral traditions, but respecting their inherent value as epistemologically different and valid forms of thought and sociological process. The power imbalance in the production of knowledge in Western versus indigenous thought remains a "Fanonian" prob-

6. Angela Cavender Wilson, "Reclaiming Our Humanity: Decolonization and Recovering of indigenous Knowledge," in *Indigenizing the Academy: Transforming Scholarship and Empowering Communities*, ed. Devon Abbott Mihesuah and Angela Cavender Wilson (Lincoln: University of Nebraska Press, 2004) 69.

7. Jan Vansina, *Oral Tradition As History* (Madison: University of Wisconsin Press, 1985) xi.

8. Ibid., xii.

9. Ibid.

Part Two—Contextual and Constructive Proposals

lem[10] because, under the current system, indigenous people are rendered subalterns. It is assumed we have nothing to give other than that which is consistently already being taken from us by force.

As Rebecca Sharpless articulates in her history of oral history, those traditions which transmitted sources of history orally prior to the Enlightenment "fell into disfavour in the scientific movement of the late nineteenth century, and there arose a prejudice against oral history that remained strong for more than fifty years."[11] Haitian historian and anthropologist Michel-Rolph Trouillot notes that around this time the solidification of history as a profession was defined by scientific positivism. He writes, "the more distant the sociohistorical process from its knowledge, the easier the claim to a 'scientific' professionalism."[12] Furthermore, Trouillot argues that all non-Westerners were classified as fundamentally non-historical, a judgment based on a western epistemology of linear and cumulative time.[13] Indeed, scientific positivism manifested itself early on in the academic objectification of First Nations. Franz Boaz is remembered for warning his students not to engage analysis put forward by their "narrators" or "informants." "Beware," he taught, "of 'intelligent Indians' who may have 'formed a theory' about the research in progress."[14] This type of overt racist cultural hegemony is now no longer politically acceptable in academic discourse. There has developed a subtle but present awareness of cultural difference and the role of epistemology in academic discourse that softens the positivism found in the modernist historical discipline. Yet scholars who study indigenous peoples still do so from a Western perspective and with little sense of a subjective connection to the lived realities of the peoples whom they study and certainly without any communicated sense of personal obligation to change the status quo of the current realities faced by their subjects. Acknowledging the dire and regrettable circumstances of indigenous

---

10. See Frantz Fanon, *Black Skin, White Masks*, trans. Richard Philcox (New York: Grove Press, 2008) ch. 4; and Nelson Maldonado-Torres, *Against War: Views from the Underside of Modernity* (Durham: Duke University Press, 2008) ch. 4.

11. Rebecca Sharpless, "The History of Oral History," in *Thinking About Oral History: Theories and Applications*, ed. Thomas L. Charlton et al. (Lanham, MD: Altamira, 2008) 8.

12. Michel-Rolph Trouillot, *Silencing the Past: Power and the Production of History* (Boston: Beacon, 1995) 5.

13. Ibid., 7.

14. Portelli, "Oral History," 30.

peoples seems to be as far as is acceptable; any further advocacy would topple "objective" scholars from their positivist pedestal.

A "Fearful Asymmetry": The Epistemological Gap between Western and indigenous

In response to what he terms a "fearful asymmetry" of ideas (the interviewer's) and accounts (the informant's), Alessandro Portelli identifies the resultant cultural hegemony that remains in terms of a hierarchy of intellect in the academy. He writes, "human beings, including 'native informants,' never speak without attempting to form an idea, a theory, of what they are speaking about, to whom, and why. The stereotype of the 'dumb Indian' at least exists in the hegemonic imagination, but the concept of a 'dumb philosopher' sounds like a contradiction in terms."[15] There persists the perception that indigenous peoples ("dumb Indians") have little right or ability to speak on their own behalf, unless they are willing to do so via the confines of traditional, objective, academic discourse. Our histories, our stories, are not credible or valued unless they can be corroborated as factually accurate and presented through the interpretive lens of a scholar who "specializes" in the study of that particular community or people.[16]

Much like earlier social and feminist history, many attempts to engage in historical reclamation of marginalized accounts of "pre-historic" life in First Nations have been well-intentioned projects by well-intentioned scholars. Yet, unless there is an attempt to reframe historical methodologies in ways that are culturally representative of the peoples studied, any production of history will fall short of being truly representative of indigenous peoples. There needs to be an attempt to define an alternative to both "oral tradition" and "oral history." One possibility is to tell history from the perspective of the ORiginAL voice. To do otherwise, in my view, perpetuates pedagogical practices and ideologies that are bent on creating patriotic citizens who believe the nationalistic myth of a history built on

---

15. Ibid., 31.

16. I refer here to "objectivity" as the legacy of Cartesian thinking that posits that, as feminist theorists Caroline Ramazanoğlu and Janet Holland state, "subjectivity contaminates the quest for truth and must be rationally controlled. If [one] could produce objective knowledge, this would give them good grounds for claiming that their knowledge is valid"; Caroline Ramazanoğlu and Janet Holland, *Feminist Methodology: Challenges and Choices* (London: Sage, 2002) 48.

colonization and manifest destiny. The dominant "newcomer" or "settler" society in north America[17] has been systematically taught to believe that there is nothing wrong with appropriation of First Nations land.[18] While Western societies have generally acknowledged since the end of World War II that imperialist expansion is no longer (overtly) acceptable, this does little to mitigate dominant interpretations of history. Instead, Western fantasies of rescue and paternalism subvert any sense of logical outrage at history, converting colonialism into a benefit of globalization whereby indigenous peoples are saved from their own primitive selves. This is particularly true in terms of the gendered subalterns and dominant misunderstandings of traditional gender relationships and sexual orientation.[19]

A methodology for discourses that engage ORiginAL perspectives can have no singular reliance on traditionally prescribed positivist sources that would achieve a balanced and "objective" methodological approach in the traditional sense of the modernist approach to history. Rather, ORiginAL voices as methodologies would be acts of resistance on epistemological grounds; they would be a rejection of the Cartesian dualism so omnipresent in contemporary academic discourse in history, Native studies, and anthropology.

Oral Becomes ORiginAL Epistemology

Oral traditions, the basis for ORiginAL voices in academic discourse, are still widely misunderstood in the Western academy. In some instances, oral traditions have been viewed primarily as records of mythological and genealogical roots of families, communities, and nations that are transmitted

17. Here I side with George "Tink" Tinker's decision in his most recent book, *American Indian Liberation: A Theology of Sovereignty* (Maryknoll, NY: Orbis, 2008), not to acknowledge the "amer-european" arbitrary division of the Americas into North and South.

18. See Mel Smith, *Our Home Or Native Land? What Government's Aboriginal Policy is Doing to Canada* (Toronto: Stoddart, 1996) and Tom Flanagan, *First Nations? Second Thoughts*, 2nd ed. (Montreal: McGill-Queens University Press, 2008).

19. This idea is explored further in Gayatri Spivak's essay "Can the Subaltern Speak?," which was originally published in Cary Nelson and Lawrence Grossberg, eds., *Marxism and the Interpretation of Culture* (Urbana: University of Illinois Press, 1988), 271–313; and later elaborated in Gayatri Chakravorty Spivak, *A Critique of Postcolonial Reason: Toward a History of the Vanishing Present* (Cambridge: Harvard University Press, 1999), wherein she discusses the dynamic of "white men saving brown women from brown men."

through family lines, ritual, and ceremony. What has traditionally been overlooked by the Western academy is that they are *also* primarily pedagogical and political. indigenous oral traditions teach communities central truths or values which are formative in right relationships with all of creation; these traditions also embody the consensus-based decision-making model that Donald Fixico has sketched in his treatment of "Indian thinking," which he describes as

> visual and circular in philosophy. Imbedded in an Indian traditional reality, this ethos is a combination of the physical reality and metaphysical reality. Listening and observing the natural environment is essential to the Indian mindset. Decision making is responsive in nature due to considering all of the physical and metaphysical factors affecting one's life. Coming to a consensus is coming to a balance of all factors so that the right decision is the best decision for all concerned.[20]

Fixico goes on to say that "[t]he power of story through the oral tradition is also explained [in] how all of this[21] transcends time, thus making time less relevant to the power of oral narrative told effectively."[22]

Rather than focusing on conforming to a Western methodology (based on what is often felt by indigenous communities to be the misappropriation of oral histories through interviews, transcriptions and archival deposits), what will allow for indigenous voices to reemerge with cultural integrity are ORiginAL methodologies defined on their own terms. It is the Western linear concepts of time and objectivity which mark our peoples with the shame of history as it currently stands. The shame of history is that countless academics have built their careers on the historical study of First Nations (and other indigenous peoples) with little or no regard for what makes them culturally and epistemologically unique. History, as told from a Western point of view, is dissociated from the present because it is by definition bounded by linear conceptions of time and progress. This makes it less useful (although not entirely useless) from an indigenous perspective because the pedagogical and political dimensions of our stories are silenced. It is, by Western standards, acceptable to research and document the smallpox epidemics, the cultural intolerance of Victorian settlers

---

20. Donald L. Fixico, *The American Indian Mind in a Linear World: American Indian Studies and Traditional Knowledge* (New York: Routledge, 2003) xii.
21. Fixico refers here to truth, multiple purposes, and teaching people to learn.
22. Ibid., xiii.

PART TWO—Contextual and Constructive Proposals

on Native lands, the residential school legacies, and other topics of study relating to indigenous peoples. In most disciplines it is intellectually inappropriate, however, to draw conclusions that judge history as in any way intrinsically linked to the contemporary reality of indigenous peoples in the Americas. Unless we (indigenous peoples) can claim our intellectual property and historical experiences through ownership and expression of indigenous epistemologies, we are left stripped of dignity because a Western worldview does not easily translate into a telling of our collective experiences of the past spilling over into the present.

Any scholarly work that puts forward claims based on ORiginAL voices will be primarily pedagogical and political—which is perhaps the defining characteristic of ORiginAL. Indeed, its very spelling, by highlighting the ORAL nature of "original" traditions in the Americas, is indeed political because it breaks the "don't talk rule" so strictly applied to the study of indigenous peoples and their lived realities as well as their entitlement to claims on what is now considered property of the state (and its private citizens and corporations). Naming indigenous scholarly voices as ORiginAL asserts the right to be pedagogical and political by virtue of the spatial claim to originality as the first peoples in their traditional territories. A methodology based on ORiginAL voice will also (in the traditions of Franz Fanon and Paulo Freire) be a decolonizing act. As Angela Cavender Wilson asserts, "A reaffirmation of indigenous epistemological and ontological foundations, then, in contemporary times offers a central form of resistance to the colonial forces that have consistently and methodically denigrated and silenced them."[23] Marxist sociologist Paul Hirst articulately reduced the theory of history to a question of epistemology when he wrote:

> Teleology and spirituality are essential mechanisms of all philosophies of history . . . It is in the philosophy of history that the past becomes a possible and rational object of knowledge. It is through the conception of historical time as a continuum that the past becomes a coherent subject.[24]

It is this conception of historical time as a continuum where past becomes subject which is ontologically different for the ORiginAL voice.

---

23. Wilson, "Reclaiming Our Humanity," 71.

24. Paul Hirst, cited in Robert Young, *White Mythologies: Writing History and the West* (London: Routledge, 1990) 60.

Jan Vansina comes close to articulating what Fixico noted as the circular properties of traditional indigenous forms of intellect. Vansina notes that in oral traditions,

> "[A]ncient things are today." Yes, oral traditions are documents of the *present*, because they are told in the present. Yet they also embody a message from the past, so they are expressions of the *past* at the same time. They are the representation of the past in the present. One cannot deny either the past or the present in them. To attribute their whole content to the evanescent present as some sociologists do, is to mutilate tradition; it is reductionistic. To ignore the impact of the present as some historians have done, is equally reductionistic. Traditions must always be understood as reflecting both past and present in a single breath.[25]

ORiginAL Must Be Political

When it comes to the connection between past and present for indigenous peoples, it is the denial of land rights that remains the most divisive issue relating to indigenous communities in English-speaking former colonies, particularly in Canada, Australia, New Zealand, and the U.S. While none of these four countries has explicitly stated as such, there is a general feeling within the international indigenous community that denial of land rights is the reason none of these four countries would endorse the 2007 United Nations Declaration on the Rights of indigenous People. In fact, these four countries were the only four to explicitly vote *against* the Declaration, with only eleven other countries abstaining and the vast majority of other countries affirming it. The BBC reported in September 2007:

> The Declaration on the Rights of indigenous Peoples calls on countries to give more control to tribal peoples over the land and resources they traditionally possessed, and to return confiscated territory, or pay compensation. The General Assembly passed it, with 143 countries voting in favour and 11 abstaining. Four nations—Australia, Canada, New Zealand and the United States—each with large indigenous populations, voted against.[26]

---

25. Vansina, Vansina, *Oral Tradition as History*, xii.
26. Online: http://news.bbc.co.uk/1/hi/in_depth/6993776.stm.

Part Two—Contextual and Constructive Proposals

Canada's decision to vote "no" was felt by many to be inconsistent with the history of colonization of what is now Canada and contemporary moves (however small) to make reparation for that colonialism. In the now-famous apology of the federal government to the victims and survivors of Indian Residential Schools on June 11, 2008, Prime Minister Stephen Harper stated, "Today, we recognize that this policy of assimilation was wrong, has caused great harm, and has no place in our country."[27] Yet admissions about the wrongness of the "policies of assimilation" perpetuated under the government act remain vague about the underlying land claims issues that secure Canada's nationhood. In fact, it was possible for Harper to acknowledge the sins of Canada's assimilationist past without actually acknowledging the colonization of the land. On September 25, 2009, just over one year after the apology, Harper announced to the G20 Summit in Philadelphia that "[w]e also have no history of colonialism. . . . So we have all of the things that many people admire about the great powers but none of the things that threaten or bother them."[28]

Shawn Atleo, Grand Chief of the Assembly of First Nations, was quick to respond to Harper's lack of connection between the residential school legacy and the suggested absence of Canadian colonialism. In a response issued October 1, 2009, Atleo stated:

> The effects of colonialism remain today. It is the attitude that fueled the residential schools; the colonial *Indian Act* that displaces traditional forms of First Nations governance; the theft of Indian lands and forced relocations of First Nations communities; the criminalization and suppression of First Nations languages and cultural practices; the chronic under-funding of First Nations communities and programs; and the denial of Treaty and Aboriginal rights, even though they are recognized in Canada's Constitution.[29]

Atleo, like other First Nations activists and scholars, does not see a separation between the different aspects of aboriginal policy in Canada, nor between the historical past and the political present. It is often that partial concessions are made in the present to make reparations for the past, but

---

27. "Prime Minister Stephen Harper's Statement of Apology"; online: www.cbc.ca/canada/story/2008/06/11/pm-statement.html.

28. "Shawn Atleo criticizes Stephen Harper over 'no history of colonialism' remark"; online: www.straight.com/article-261089/shawn-atleo-criticizes-stephen-harper-over-no-history-colonialism-remark .

29. Ibid.

then the autonomy of the First Nation is never nearly complete because history and politics become segmented and disconnected from each other. I use the term "concessions" here intentionally, since the power almost always rests in the state, and not in the First Nation. This is what Alan Noël refers to as "autonomy with a footnote"—that is, "the *negative autonomy* of the non-participant."[30]

ORiginAL Spatiality

It is important at this juncture to consider indigenous epistemologies and what precisely governs an indigenous claim to the land, for this argument is deeper than property rights. In his book *God Is Red*, Vine Deloria, Jr., writes about the problems of interpretation—epistemological and hermeneutical—that happen when cross-cultural dialogue happens between indigenous and non-indigenous populations:

> When the domestic ideology is divided according to American Indian and Western European immigrant . . . the fundamental difference is one of great philosophical importance. American Indians hold their lands—*places*—as having the highest possible meaning, and all their statements are made with this reference in mind. Immigrants review the movement of their ancestors across the continent as a steady progression of basically good events and experiences, thereby placing history—*time*—in the best possible light.[31]

According to Deloria, this is particularly apparent when it comes to the discipline of ethics. He notes how Western thought, once it has dealt with the concept of time or temporality, has relatively no concern for spatiality at all. The practice of ethics in the academy, he says, "seems to involve an abstract individual making clear, objective decisions that involve principles but not people. . . . Spatial thinking requires that ethical systems be related directly to the physical world and [that] real human situations,

---

30. Alan Noël, as quoted in Fiona MacDonald, "The Manitoba Government's Shift to 'Autonomous' First Nations Child Welfare: Empowerment or Privatization?" in *First Nations, First Thoughts: The Impact of indigenous Thought in Canada*, ed. Annis May Timpson (Vancouver: University of British Columbia Press, 2009) 182.

31. Vine Deloria, Jr., *God is Red: A Native View of Religion* (Golden, CO: Fulcrum, 1992) 63 (emphasis added).

PART TWO—Contextual and Constructive Proposals

not abstract principles, are believed to be valid at all times and under all circumstances."[32] George "Tink" Tinker echoes Deloria here, positing four fundamental cultural differences between indigenous cultures and the Western cultures that racialize them: "spatiality as opposed to temporality; attachment to particular lands or territory; the priority of community over the individual; and a consistent notion of the interrelatedness of humans and the rest of creation."[33]

When indigenous bodies are suffering, in order for erotic or spatial morality to govern our ethical discernment and processes, spatiality must be articulately expressed in terms of how reconciliation and justice are to be achieved. While abstract philosophical morality seems to be substantially distinct from politics or economics, it cannot be for an embodied, spatial indigenous morality. If, as Hirst has argued, spirituality and teleology are inseparable from the philosophy of history, this must be true for ORiginAL methodologies as well.

Taiaiake Alfred has argued for what, in his Mohawk language, is called *Wasáse*, or the "new warrior's path." *Wasáse* is an "Onkwehonwe [original peoples] attitude, [a] courageous way of being in the world—all come together to form a new politics in which many identities and strategies for making change are fused together to challenge white society's control over Onkwehonwe and our lands."[34] He goes on to describe *Wasáse* as "an ethical and political vision, the real demonstration of our resolve to survive as Onkwehonwe and to do what we must to force the Settlers to acknowledge our existence and the integrity of our connection to the land."[35]

Both Alfred and Tinker argue for the acknowledgment of indigenous survival that is not only temporal but spatial—Alfred from a strictly political perspective; Tinker from a politico-theological angle. Tinker states, "An American Indian theology must necessarily be a political theology, especially if we take political in its broadest sense to indicate the cultural life of a community."[36] He rightly identifies the failure of theology to identify the spatiality of indigenous peoples as having a distinct quality which separates

---

32. Ibid., 73.

33. Tinker, *American Indian Liberation*, 7.

34. Taiaiake Alfred, *Wasáse: indigenous Pathways of Action and Freedom* (Peterborough: Broadview, 2005) 19.

35. Ibid.

36. Tinker, *American Indian Liberation*, 1.

us over and against other marginalized peoples in the context of what are now "Canadian" and "American" societies:

> What indigenous communities want most of all is to have our cultural differentness recognized and respected as signifying distinct political entities based on specific land territories. To reduce us to some notion of class is to obviate that differentness and to replace our community identity with participation in a general class struggle for mere economic sufficiency. Such a movement must eventually impose notions of value, ethics, and aesthetics on indigenous communities, just as the colonizer governments have always done. Only this time, the imposition is from a more liberal side of the colonizer with the "good intention" of building solidarity among a presumed class for the sake of the economic well-being and even survival of the class as a whole.[37]

Spatiality in the Academy

In his book *The Land*, Walter Brueggemann writes that "land" refers "to *actual earthly turf* where people can be safe and secure, where meaning and well-meaning are enjoyed without pressure or coercion."[38] Because the academy is not a nation-state that can grant access to land or the right of return for indigenous peoples, space *within the academy* is what is at stake for recognizing the spatial-orientation of indigenous peoples. ORiginAL voices present a justice challenge to the academy that reorients discourse from traditionally positivist accounts to more politically and pedagogically oriented views that are spatially grounded in the lived experiences of indigenous peoples.

Theologically there can be an argument for ORiginAL methodologies in the academy. Paul Tillich's *Love, Power, and Justice* is helpful in understanding the interconnectedness of justice and power. He writes that, "justice was defined as the form in which power of being actualizes itself in the encounter of power with power."[39] Given that his understanding of the interaction of power of being with/against power of being is termed

---

37. Ibid., 23.

38. Walter Brueggemann, *The Land: Place as Gift, Promise, and Challenge in Biblical Faith*, 2nd ed. (Minneapolis: Fortress, 2002) 2.

39. Paul Tillich, *Love, Power and Justice: Ontological Analyses and Ethical Applications* (London: Oxford University Press, 1954) 67.

Part Two—Contextual and Constructive Proposals

compulsion, it is important to understand how compulsion becomes the Mis/Use of power. To say that there is mis/use of power highlights the fact that, according to Tillich, justice exists as a possibility within power, and that therefore there is the potential to either use or misuse power in any relationship between beings. He writes, "The answer must be: it is not compulsion which is unjust, but a compulsion which destroys the object of compulsion instead of working towards its fulfillment. It is not compulsion which violates justice, but a compulsion which disregards the intrinsic claim of a being to be acknowledged as what it is within the context of all beings."[40]

In Tillich's thought, *Kraft* is the teleological power of potentiality which pervades the universe; *Mächtigkeit* is the power of form in all existence.[41] The realization of *Kraft*, or the potentiality of being, as *Mächtigkeit* is the embodiment of justice through the recognition of each being's intrinsic claim of being. Therefore the Mis/Use of power is determined by whether there is a recognition of that intrinsic value in the compulsion of power of being with/against power of being. Tillich goes on to say that "a power structure in which compulsion works against the intrinsic justice of its elements is not strengthened but weakened."[42] In other words, if power is sought solely for the value of power, and not for the self-expression of God's Wisdom through the intrinsic power of being, then injustice is unavoidable. When this happens, domination occurs within the distributive systems of society—*Macht* becomes the power of relationship between the dominating/dominated.

Perhaps this theological argument for determining the existence of justice can be applied to epistemological concerns. If indigenous scholars have the inherent capability of determining their own methodologies on their own terms, then the refusal of the academy to acknowledge ORiginAL voices becomes a matter of power relationships in the production of knowledge. Much work has been done by culture theorist Michel Foucault and the descendents of his intellectual projects in this vein. The argument here is not to determine whether power is involved in the production of knowledge, but rather whether the academy is yet capable of enough self-examination to ask whether marginalized—ORiginAL—voices are

40. Ibid.

41. Kyle A. Pasewark, *A Theology of Power: Being Beyond Domination* (Minneapolis: Fortress, 1993) 273–85.

42. Tillich, *Love, Power and Justice*, 67.

inherently valued. Trouillot contends that the academy does not yet see the power struggles involved in the positivism that it refuses to admit exists. He writes, "[t]he positivist position dominated Western scholarship enough to influence the vision of history among historians and philosophers who did not necessarily see themselves as positivists . . . Within that viewpoint, power is unproblematic, irrelevant to the construction of the narrative as such."[43]

Saving ORiginAL

In the opening pages of *Indecent Theology*, Marcella Althaus-Reid speaks of the destruction of the indigenous Grand Narratives, especially during the active and overtly violent context of the history of Latin America and the brutalization of indigenous peoples by the Conquistadors. She writes:

> [T]he destruction of the Grand Narratives of the Americas did not come as the result of a hermeneutics of suspicion, or the realization of the trace in the text, that element which is a movement leading us towards what the text tries to occult, hide and negate. No, economic exploitation was the deconstructive clause, the doubting interrogation of naturalized, assumed authoritative narratives.[44]

While the context about which she speaks is somewhat different, the effects of ethnocidal/genocidal colonization of the indigenous inhabitants of all the Americas share common elements. Althaus-Reid's critique of the economic deconstruction speaks to the sexual mutilation of the indigenous peoples of Latin America, but it was also the clash of economic systems between the colonizers and the peoples of the Pacific Northwest, which provoked much of the European labeling of "lazy Indians" and "uncivilized nomads."

The implication of the colonizers' intent is obvious when Christianization was not seen as separable from enculturation. It was not acceptable for the Christian Grand Narratives to be simply absorbed into our cultures; the cultural views of an "enlightened" Christendom were viewed

---

43. Trouillot, *Silencing the Past*, 5.
44. Marcella Althaus-Reid, *Indecent Theology: Theological Perversions in Sex, Gender and Politics* (New York: Routledge, 2000) 16.

PART TWO—Contextual and Constructive Proposals

as supercessionist or more advanced, and therefore superior. Althaus-Reid describes the process:

> Cultural, religious, socio-political discourses, economy and science, and philosophical cosmovisions which defined identity, meaning and patterns of social organization and sexual constructions were obliterated from the earth. Even language was erased. "Tongues" were lost; mother tongues were buried while human tongues were cut from mouths. Women's tongues were silenced for centuries. What survived entered into a covenant of silence, and since then it has never fully spoken again.[45]

Although Althaus-Reid argues that the mother tongues of the indigenous peoples in the Americas were buried and erased, I argue that there exists a cultural memory in the subconscious collective which speaks to the trauma of a grand narrative deconstructed virtually overnight; there is a growing and urgent need to speak a truth that we no longer know exactly how to articulate.

Conclusion

If Vansina's statement I quoted at the beginning of this essay is correct, it is not yet explicit enough to encapsulate the fully spatialized lived realities of indigenous communities who form the "oral traditions" that Vansina studies. There is nothing that articulates the generations of trauma carried in those memories. Rather, he presents a tidy and still romanticized belief that somehow those among us who are trained in "the old way" (or who work towards the prevention of language loss and towards cultural reclamation) know how to do this in ways that are "purified" of western contamination. But the cleansing of Western contamination also sterilizes the present from the damage done in the past—as though there were no division between past and present. The work of Native Canadian novelist Lee Maracle speaks to the context of a people devastated through the experience of colonization:

> Grace has left their bodies. They are rendered stiff and tense by the knot of shame that sits stuck in their throats. It needs to be expressed, pushed up and out so they may sing again, but five centuries of "Hush, don't cry" holds the expression of their shame still. Under it lies a dangerous grief. They now tread heavily upon

45. Ibid., 11.

the back of their mother. Lunging from place to place, they plant seeds but don't bother to watch them grow. They water nothingness as though this water will somehow recreate life without their participation. Many have acquired the jerky movements, the bad skin and the hard, strident song-less voices of the newcomers. Their world has lost its future. Cut off from considering their past, they list in the momentary context of the present. Consideration requires a spiritual sensibility, one that sees life from all its jewel-like angles. [They] don't see life; they barely feel their existence. They avert each other's gaze. The reflection of grief and shame in the eyes of others mirrored back at them is too terrifying to contemplate. They mark time. Time is the enemy of the dispirited. [They] wander aimlessly, killing time in small pieces.[46]

When indigenous communities have no way to take ownership of their histories through our own inherent epistemological positions, we remain, in Maracle's words, cut off from considering our past . . . "[listing] in the momentary context of the present."[47] It is an act of protest, then—a political statement of ORiginAL voices—to argue for a methodology that allows for First Nations to gather together (in jerky movements) the lost yet still subconscious collective knowledge of our history and attempt to express it in a way that has meaning within our own epistemological constructions.

---

46. Lee Maracle, *Daughters Are Forever* (Vancouver: Raincoast, 2002) 25.
47. Ibid., 24.

7

Accompanying el Señor de los Milagros

The Early Processional Theology of Diego Irarrázaval

MARIO DeGIGLIO-BELLEMARE

"[La religión popular es una] religión del pan de cada dia." [1]

IN THE MID- TO late 1970s, Diego Irarrázaval began to develop an innovative processional theology rooted in the religious practices of the *pueblo* (the people), commonly known as popular religion in Latin America and the Caribbean. Central to this development was Gustavo Gutiérrez's early insistence on the complex and contested phenomenon of popular religion as an area in need of research and analysis for the development of liberation theologies in Latin America. In 1979 Gutiérrez wrote that "one of the values of the people of Latin America is popular religion."[2] A few years prior to this publication, Gutiérrez foregrounded popular religion as an area requiring special attention and elaboration at the Instituto Bartolomé de Las Casas, in Lima, Perú. Irarrázaval, who had fled the Pinochet dictatorship because

---

1. "Popular religion is a religion of everyday bread." See Irarrázaval, "Cristo Morado: Señor de los maltratados," in *Cristo crucificado en los pueblos de America Latina: Antología de la religión popular*, ed. Frans Damen and Esteban Judd Zanon (Quito: Abya-Yala, 1992) 305–27.

2. Gustavo Gutiérrez, *The Power of the Poor in History*, trans. R. R. Barr (Maryknoll, NY: Orbis, 1983) 193.

he had been active with the Christians for Socialism in Chile, was invited by Gutiérrez to the newly founded Instituto to help develop the study of popular religious practices from a liberationist perspective.

This chapter will examine Irarrázaval's pioneering text, *Cristo Morado: Señor de los maltratados*, which was published in Perú in 1977. This text constitutes an important breakthrough in liberationist readings of popular religion utilizing a social-scientific approach. This early liberationist reading of popular religious practices in Perú complicates a predominant notion held among theologians that liberationists simply disparaged popular religion in the 1970s and 1980s.[3] While some liberationists did disparage popular religion, recounting the history of liberation theologies in this way obscures the important theology developed by Irarrázaval (and others) at this time. Such a monolithic account also tends to reinforce the notion that in the early 1990s, as suggested by Pablo Richard, an "axial shift" from economic to cultural categories took place in liberation theologies.[4] Irarrázaval has spent his whole life studying popular religion in Perú from a

---

3. María Pilar Aquino, who is originally from México and who acknowledges the important influence of liberation theologies on Latino/a theologies, has written that liberation theology "has disdained popular Catholicism in theological epistemology, in spite of it being the omnipresent expression of faith of the people throughout the continent" ("Theological Method in U.S. Latino/a Theology," in *From the Heart of Our People*, ed. Orlando O. Espín and Miguel H. Diaz [Maryknoll, NY: Orbis, 1999] 16). Aquino is following Orlando Espín's comments that even "liberation theologians have tended to downplay popular religion's role in the Church" (*The Faith of the People: Theological Reflections on Popular Catholicism* [Maryknoll, NY: Orbis, 1997] 64). Espín has made some very important contributions on popular religion in theology, but oddly, he footnotes the work of Galilea and Scannone as examples of this tendency of downplaying popular religion. While Scannone is much more nuanced in his understanding of popular religion than Galilea, these two Latin American theologians hardly downplayed the role of popular religion. In fact, the opposite is true. See also R. S. Sugirtharajah, who writes that "liberation hermeneutics is still stuck with some vices of the modernistic project— excessive textualism, disparagement of major and popular religion. . . ." (*Postcolonial Criticism and Biblical Interpretation* [Oxford: Oxford University Press, 2002] 103). While I fully appreciate Sugirtharajah's development of postcolonial hermeneutics, his reading of Latin American liberationist hermeneutics here is reductive.

4. See Pablo Richard et al., "Challenges to Liberation Theology in the Decade of the Nineties," in *New Face of the Church in Latin America*, ed. Guillermo Cook (Maryknoll, NY: Orbis, 1994) 245–58. Juan Carlos Scannone also argued this point: "a comparison of them [the El Escorial meetings of liberation theology in 1972 and 1992] illustrates at least an 'axial shift' (*desplazamiento de eje*) from the socio-economic to the socio-cultural perspective, without, however, neglecting the former" ("'Axial Shift' Instead of 'Paradigm Shift,'" in *Liberation Theologies on Shifting Ground*, ed. G. De Schvijver [Leuven: Leuven University Press, 1998] 87).

Part Two—Contextual and Constructive Proposals

liberationist perspective: in Lima and Chimbote in the 1970s, and in the Andean mountains from 1981 to 2004. His early processional theology lays down a foundation for the lifework of a theologian who always insisted that a critique of power asymmetries in history cannot be divorced from the everyday *culture(s)* of processional peoples.

The Peruvian Context in the 1970s

Argentinean theologian Juan Carlos Scannone noted in the late 1990s that "there appeared in liberation theology, including its main current, an ever growing interest in popular religion."[5] Under the influence of Gutiérrez, this "growing interest" in popular religion took root in Perú in the 1970s. A project was initiated in 1979, the "Proyecto de investigacíon sobre la religiosidad popular en el Perú," which assembled a country-wide team of researchers, including anthropologists, sociologists of religion, and theologians, who responded to "the recommendation that was made at the Second Latin American Bishops Conference [CELAM] (Medellín, 1968) to study the forms of popular religion for the purpose of pastoral ministry" within poor and marginalized communities.[6] Although the project remains partly unfinished, the study was, at the time of its publication, one of the most comprehensive studies on popular religion in Latin America. The results are based on five years of research, consisting of over 2,000 responses to surveys by people in all regions of Perú, and over one hundred in-depth interviews and biographies on the place of popular religion in the *cotidiano* of poor people's lives. As a student of the anthropologist Manuel Marzal, a specialist in Andean religions, the coordinator of the project, José Luis González, gave special attention to a cultural analysis of popular religion in Perú while holding fast to a liberationist option for the poor and excluded.

Popular religious practices in Perú are imbued with Quechuan and Aymaran perspectives, and these important indigenous perspectives opened the doors for anthropological trajectories to take root in theology. Also, responding to the recommendations made at the Medellín meeting, the Catholic bishops of southern Perú had founded the Instituto Pastoral Andina (IPA) in Cusco, in 1969. The IPA is a research center that studies Andean cultures, both Quechuan and Aymaran, in order to assist pastoral

---

5. Scannone, "Axial Shift," 92.

6. José Luis González, *La religión popular en el Perú* (Cusco, Perú: Instituto de Pastoral Andina, 1987) 15.

ministries in empowering indigenous communities to become subjects of their own histories. The IPA has published ethnographic research material, and has been at the forefront in educating pastoral agents about cultural and socio-political issues in the Andes. The IPA has also worked very closely at the grassroots level with women, youth, and rural peoples. The anthropological research done at the IPA was very important for the study of popular religion in Perú insofar as it enriched the early research in the mid 1970s, which tended to be informed by a social-scientific approach with a strong emphasis on structural-economic issues.

The *"Proyecto de investigacíon"* also helped to precipitate the founding of the Instituto de Estudios Aymaras, in Chucuito (on the shores of Lake Titicaca in the Altiplano), which also sought to promote the study of Aymaran culture utilizing anthropological research.[7] Hence as early as 1979, anthropological methods were being utilized to understand the role of popular religion in Latin America. This is important to note, because some commentators tend to draw too starkly a methodological shift from socio-political analyses to cultural analyses in the late 1980 to early 1990s.[8] It is true that the late 80s and early 90s was a significant time for Latin America and the Caribbean, and the world more generally; it is a time that corresponds, among other developments, with the fall of the Berlin wall, the first invasion of Iraq, the defeat of the Sandinistas, the assassination of the six Jesuits and their two friends in San Salvador, and the 500th year commemoration of the conquest of the Americas. And while important shifts certainly occurred at this time, framing the history in these terms tends to veil an interest in culture already present within the so-called *dependentista* stream of liberationist hermeneutics as early as the late 1970s.

DIEGO IRARRÁZAVAL: THEOLOGIAN OF ACCOMPANIMENT

Born in Chile in 1942, Diego Irarrázaval was forced to flee the Pinochet dictatorship in 1974. Before his departure, Irarrázaval was a leader in Santiago

---

7. One of the founders of the Instituto was Curt Cadorette, an American Maryknoll priest, and one of the researchers on the *Proyecto de investigacíon sobre la religiosidad popular en el Perú*. He was joined by Diego Irarrázaval in 1981, also on the research team of the *Proyecto*, who later served as the Instituto's coordinator until its closure in 2004. Irarrázaval moved back to Chile after 29 years in Perú. See Irarrázaval's moving tribute to his Peruvian friends in "Gracias a Dios y a ustedes," *Páginas* 188 (2004) 82–84.

8. Richard et al., "Challenges," 251–52.

Part Two—Contextual and Constructive Proposals

"along with Sergio Torres, Gonzalo Arroyo, and Pablo Richard" of the Christians for Socialism, an organization that argued that there was no incompatibility between the Christian gospel and the emerging socialist project in Chile. Christians for Socialism encouraged Christians to be involved in the programs conceived by the left-leaning Allende government. But the U.S.-backed Pinochet coup on September 11, 1973, that ousted the Allende government constrained these aspirations. Irarrázaval's involvement with the Christians for Socialism helped shape in him a more militant form of Catholicism, which sought to liberate Latin American society from its state of dependency within a center-periphery world capitalist system. In 1975, he was invited to work in Perú by Gustavo Gutiérrez. In Perú, Irarrázaval revealed a new appreciation of the everyday religious practices of ordinary people. Irarrázaval's life and context cannot be divorced from his scholarly research and pastoral work. He is not a traditional scholar and does not work primarily within academic institutions. Like many liberationists, he has always sought to immerse himself in the daily lives of excluded peoples. He represents a great example of a grassroots theologian who lives an incarnational Christian life by embodying the liberationist ideal of opting for the poor and excluded. Over the years he has demonstrated an increasing preoccupation with working in dialogue with other "new (and newer) voices" in theology, such as feminist theologies, indigenous theologies, black theologies, ecological theologies, and theologies springing out of popular movements. Irarrázaval calls this dialogic work towards liberation "communion in plurality," where convergences and meeting points collide in a deepening pluralism that calls to mind the Spirit-imbued experience of the Pentecost.[9]

Irarrázaval was ordained a priest in the order of the Congregation of the Holy Cross.[10] He holds a master's degree in theology from the Divinity School of the University of Chicago, but did not pursue academic work at the doctoral level. Among his principle teachers have been the poor

9. Irarrázaval, *Inculturation: New Dawn of the Church in Latin America*, trans. P. Berryman (Maryknoll, NY: Orbis, 2000) 10.

10. This is same order that accepted, in 1870, Alfred Bessette, as a lay brother into their ranks. Before entering the religious order, Bessette was an uneducated doorkeeper at le Collège Notre-Dame in Montréal, which was founded by the Congregation of the Holy Cross. Better known by his religious name, Frère André, this man is the source of a rich tradition of popular religion in Montréal. Upon visiting the Oratoire St-Joseph in Montréal, which was built in honour of the popular healer, Irarrázaval related to me that he had much respect for Frère André's healing abilities, which he compared to the practices of the Aymaran and Quechuan peoples of Perú.

Aymaran and Quechuan peoples of the Altiplano, especially in and around the small village of Chucuito, on the shores of Lake Titicaca, along the Bolivian border, where he worked as a priest and researcher. Irarrázaval spent twenty-three years in Chucuito, most of the time as a parish priest and coordinator of the Instituto de Estudios Aymaras. Irarrázaval left the Altiplano and returned to Chile in 2004. Irarrázaval is a proficient writer. Since the early 1990s, he has published over fifteen books of theology and become a major voice in the development of liberation theologies in Latin America and the Caribbean. He has also published papers and articles on a wide variety of topics, including popular religion, inculturation and syncretism, religious humor, indigenous religious systems, feminism and eco-justice, and religious pluralism. Only his book, *Inculturation: The Dawn of the Church in Latin America* (2000), has been translated into English, thus making Irarrázaval's work relatively unknown within the academic circles of the so-called First World. In 2001, Irarrázaval was elected president of EATWOT (Ecumenical Association of Third World Theologians) in Quito, Ecuador. His EATWOT tenure ended in 2006. He is presently a board member of the international journal of theology, *Concilium*, and part-time on the faculty at the Redemptorist-run Instituto Superior De Teología y Pastoral Alfonsiano, in Santiago, Chile.

Critiquing Religious Oppression

In his book *Popular Religion and Liberation*, Michael Candelaria wrote that as a member of the Christians for Socialism, Diego Irarrázaval "berated popular religion as a false praxis."[11] Candelaria quoted from an article written by Irarrázaval in 1975, entitled *"Cristianos en el proceso socialista"*: "[Popular religion] appears as a false practice of liberation, because it departs from the consciousness and struggle of the oppressed. It is a false practice because it does not break free from the chains that enslave the people."[12] However, Candelaria's characterization of Irarrázaval as "berating" popular religion must be understood in context. It is important to remember that during the early 1970s in Chile, the members of Christians for Socialism were preoccupied with demonstrating to Christians, especially

11. Michael R. Candelaria wrongly characterized Irarrázaval as being a "liberation theologian from Peru." *Popular Religion and Liberation: The Dilemma of Liberation Theology* (Albany: SUNY Press, 1990) 7.

12. Ibid., 7.

PART TWO—Contextual and Constructive Proposals

Catholics, that they could be both faithful Christians and Socialists. They were also attempting to demonstrate to the radical groups they sought to form alliances with that Christianity could be revolutionary and socialist. The members of Christians for Socialism argued that religion was a crucial and necessary element in the transformation of Latin America and the Caribbean from its state of dependency on imperial powers. They argued that *all* forms of religion, especially "official" forms, should be transformed. During this particular moment, these Christians developed a critical consciousness about how hegemonic religion could impede the revolutionary process.[13] Hence, a Marxist critique of religious oppression moved to the center of leadership discourses, which targeted the church of Christendom in Latin America and the Caribbean because of its history of blessing elite structures.[14]

Some liberationists were influenced in part by the idea of ideological domination, and were particularly attuned to the ways subaltern peoples internalized this domination in their religious practices. Religious practices that centered on the cross were an area of deep suspicion, because they were perceived by Marxists and Socialists as blessing colonial triumph and fatalism about one's own suffering in the world. In a later book, Irarrázaval said this about his perspective on popular religious practices while in Chile, especially the cross-centered practices of Good Friday: "on this matter I can confess that during many years I loathed those rites and did not see in them the contents of the faith, but in this" and in so many other areas "the people have taught me much*."[15] For many radical Latin Americans in that period, especially Marxists, religion was seen to be within the hegemonic control of the ruling classes and was dismissed as reactionary. Religious displays that

---

13. Pablo Richard explained that the concern in the early 1970s within these circles in Chile was to "orient popular religion toward a socialist dimension*" (*Origen y desarrollo del movimiento Cristianos por el Socialismo: Chile, 1970–1973* [Paris: Centre Lebret, 1975] 147).

14. As David Fernández Fernández notes in his history of the Christians for Socialism movement in the early 1970s, some of the people he interviewed in Santiago "experienced the CpS (Cristianos por el Socialismo) as a vanguard of the revolution with a strong sectarian flavour" ("Oral History of the Chilean Movement 'Christians for Socialism,' 1971–73," *Journal of Contemporary History* 34 [1999] 293).

15. Irarrázaval, *Teología en la fe del pueblo* (San José: Costa Rica: Departamento Ecumenico de Investigaticiones, 1999) 70. I use the asterisk (*) at the end of quotes to signify my own translations from the Spanish. Many of the works used in my research have not been translated into English. If works already exist in translation, I use the published translations unless indicated by an asterisk.

exhibited conquered or oppressed peoples, especially indigenous peoples, carrying the cross were often met with disgust and disdain by progressives and radicals. This was perceived as the ultimate symbol of the ongoing spiritual and material conquest of Latin America and the Caribbean. But as I will show below, Irarrázaval quickly shifted his perspective and would later argue that for "the people" of Latin America and the Caribbean, the cross is "the principal religious symbol*."[16]

After his arrival in Perú, Irarrázaval faced a context where "the church wanted to be able to connect their pastoral work more concretely with the people's context and experience."[17] Irarrázaval arrived in Perú shortly after the publication of an important study by Raúl Vidales and Tokihiro Kudó, *Práctica religiosa y proyecto histórico* (1975),[18] which sought to highlight the liberative dimensions of popular religion present in the emergent classes. As I mentioned already, Gutiérrez had invited Irarrázaval to go to Chimbote, in northern Perú, specifically to study popular religion within a liberationist perspective. Hence the context in Perú was much more receptive to popular religion than his earlier experiences had been in Santiago. This was partly due to the culturally indigenous stamp, with its radically different and diverse traditions, that shapes the Peruvian context.

In an interview with Irarrázaval in 2001, I asked him how his work on popular religion from 1976 onwards (in Chimbote, Perú) was perceived at the time, considering that some liberationists rejected popular religion. His answer was quite revealing of a liberation theologian for whom a critique of religious oppression is central: "Yes, that critical perspective continues. And I'm so happy that it does, because it is not simply a critique of popular religion but a critique of all forms of religion that are oppressive."[19] This critical approach was very prominent in the context of the 1970s, because many Latin American Christians made the radical move of opting for the poor: religious educators left elite schools for the barrios; pastoral workers opted for marginal areas; priests focused their energies on building CEBs in

---

16. Irarrázaval, "La cruz de un pueblo crucificado," in *El Señor de los Milagros: Devoción y liberación*, ed. Diego Irarrázaval and Jeffrey Klaiber (Lima: Instituto Bartolome de Las Casas, 1998) 41.

17. Mario Bellemare, "The Feast of the Uninvited: Popular Religion, Liberation, Hybridity," PhD diss., Univ. of St. Michael's College, Toronto, 2008, 306.

18. Raúl Vidales and Tokihiro Kudó, *Práctica religiosa y proyecto histórico* (Lima: Centro de Estudios y Publicationes, 1975).

19. Bellemare, "Feast," 307.

PART TWO—Contextual and Constructive Proposals

rural areas; and some bishops opted to speak with, and help give voice to, the voiceless and excluded.

The 1970s were a time of unprecedented change for religious institutions, for men and women religious, and for lay and ordained Catholics in Latin America and the Caribbean. After many years of reflection, those who had switched sides, so to speak, became keenly aware of the colonial framework that underlined the Catholic presence in the region. This entailed a sharp critique of all forms of religious oppression and alienation. And they found in the Bible, in both the Hebrew and Christian scriptures, a solid framework of prophetic criticism of religious oppression, especially one's own beloved traditions.[20] Because of a long history of sharp stereotypes fashioned by elites within modern liberal perspectives, popular religion was interpreted as a phenomenon of mass superstition and ignorance. Elite liberal discourses argued that popular religion was irrational and anti-modern, and therefore the "mass" character of popular religion was dismissed. Some liberationists leveled their critique against the impact of hegemonic religion on popular religion more specifically. But Irarrázaval's work demonstrates that this exclusively negative reaction was short-lived among discerning liberationists. By the mid-1970s, Irarrázaval had moved from a position of critical evaluation to one of critical openness.

¡Un pueblo caminando con el Cristo Morado!

In the 2001 interview, Irarrázaval stated that "popular religion was clearly something I was concerned about before I arrived to Perú."[21] Also, he made his decision to go to Perú after he was invited "to do research on how people practice their faith at a popular level."[22] Irarrázaval's move to Perú to work with Gutiérrez at the Instituto Bartolomé de las Casas, in Lima, confirms that a serious interest in popular religion was developing among these early liberationists in the mid-1970s. Upon arriving in Perú, Irarrázaval made his way north to the coastal fishing town of Chimbote to research

---

20. Rosemary Radford Ruether defined prophetic criticism as a critique that originates from within a tradition. She noted, "[t]hus our own critique of scripture for failing to live up to its own prophetic promise reflects and is rooted in the self-criticism that goes on in, and is basic to, biblical faith itself." *To Change the World: Christology and Cultural Criticism* (London: SCM, 1981) 5.

21. Bellemare, "Feast," 306.

22. Ibid.

popular religion. Irarrázaval stated that there "was a sector in the church at the time in Chimbote that was interested in [popular religion] and had begun a study of these things before I arrived."[23] Two years later, Irarrázaval produced his first book, *Religión del pobre y liberación en Chimbote* (1978),[24] a theological study of popular religious practices with a methodological focus that prioritized the social sciences, especially sociology.

The engagement with a social science perspective by progressive Catholic scholars and theologians in a post-Vatican II context was significant. Many theologians turned to the social sciences as a way of articulating an alternative to the highly abstract philosophical paradigm that had been entrenched in traditional systematic theology.[25] For Irarrázaval, a more empirical sociological/anthropological/historical approach meant that, instead of attempting to formulate theories about the role of "the people" in Latin American society, he developed a method called the "*acción-teórica*," where he collected interviews in communities with practitioners of popular religion.[26] Irarrázaval asserted that this was a "new approach" in the *doing* of theology:

> [I]n this actual decade, we are seeing a new approach being developed toward the religion of the people and toward its evangelization. It is the posture of pastoral teams and organic theoreticians who are acting in relation to the history of the popular classes, within the perspective of the theology of liberation*.[27]

This was scientific research rooted in concrete pastoral work, which did not claim to be objective or neutral. Emphasizing wider concern for liberation among the pastoral teams he worked with, Irarrázaval conceptualized a perspective which is "characterized by its approach to the religious factor within the project of liberation of the poor*."[28] He affirmed that "the intention is an interdisciplinary focus appealing in particular to sociological, anthropological, historical, and theological elements; its scientific rigour responds to the interests of the oppressed classes . . . *"[29] In his research,

23. Ibid.

24. See Irarrázaval, *Religión del pobre y liberación en Chimbote* (Lima: Centro de Estudios y Publicaciones, 1978).

25. See, for example, Gregory Baum, *Religion and Alienation: A Theological Reading of Sociology* (Mahwah, NJ: Paulist, 1975).

26. Irarrázaval, *Religión del pobre*, 35.

27. Ibid., 30–31.

28. Ibid., 31.

29. Ibid.

Part Two—Contextual and Constructive Proposals

Irarrázaval concretely found a "people" deeply engaged in the creation of their own popular religious symbols and practices.

In his investigations, Irarrázaval began formulating a perspective on popular religion as the action of a people walking forward, on life's pilgrimage, with the people's own images, songs, dances, and *fiestas*. This became for him an important hermeneutical key for understanding popular religion in the daily life of Latin American peoples, and was an aspect that concretely resonated with the world of popular religion, with its many processions, pilgrimages, and *fiestas*. Irarrázaval sought to move beyond paternalistic prejudices that imposed themselves on the faith of "the people," such as vanguardist (Marxism: popular religion = alienation), elitist (liberal: popular religion = superstition), and conservative ("official" church: popular religion = idolatry) perspectives. As I will explain below, Irarrázaval's approach emphasized eschatological hope in the image of a forward-moving people.

¡Un pueblo caminando con el Cristo Morado![30] was how Irarrázaval framed Perú's most important feast: *El Señor de los Milagros* (October 18). In 1977 Irarrázaval wrote a pioneering article from a liberationist perspective on the processional movement of "the people" in the devotion to the *Señor de los Milagros*. Entitled "*Cristo Morado: Señor de los maltratados*," it is one of the most important early liberationist appraisals of popular religion to surface in Latin America and the Caribbean. As in his study about Chimbote, the article drew upon the more empirical methods and findings of sociology, anthropology, and history in order to lay out concretely the tapestry of religious experiences that make up this stunning feast day. In reporting on interviews with practitioners, Irarrázaval demonstrated that this feast day meant very different things to the millions of Peruvians who participate in it. According to Irarrázaval, the feast is especially popular with Aymaran and Quechuan peoples, who, among other reasons, strongly identify with the feast because of its humble origins among enslaved peoples. Hence, for Irarrázaval, it is a feast that belongs to all the oppressed and *maltratados* of Perú. The legend of the image is rooted in the anti-colonial practices of Black slaves who saw in the crucified One a man of sorrows like themselves and worshipped him according to their own cultural traditions brought to the Americas on slave boats.

---

30. "A people walking with the purple Christ."

According to a church booklet, entitled *Historia de la sagrada imagen del Cristo de Pachacamilla*,[31] the legend of the origins of the feast dates from the mid-seventeenth century, in Pachacamilla, on the outskirts of Lima, where Black slaves from Angola and elsewhere in Africa, began to sing, dance, and pray together before an image of the crucified Jesus painted by one of the slaves. The colonial and ecclesial authorities became alarmed by the ecstatic power of these practices, and attempted to put a stop to them for fear that they could irrupt into something more rebellious. But the devotion grew too rapidly. As Irarrázaval explained, like most systems of power that seek to maintain hegemonic control, the ecclesial authorities attempted to incorporate the rituals into the colonial order.[32] People attributed many miracles to the image, especially as protection against earthquakes. To this day, the feast's fraternal associations, or brotherhoods, link their origins to the first Black slaves who gathered before the image. Because of its multiple usages within the colonial order by dominant groups, which often domesticates its initial anti-colonial impetus, Irarrázaval argued that there are multiple and even contradictory interpretations of the *Milagros* feast in Perú. Like all cultural and religious symbols and texts, popular religion was for him always multiple, polyvalent, and open-ended, with shifting meanings and interpretations arising from different social locations throughout history.

Irarrázaval's Typologies

Irarrázaval delineated four different interpretations of the *Milagros* feast. But Irarrázaval specifically focused on this one feast, rather than on popular religion more generally. Irarrázaval did not posit these interpretations as all-encompassing paradigms, but situated them in relation to the actual feast of *El Señor de los Milagros*. In the early 1980s, Irarrázaval argued that "popular religion does not exist. There only exists, and one can only study, the religious practices of concrete subjects in specific social conditions*."[33] In other words, abstract definitions that are divorced from history will

---

31. Anonymous popular booklet purchased at the Iglesia de la Nazarenas, in Lima, with no publication date.

32. Irarrázaval, *Cristo Morado*, 307.

33. Irarrázaval, "Prologue," in Tokihiro Kudó, *Práctica religiosa y proyecto histórico*, vol.2: *Estudios sobre la religión popular en dos barrios de Lima* (Lima: Centro de Estudios y Publicationes, 1980) 12.

PART TWO—Contextual and Constructive Proposals

always fall short of the powerful complexity, the plural realities, and the symbolic density that is constitutive of popular religion. Accordingly, Irarrázaval identified these approaches to *El Señor de los Milagros* as "partial interpretations*."[34] According to him, because there is no such thing as an abstract phenomenon called popular religion, no single interpretation can do justice to the complexity of this feast. And while practitioners cling to tradition, they also re-shape the feast in response to the changing context in ways that are often imperceptible, especially to outsiders.

As I mentioned above, Irarrázaval wrote "*Cristo Morado: Señor de los maltratados*" in 1977, at a time when Lima had already experienced a surge of rural migrants (750,000 by the end of the sixties), which lead to the creation of *pueblos jóvenes* around its core.[35] Latin America more generally was experiencing a massive influx of rural peoples into the major cities in this period.[36] Regional diversity in tightly knit urban communities generated by rural migrants from all over the country was reflected in a shifting tapestry of devotions surrounding the feast. In this article, Irarrázaval argued that what is truly "significant [about this feast] is how a mutation occurred at the symbolic level*."[37] For example, Irarrázaval wrote, "[t]he Lord of the slaves went to being Lord of all races and classes, even though the devotion was strongly marked by the experience of the poor*."[38] This mutation happened in part because the feast was appropriated by the dominant classes and redeployed as a national feast. But a feast such as *El Señor de los Milagros* never has only one single over-arching meaning. For Irarrázaval, a processional "people" on the move making history is also making and re-making its devotions anew.

In order to highlight the multiplicity of perspectives on the *Milagros* feast, Irarrázaval delineated four approaches. He identified the first approach as the "evangelical interpretation." This interpretation conceived of popular religious practices as a form of idolatry, where images are

34. Irarrázaval, *Cristo Morado*, 311.

35. Thomas E. Skidmore and Peter H. Smith, *Modern Latin America*, 5th ed. (New York: Oxford University Press, 2001) 206.

36. The Latin American continent has experienced a massive shift in the last 50 years, going from what was a predominantly rural continent to an urban one. Berryman notes, "the typical Latin American living today is not a peasant but lives in the city. Indeed, 72 percent of Latin Americans are urban." *Religion in the Megacity* (Maryknoll, NY: Orbis, 1996) 4.

37. Irarrázaval, *Cristo Morado*, 309.

38. Ibid., 309.

worshipped instead of God.[39] Irarrázaval was referring to fundamentalist (*integrista*) interpretations that seek to defeat what is considered sinful pagan-like practices, in order to establish instead a biblical truth and a type of salvation that is individualistic and other-worldly. The second approach, according to Irarrázaval, is the "traditionalist perspective." It is characterized by a dichotomy between "official" and "popular." For Irarrázaval, this perspective is "the one that carries the most weight in Peruvian society*."[40] Irarrázaval argued that, because El Señor de los Milagros had become an unofficial national feast, ecclesial authorities "attempt to defend popular religion in order to promote a spiritual doctrine of personal piety that merges with the social order*."[41] In this perspective, the ecclesial authorities also attempt to control the meaning of the symbols related to the image (sun, moon, Father, Christ, Holy Spirit, Mary) by interpreting them in ways that are divorced from the people's own this-worldly everyday concerns. Most importantly, there is an imposition in this perspective of "practical recommendations, of a pietistic type, but with obvious political implications*."[42]

The third approach is the "functionalist perspective." This is an interesting proposal coming from a theologian like Irarrázaval, who at this time, was heavily invested in social science perspectives. Irarrázaval wrote that this perspective "uses the social sciences and appeals to modern theology. This is the case with the influential observations contributed by Manuel Marzal*."[43] Irarrázaval argued that the functionalist perspective has many positive features, such as laying out the social functions of this feast for the identity of a people who share a common religious vision. The functionalist perspective is positive in that it tends to highlight the importance of popular religion as a journey of life for individuals in limited situations, and because it attempts to understand Peruvian culture, with its religious inheritance, in light of its public acts of worship, *fiesta*, and communitarian encounters.[44] However, the functionalist perspective is limited, argued Irarrázaval, insofar as it does not "sufficiently go into the specific and profound fibers of the faith of the people, with its alienation and its symbolic

---

39. Ibid., 311.
40. Ibid., 312.
41. Ibid., 313.
42. Ibid.
43. Ibid., 314.
44. Ibid.

resistance*."⁴⁵ For Irarrázaval, this had the effect "of diminishing the historical amplitude of the 'encounter of God in Jesus Christ' in the terms of dominant individualism*."⁴⁶

The fourth partial interpretation of *El Señor de los Milagros* is what Irarrázaval called the "reductionist perspective." Here Irarrázaval was critical of attempts to reduce the figure of *El Señor de los Milagros* to a present-day revolutionary. Again, Irarrázaval did not shy away from critiquing a perspective close to his own (especially considering that he is coming from a context of militancy with the Christians for Socialism and working within a liberationist framework). For Irarrázaval,

> the objective of this perspective in the end is to legitimize a "humanist and Christian socialism," and through this manipulate the religion of the poor. . . . That's why the Christians who participate in the gestation of this socialist project do not need to put forward such distortions of the faith.*⁴⁷

Here Irarrázaval was critiquing the facile attempt by some vanguardists who equated Jesus with a modern revolutionary who overcomes capitalism. This was not the Jesus that Irarrázaval had encountered in the feasts of the poor and excluded, but a construction of the vanguardist kind that sought to instrumentalize Jesus for its own purposes. For Irarrázaval, the Purple Jesus belongs to "the people," not to an elite few who use the idea of "Jesus the revolutionary" to establish links with the so-called church sectors. Irarrázaval argued that "highlighting the liberative dimension of the gospel" must be deeply rooted in the faith of "the people" who "accompany Christ" in their daily lives.⁴⁸ Irarrázaval regarded "the people's" faith as a place from which to construct a theology of liberation. However, liberation could never be an imposition of the elites, but a dimension emerging from within "the people's" own accompaniment with Jesus in their feasts, processions, and pilgrimages.

45. Ibid., 315.
46. Ibid.
47. Ibid., 316.
48. Ibid.

A Church Moving Forward

Irarrázaval argued for an approach that appreciates the feast on its own terms: one that accompanies those who are accompanying the processional Christ. As I mentioned earlier, Irarrázaval's central notion for this feast is pilgrimage. Irarrázaval explained that when the procession stops and pauses, every new movement forward is punctuated with the words: "let us move forward brothers!*"[49] "This gesture," added Irarrázaval, ⊠with its significance of ecclesial movement, suggests an actual demand. The practitioners of the Purple Christ are announcing the gospel, because the poor masses have the right and the duty to show publicly their profound experience of Christ*."[50] For Irarrázaval, the practitioners of this feast are not simply objects of the evangelization process, namely from the clerical class down to the laity through the rituals, but are subjects of the evangelical process, whereby their own experience of Christ is announced as an eschatological journey, a movement forward, a life's pilgrimage toward a different tomorrow.

The lay practitioners of this popular religious feast are thus not simply partaking in the traditions of the church; they are moving the church forward in history and are announcing themselves as church. A practitioner whom Irarrázaval interviewed in the streets said very succinctly: "And to be in a procession, one feels a deep harmony of being accompanied*."[51] This sense of accompaniment is not simply in relation to Christ, but also in the manifestation of Christ in history: the church. Another person is quoted as saying: "*El Señor de los Milagros* forms a brotherhood with all the workers, a sort of temple*."[52] Here Irarrázaval was pointing to the lay ecclesiology being proclaimed by the poor and marginalized in the procession of *El Señor de los Milagros*.

Irarrázaval was very careful to remind his readers that there will always be very clear variations in how the feast is experienced in Perú. One cannot forget the ways in which those who hold to the "traditionalist" perspective attempted to use the feast to legitimize an oppressive and dehumanizing

---

49. Ibid. At this time, Irarrázaval did not critique the patriarchal framework of these so-called "brotherhoods," but they were then, and are still today, dominated by men. In dialogue with feminist theologies, Irarrázaval has become more conscious of gender asymmetries in his theology.

50. Ibid., 316–17.

51. Ibid., 322.

52. Ibid.

Part Two—Contextual and Constructive Proposals

social order. Hence for Irarrázaval, the processional pilgrimage of the people has two trajectories, one from above and the other from below. In the former, the procession is a mass of individuals lead by the dominant class. The groups with power transform the faith of the people into a worship of the political-national. But in the one from below, "the procession is an act of the masses, where the mistreated who accompany Christ express their collective yearning for liberation*."[53] Here Irarrázaval is expressing much more than the double dimension paradigm of the CELAM bishops at Puebla conference (1979), where popular religion is defined as having both positive (cultural matrix, human dignity, etc.) and negative (superstition, syncretism, etc.) aspects woven together. This kind of analysis can lead to a "traditionalist" posture of imposed purification, whereby the "official" church is called upon to evangelize the deficient aspects and purify the contaminated aspects of the faith. Irarrázaval's characterization of different trajectories from below and from above challenges the double dimension perspective adopted later at Puebla. In Irarrázaval's processional perspective, the people in the processions are not reduced to objects of evangelization whose practices have aspects that are orthodox and deficient. The processional people are moving forward as subjects of history, not in a progress narrative, but as a church yearning for liberation. The processional people, *los maltratados con su fe firme y sencilla*,[54] incarnate eschatological hope, and everyone (the universal) is called to follow them (the specific poor ones), including the clerical class.

With this important article in 1977, Irarrázaval began to enter the world of popular religion on its own terms using a multifaceted social-scientific approach focused on the hopes and aspirations of the popular classes. In shifting to this processional perspective, where "the people" walk in solidarity with their Purple Jesus, Irarrázaval was clearly developing what Scannone called the "emergent class" perspective in his own work on popular religion.[55] This paradigm was characterized by its focus on popular religion as a strategy of resistance for subaltern peoples making history. Irarrázaval attempted to delineate articulations of the feast that belonged to "the people" from those that were instrumentalizing popular religion for

53. Ibid., 326.

54. I am using Irarrázaval's language here: *the maltreated ones with their simple and firm faith*.

55. Juan Carlos Scannone, *Evangelización, cultura, y teología* (Buenos Aires: Guadalupe, 1990) 163.

their own purposes. Through close contact with participants and through his own participation in their processional feasts, Irarrázaval critiqued attempts to control or purify popular religious practices from the "official" church sectors to the discourses of some left-wing vanguards. Similar to Gutiérrez, who insisted that "the religious experiences of the people are charged with values of protest, resistance, and liberation."[56] Irarrázaval sought to highlight these aspects in his research without romanticizing everything that comes from the "the people." He continued to utilize this approach after he moved to the Altiplano in the early 1980s to become the coordinator of the Instituto de Estudios Aymaras, while developing a more deeply rooted anthropological method focused on the cultural systems of Aymaran and Quechuan peoples. There is another story to tell here, one that features *fiesta* (feast) and *sanación* (healing) as integral parts of a theology informed by the everyday pilgrimages of Andean peoples. But for the purposes of this chapter we will have to stop at 1977.

I have shown that as early as the mid to late 1970s, Irarrázaval argued for (and hoped for) a newly transformed Latin America and Caribbean rooted in the everyday cultures and popular religious practices of subaltern peoples. Irarrázaval's theology was deeply rooted in the peoples' processional movement of walking forward in history. He worked very closely with ordinary lay people, as a pastor and as a researcher who utilized a social-scientific approach in order to partially tap into their daily wisdoms. Irarrázaval is an example of a liberationist who had a broader and more nuanced understanding of oppression and liberation, one that was clearly forged in the festive everyday cultures of excluded peoples. Irarrázaval understood that accompaniment was the way forward with a *pueblo* whose own religious practices constituted a framework for liberation. This perspective of accompaniment has proved to be a lasting one. As part of an ongoing dialogue with feminist, indigenous, black, and Latino/a voices, the work undertaken by liberationists such as Diego Irarrázaval on popular religion has helped secure a trajectory for a more complex and nuanced understanding of religious pluralism in the contemporary Latin America and the Caribbean context.

---

56. Gutiérrez, *Power of the Poor*, 193.

8

The Church and Indigenous Cultures

Beyond the Violent Encounter with "Modernity"

MICHEL ANDRAOS

> Modernity's recent impact on the planet's multiple cultures . . . produced a varied "reply" by all of them to the modern "challenge." Renewed, they are now erupting on a cultural horizon "beyond" modernity.
>
> —Enrique Dussel

INTRODUCTION

THIS CHAPTER CONCERNS CHURCH and culture, and will focus mainly on some recent developments in the cultural encounter between the church and indigenous peoples within the Roman Catholic Diocese of San Cristóbal de Las Casas, Chiapas, Mexico. The pastoral practice of this local church since the 1970s, I believe, presents an alternative to the dominant model of mission theology that was the product of the colonial, violent cultural encounter of Western Christianity and indigenous peoples. This violent encounter, which characterized most indigenous peoples' experience of modernity, is still part of their lived reality in many parts of the world.[1] Their cultures have been demonized and excluded from the process of constructing the new society, civilization and church.

The main reason for my choice to write on this topic as part of this collection in honor of Lee Cormie is that I began this research under Cormie's direction in the mid 1990s when I started writing my doctoral dissertation.[2] My research continued since, and my thinking on this topic has evolved in a variety of new directions, which helped me connect the struggle of the indigenous peoples of Chiapas to other similar struggles around the world. I am more convinced today than when I began my research of the relevance of this case study and its potential contribution to current debates on church and culture, as I will explain in more detail below. The story I tell here is one of interaction between "faith, theology and concrete, historical hope," to use one of Cormie's cherished theological preoccupations.[3] For the most part, this story is still untold, under-studied, and marginalized in the global church.[4]

1. The term "modernity" as used in this article refers to the period that began with the conquest of the American continent by the Europeans as of 1492. There is no one agreed-upon interpretation of modernity. From a Eurocentric perspective, many authors talk about modernity in relation to the Enlightenment in 18th-century Europe, while several Latin American scholars refer to 1492 as the starting point of a new period in world history and the beginning of a re-configuration of the old systems of global relations with now Europe in the center. See also Enrique Dussel, *The Invention of the Americas: Eclipse of "the Other" and the Myth of Modernity*, trans. Michael Barber (New York: Continuum, 1995); idem, "World System and 'Trans'-Modernity," *Nepantla: Views from South*, 3/2 (2002) 221.

2. Michel Andraos, "Praxis of Peace: The Pastoral Work and Theology of Bishop Samuel Ruiz and the Diocese of San Cristóbal de Las Casas, Chiapas, Mexico," PhD diss., University of St. Michael's College, Toronto, 2000—available online from the National Library of Canada: www.collectionscanada.gc.ca/obj/s4/f2/dsk2/ftp02/NQ54044.pdf.

3. Lee Cormie speaks about this theological theme in many of his works. One article, which has particularly influenced my thinking on this topic, is "Seeds of Hope in the New World (Dis)order," in *Coalitions for Justice: The Story of Canada's Interchurch Coalitions*, ed. Christopher Lind and Joe Mihevc (Ottawa: Novalis, 1994) 360–77.

4. Despite the international attention on Chiapas since the indigenous uprising in January of 1994, there are still very few theological works on the experience of this local church, especially in the English language. The new book by Richard Gaillardetz, *Ecclesiology for a Global Church: A People Called and Sent* (Maryknoll, NY: Orbis, 2008) is the only theological work I am aware of that takes the experience of the Diocese of San Cristóbal seriously in its discussion on global ecclesiology. See also Michel Andraos, "Indigenous Leadership in the Church: The Experience of the Diocese of San Cristóbal de Las Casas, Chiapas, Mexico," *Toronto Journal of Theology* 21 (2005) 57–65; and Richard Gaillardetz, "Accountability in the Church: Report from Chiapas," *New Theology Review* 19 (2006) 33–43.

PART TWO—Contextual and Constructive Proposals

The first part of this article will examine the stages and context of the developments of an emerging mission theology through exploring the evolving personal experience and theological perspectives of Samuel Ruiz García, bishop of the Diocese of San Cristóbal between 1960 and 2000. Ruiz's personal transformation story and his impressive pastoral and theological contributions are a witness to an era of profound change and a movement of hope in the church. The second part will look at some new intercultural experiences of this local church and their potential contribution to the universal church and to current debates on culture as we advance into the twenty-first century.

AN EMERGING PARADIGM OF MISSION THEOLOGY IN LATIN AMERICA[5]

A new mission theology emerged in many parts of Latin America around the time of the Second Vatican Council (1962–1965) and the meeting of the Latin American Bishops (CELAM II) in Medellín, Colombia (1968). The new theology challenged the old colonial models of mission that were operative in the church for several centuries.[6] Wherever the gospel was proclaimed to indigenous people in the "New World," notes Bishop Ruiz,

> with it came a new culture, namely the Western culture, and it was imposed on people as the only way of living the Christian faith. This imposition, therefore, created a real and visible cultural and religious schizophrenia with obvious symptoms among all the Native peoples in the continent.... We realized that their marginalization, poverty and misery were not the result of their free choice but rather were the result of a process in which we are involved and which we need to rethink.[7]

---

5. A shorter version of part II of this chapter was published online by *Learn@CTU* in memory of Bishop Samuel Ruiz shortly after his death on January 24, 2011.

6. For a description of the relationship between the Catholic Church and the indigenous people of Southern Mexico, see John D. Early, *The Maya and Catholicism: An Encounter of Worldviews* (Gainesville: University Press of Florida, 2006).

7. Michel Andraos, ed. and trans., *Seeking Freedom: Bishop Samuel Ruiz in Conversation with Jorge S. Santiago on Time and History, Prophecy, Faith and Politics, and Peace* (Toronto: Toronto Council of the Canadian Catholic Organization for Development and Peace, 1999) 18–19.

A different approach to missionary work among indigenous peoples that began in the 1970s in dioceses such as San Cristóbal, among other places, informed and shaped a new mission theology. One of the key factors that contributed to this development is the interaction of some missionaries and pastoral leaders, including Ruiz, who was a new bishop then, with the anthropological movement at that time. This anthropological movement critiqued the Eurocentric missionary work of the church in Latin America and developed an alternative anthropology in support of the liberation of indigenous peoples. The interaction between pastoral workers and anthropologists from this movement gave an impetus for the development of a new mission theology.[8] Tracing in the following paragraphs the stages and context of the radical transformation of Ruiz's missionary approach, particularly as a result of his new understanding of the cultures of indigenous peoples, helps us better understand the significance of this new relationship between the church and local indigenous communities.

"When I came [to Chiapas]," recounted Bishop Ruiz, "I saw the churches full of Indians, but it was only later that I realized the sad reality of these people which provoked my conversion."[9] "My eyes were open," he said, "but I was sleeping."

> I traveled through villages where bosses were scourging debt-slaves who did not want to work more than eight hours a day, but all I saw were old churches and old women praying. "Such good

---

8. In a paper presented at the First International Colloquium in memory of anthropologist Andrés Aubry in San Cristóbal de Las Casas, December of 2007, Jorge Santiago outlined the history of the interactions between the anthropological movement that emerged in the 1970s and the missionaries and pastoral agents who worked in some dioceses of Mexico that have high indigenous population. Santiago notes that shortly after the *Encuentro de Antropólogos en Barbados* in 1971 and the declaration in support of the liberation of indigenous peoples that followed, several meetings took place between anthropologists and pastoral workers, both in Chiapas and the rest of Mexico. Bishop Ruiz, along with Andrés Aubry who worked closely with him and the pastoral agents of the Diocese of San Cristóbal since the early 1970s, participated in many of these meeting which, according to Santiago, had a significant influence on Ruiz's new understanding of culture and the subsequent development of his mission theology. See www.coloquio-internacionalandresaubry.org/aubry.html (accessed December 20, 2007). See also the interview of Santiago with Ruiz on this topic in Andraos, *Seeking Freedom*, 15-18.

9. Carlos Tello Díaz, *La Rebelión de las Cañadas* (Mexico City: Cal y Arena, 1995) 58–59. Unless indicated otherwise, all quotations from sources in the Spanish language are the author's translation.

PART TWO—Contextual and Constructive Proposals

> people," I said to myself, not noticing that these good people were victims of cruel oppression.[10]

This blindness to social realities did not last very long. A few years later, the new bishop began to ask himself a fundamental question: What has the church been doing during all these years of evangelization, if the indigenous communities continue to be marginalized the same way as in colonial times?[11]

I will turn now to some of Bishop Ruiz's writings in the late 1960s and early 1970s in order to examine some of the key theological turning points that influenced the future development of his theology and pastoral ministry. One of the earliest available theological works by Bishop Ruiz is a paper that he presented at the Medellín meeting.[12] This paper comprises a critique of the missionary work of the Catholic Church in Latin America and the church's pastoral approach to indigenous peoples and their cultures.

On the topic of the presence of the Catholic Church in Latin America in general, Bishop Ruiz pointed out that "we must put an end to the myth that Latin America is a Catholic continent. If the Church is a 'community of faith, hope and charity,' this vision is not carried out in Latin America."[13] He pointed to several areas, including religion and culture, where he saw a juxtaposition of opposing social realities.

One aspect of his paper that is particularly pertinent to this essay is his analysis of the "Indian situation." Indigenous peoples, he argued, are marginalized at all levels. Generally, churches in their pastoral work either support their total integration, which is assumed to mean the death of their culture, or they go to the other extreme, that is, "promote a charitable and welfare-type assistance which does not take into consideration marginality and underdevelopment, and which does not see the necessity of basing

---

10. Gary MacEoin, *The People's Church: Bishop Samuel Ruiz of Mexico and Why He Matters* (New York: Crossroad, 1996) 26; see also Carlos Fazio, *El Caminante* (Mexico City: Espasa Calpe, 1994) 105–6.

11. Fazio, *El Caminante*, 101.

12. Samuel Ruiz, "Evangelization in Latin America," in *The Church in the Present-Day Transformation of Latin America in the Light of the Council, Second General Conference of Latin American Bishops, I, Position Papers* (Bogotá: General Secretariat of CELAM, 1970) 155–77.

13. Ibid., 155, 158. In the same vein, Bishop Ruiz commented in an address to a group of university students in Mexico City in 1995 saying, "I often wondered what has the church done here in 500 years?" Samuel Ruiz, *Reflexiones Pastorales ante Universitarios* (Mexico City: Universidad Iberoamericana, 1995) 12.

this help on Indian values, cultures, and ways of thinking."[14] The paper also pointed out that the present ways of evangelization were destroying indigenous cultures.

In his subsequent pastoral work and theological reflections, Bishop Ruiz continued to give special attention to the areas of faith, evangelization, and cultures. Since the early 1970s, he became convinced that divine salvific work is present in other cultures, and that it is necessary for the church to enter into honest dialogue with other peoples and their cultures in order to discover and learn about this divine presence. He began, then, to consider this dialogue as an essential part of the missionary work of the church. In his view, this was the important contribution of the Vatican II document *Ad Gentes*, and he had no illusion concerning the difficulty of this task.[15] "The missionary church," he argued,

> is facing a delicate and difficult work: the study and accurate, positive and sympathetic knowledge of non-Christian religions. The church has to see in these religions a divine element and a presence of God (Vatican II, *Ad Gentes*, 9 b et 11 b); and more so, to know that the Word of God, before he became flesh in order to save and gather up all things in himself, was already in the world, as the "true light that enlightens every man" (Jn 1,9 and *Gaudium et Spes*, 57).[16]

According to Bishop Ruiz, there are not two parallel histories in the world, one sacred and one profane. He learned from his work with indigenous communities that God's work is revealed in the history of all peoples and that God's Spirit is present in all cultures—the Spirit was at work in the world before Christ.[17] In Ruiz's view, this is an important theological foundation for inter-religious and intercultural dialogue. Making reference to *Ad Gentes, Gaudium et Spes*, and to the letter to the Ephesians, he asserted:

> If there is only one history of salvation and this history includes all peoples of all times, then God has already acted and is still acting

14. Ruiz, "Evangelization in Latin America," 166.

15. See the commentary by Bishop Ruiz on this topic in Felipe J. Ali Modad Aguilar, SJ, *Engrandecer el Corazón de la Comunidad: El Sacerdocio Ministerial en una Iglesia Inculturada* (Mexico City: Centro de Reflexión Teológica, 1999) 5.

16. Samuel Ruiz, "Le Monde d'Aujourd'hui Interpelle la Théologie," in Samuel Ruiz et Edgard Beltran, *L'Utopie Chrétienne, Libérer l'Homme* (Québec: Edition Départ, Entraide Missionnaire, 1971) 24.

17. Samuel Ruiz and Javier Vargas, "Pasión y Resurrección del Indio," *Estudios Indígenas* 2/1 (1972) 35–48.

PART TWO—Contextual and Constructive Proposals

>today in all cultures. The presence of God, and the presence of the Word (the seeds of the Divine Word) appear in the multiple cultural riches and values that are rays of the supreme Truth (*Ad Gentes*, 9 b, 11 b; *Nostra Ætate*, 2 b; *Gaudium et Spes*, 38). These values that prepare the way for the gospel, which are either implicitly salvific, ascetic or mystical, were present prior to the preaching of the gospel (*Ad Gentes*, 3 a; 18 b; *Gaudium et Spes*, 92 d).[18]

Vatican II, notes Bishop Ruiz, affirmed these theological principles and opened the way for a genuine religious and cultural dialogue. The church is called to act on this by engaging in dialogue with other cultures to discover their religious and spiritual richness. Part of the church's work of evangelization, then, insisted Ruiz, is to dialogue with cultures and learn about God's salvific presence in them. In this sense, the church is called to be a servant to the world, and not to act as its master by imposing a foreign culture on other peoples. These aspects of a theology of history and a theology of culture have been clear in Ruiz's mind since the early 1970s. They provided a theological foundation that guided and supported his pastoral practice.

It is important to clarify what Ruiz means by "culture" in order to understand the significance of the above claims. Culture, according to him, is the totality of expressions that members of a determined ethnic group formulate in their relationship to the transcendent, to each other, and to their physical environment. He compares culture to the dignity of the human person: culture should be respected in the same way the individual human dignity should be respected. In other words, cultural symbols represent the collective dignity of a people. Following from this, Bishop Ruiz asserts that culture is sacred and that its destruction can never be justified. Cultural elements should never be changed by external agents (e.g., missionaries) without the consensus of the community—even if the changes are minor. Learning to understand and respect another culture is the cross of the missionary, he added.[19]

"What does it mean, then, to evangelize?" asked Bishop Ruiz. "If there is only one history," he asserted, "it is logical to conclude that God's work of

18. Samuel Ruiz, "Ecclésiologie et Engagement Pastoral," in Ruiz and Beltran, *L'Utopie Chrétienne*, 63–64.

19. Ruiz and Vargas, "Pasión y Resurrección del Indio," 37; see also Samuel Ruiz, "Testimonio de Mons. Samuel Ruiz: 25 Años Caminando con los Pueblos Indígenas," in *Signos de Nueva Evangelización: Testimonios de la Iglesia en América Latina 1983–1987*, ed. Carmen Lora et al. (Lima: Centro de Estudios y Publicaciones, 1988) 114.

salvation has always been active in the bosom of each culture." To evangelize, then, is to discover and affirm this reality. Bishop Ruiz identifies three stages of evangelization: (1) to understand and believe in this salvific presence of God in history; (2) to be personally incarnated in a culture through an authentic sharing of peoples' experience; and (3) to affirm through internal proper cultural expressions with the community the salvific work of God in its history.[20]

Since the early 1970s, Bishop Ruiz, among many others, concluded that the missionary work of the church among indigenous communities was destroying their cultures in the name of the gospel. Destroying a people's culture is trampling on their dignity and pride, and humiliating them as a people. This kind of missionary work is not acceptable according to the gospel message and to Christian tradition as emphasized by Vatican II and Medellín.[21] "The missionary may only stay," asserted Bishop Ruiz, "on the condition of developing pastoral action which promotes the liberation of the people. But that will be something totally different from what is understood as missionary work now."[22] A new accent emerged in the development of his theology: liberation of the people is integral and it includes the liberation of their culture.

A second key theme that developed in his theology in the 1970s is the salvific work of God in concrete history. This theme is linked to the social role of the church, inculturation and incarnation of the gospel message. The incarnation of the church in a specific culture, he affirms, is also an incarnation in a specific historic process here and now. The purpose of this incarnation is to transform history and make it a history of salvation. "The church," notes Bishop Ruiz, "does not have as a goal the creation of a universal mono-culture."[23] This means for the church, he explains, a concrete historic contextual commitment in an alternative process to transform social reality. The Church, he asserts, should not be behind history, but rather moving it ahead.[24]

20. Ruiz and Vargas, "Pasión y Resurrección del Indio," 42–43; see also Ruiz, "Testimonio de Mons. Samuel Ruiz: 25 Años Caminando con los Pueblos Indígenas," 114.

21. See Vatican II, "Church in the Modern World," Nos. 53–62.

22. Ruiz and Vargas, "Pasión y Resurrección del Indio," 37–38; see also Ruiz, "Ecclésiologie et Engagement Pastoral," 66.

23. Ruiz, "Ecclésiologie et Engagement Pastoral," 67.

24. Samuel Ruiz and Edgard Beltran, "Les Grandes Options Pastorales du Missionnaire d'Aujourd'hui," in Ruiz and Beltran, *L'Utopie Chrétienne*, 95–97; see also Samuel Ruiz, *Los Cristianos y la Justicia en America Latina* (Lima: MIEC-JECI, Secretariado Latinoamericano, 1973) 12–13.

Part Two—Contextual and Constructive Proposals

The story of Ruiz's transformation outlined above is symbolic of a significant historic moment of cultural change in the church and the world at large. He is a Vatican II and a Medellín bishop who was both transformed by these events and made a difference by becoming a key player in transforming a diocesan pastoral process and mission theology in the Latin American church. The importance of Ruiz's transformation story is not only that he became an important bishop who made a difference, but that he also became a model of pastoral leadership in the church, particularly in relation to indigenous peoples. In the following section, I will focus on some areas of transformation in the Diocese of San Cristóbal that are also the result of a cultural dialogue between the local church and indigenous peoples.

Toward the Twenty-First Century

In *The Invention of the Americas*, Enrique Dussel notes:

> By controlling, conquering, and violating the Other, Europe defined itself as discoverer, conquistador, and colonizer of an alterity likewise constitutive of modernity. Europe never discovered (*descubierto*) this Other as Other but covered (*encubierto*) the Other as part of the Same: i.e., Europe. Modernity dawned in 1492 and with it the myth of a special kind of sacrificial violence which eventually eclipsed whatever was non-European.[25]

What was eclipsed during the last 500 hundred years has been resisting and irrupting again and again, as Dussel notes in the epigraph of this article. On January 1, 1994, using again an example from Chiapas, the Zapatistas made known to the whole world their loud cry: "Today We Say Enough is Enough!"[26] "We are a product of 500 years of struggle," they said and describe their historical resistance and ongoing struggle for justice against slavery and a sequence of imperial powers, which they consider the main cause of their misery.

Similar voices of protest were also echoed in several diocesan pastoral documents. In 1993, one year before the Zapatista uprising, the Diocese of San Cristóbal had issued a pastoral letter, *En Esta Hora de Gracia* (In this

25. Dussel, *Invention of the Americas*, 12.

26. See the First Declaration from the Lacandon Jungle of the Zapatista National Liberation Army (EZLN) "Today We Say Enough is Enough!" in *Zapatistas, Documents of the New Mexican Revolution* (New York: Autonomedia, 1994) 49.

Hour of Grace), which was collectively prepared by the pastoral agents of the diocese, including many indigenous representatives. The letter outlined the history of the struggle of indigenous peoples and the main stages of four decades of diocesan pastoral work, which, despite the efforts of solidarity, failed to bring any significant systemic change that would improve the miserable social, economic and cultural situation of these communities.[27] The document describes the atrocities committed against the indigenous communities and argues that, "in the name of modernization, globalization and free trade, these communities were being deprived of land, justice, education, democracy and the basic conditions needed for living a decent life. Their economic survival has become impossible."[28]

From the midst of these irruptions of struggle and protest new alternative movements are emerging, both in civil society and the church, which are forcing a dialogue in order to transform the old relations created by centuries-old patterns of cultural violence. The San Andrés Accords of peace that focus mainly on indigenous rights and culture, which were signed by the government of Mexico and the Zapatistas in February of 1996, are one of the best expressions of cultural dialogue for peace between the indigenous peoples of Mexico and the rest of the country. According to Navarro and Herrera, this agreement, which is the result of two years of deliberations between the two parties that included wide and intensive consultations of the indigenous communities and civil society, has as its "central proposal the end of inequality, discrimination, exploitation and political exclusion of indigenous peoples."[29] For the indigenous communities, the proposal their representatives presented at San Andrés became an impetus for a social movement for building a new society and new cultural relations with the rest of the world. This movement evolves mainly around strengthening indigenous autonomy and the institutional structures that sustain it in areas such as education, healthcare, economy and culture. Discussing in detail the progress and challenges of this new social project is outside the scope of this article. However, it suffices here to say that in many indigenous societies, in the Americas, and other places, the waves of cul-

27. Samuel Ruiz, *En Esta Hora de Gracia* (= "In This Hour of Grace"), a pastoral letter (*Origins* 23/34 [February 10, 1994] 591–602).

28. Andraos, "Praxis of Peace," 79–80.

29. Luis Hernández Navarro and Ramón Vera Herrera, eds., *Accuerdos de San Andrés* (Mexico City: Era, 1998) 9. This accord was never implemented by the Mexican federal government for a variety of political reasons, which could not be discussed here because they are outside the scope of this chapter.

PART TWO—Contextual and Constructive Proposals

tural protests, which irrupted over the past decades, are producing several alternative movements that challenge modernity's exclusion and violence and are opening new horizons for thinking about the possibility of another world in which there is room for all peoples, as one often hears reiterated in Chiapas and elsewhere.

In terms of the Catholic Church in Chiapas, the transformation of the old cultural relations is taking place at many levels. I will mention only two areas of relevance to our topic, which in my opinion also have implications for the wider church. The first area is the development of the concept and practice of *Iglesia autóctona* (autocthonous church); and the second area is the emergent *teología india* (Indian theology). A few comments on each area are in order.[30]

"*Iglesia autóctona*" is the term used in the Diocese of San Cristóbal to describe the ecclesial communities that have a distinct indigenous cultural character and organizational structure for pastoral service and leadership. The documents of the III Diocesan Synod (1995–1999) in the first section define *Iglesia autóctona* as "a church that is rooted in the place where it is located, that realizes itself and develops assuming the local culture, and not a church that comes from outside, that belongs to another culture, and that only makes external adaptations."[31] This achievement is the result of a long and arduous cultural dialogue between the indigenous communities and the hierarchy of the local church. The diocese is now committed to promoting this pastoral process and has integrated it in its short-term and long-term pastoral plan.[32]

The second area is the emergent movement of *teología india*, which is still in its initial stages. This movement is also the result of an intercultural theological dialogue between the indigenous communities and their theologians, on the one side, and Western Christian faith and theology represented by the church hierarchy and its theologians, on the other. What we mean by *teología india*, notes indigenous theologian Pedro Gutiérrez Jiménez, is

---

30. Andraos, "indigenous Leadership in the Church," 64. For a more detailed explanation of these movements, see Andraos, "Praxis of Peace: The Pastoral Work and Theology of Bishop Samuel Ruiz and the Diocese of San Cristóbal," 70–118.

31. Andraos, "indigenous Leadership in the Church," 64. See also Gaillardetz, *Ecclesiology for a Global Church*, 159–62.

32. For a recent articulation of the diocesan commitment to the development of *Iglesia autóctona*, see Diócesis de San Cristóbal de Las Casas, *Plan Diocesano de Pastoral* (Diocese of San Cristóbal de Las Casas, 2004) 23–30.

the set of religious experiences and knowledge that we Indian peoples possess and with which we explain our experience of faith, our harmonious [relationships] with others and with all of the cosmos.... These theologies have accompanied our origin and our civilization as peoples, have generated and fed our resistance against projects of conquest and colonization, and have accompanied today our resistance against the neoliberal system and fed our proposal of a more human and divine society for all. Our theologies seek to strengthen our heart so that we as peoples do not shrivel away under the power of the system of death.[33]

Rethinking the structure of the local church in order to fully include the cultural "Other," in this case the indigenous, and making room for more than one cultural theology are only two among many other initiatives that are the result of a new intercultural dialogue between the indigenous communities and the local church that has just begun. There are many challenges on the path of this new intercultural dialogue, but the determination of the indigenous communities and their leadership is very strong and is rooted in a broader cultural and historical movement of change, which seems to be irreversible.

Ricardo Robles, a Jesuit theologian who worked and lived for several years with the indigenous peoples of Mexico, suggests that the process that began in Chiapas since the 1960s gave an impulse to creative theological insights and profound inter-religious dialogue about God and history reaching far beyond Chiapas. A broad movement emerged from this pastoral process that has awakened the spirit of other indigenous peoples in Mexico, won their support, and united their efforts. This, asserts Robles, nurtured the capacity of many indigenous groups to proudly and confidently say since the 1990s "We are equal, therefore we have the right to be different."[34]

---

33. Pedro Gutiérrez Jiménez, "Flowers and Fruits of Our Maya-Christian Spirituality and Theology," paper presented at the Latin American Congress on Religion and Ethnicity, Institute for Intercultural Studies and Research, San Cristobal de Las Casas, Chiapas, Mexico, January 11, 2005. An English translation and a copy of the Spanish original were given to the author by Pedro Gutiérrez Jiménez.

34. Ricardo Robles, "El Obolo de los Pueblos Indios para el Tercer Milenio," in *Christus*, Mexico City, 712 (1999) 18–28.

Part Two—Contextual and Constructive Proposals

Conclusion

The current debates on the clash of cultures, religions, and civilizations at a global scale, raise central questions to the religions of the world and all of humanity about how to relate to the cultural and religious "Other," both within the same society (and church), and between states, regions, and continents. The violent cultural pattern created as a result of the encounter with European modernity certainly cannot continue. It has been a main obstacle to world peace and has to change. The story of the emergent intercultural dialogue that has just begun between a local church and indigenous peoples hopefully opens a horizon of hope for imagining a new relationship beyond this violent encounter.

I began this essay by mentioning one of Lee Cormie's cherished theological questions that inspired this writing, namely, the question of faith, theology, and concrete, historical hope. I would also like to end by mentioning what for me has been a profound theological insight I learned from Cormie: reading the signs of the times, or in his words, "reading the movements of the Spirit in history." In my opinion, one of Cormie's important assertions is that theology's main contribution is to name the old and new experiences of the Spirit in history and recognize the genuine signs of hope for the world in these movements of resistance and hope for another, better world.[35] The story in this chapter is one of many episodes of resistance and hope that another world is possible.

---

35. Lee Cormie, "Movements of the Spirit in History," in *Talitha Cum! The Grace of Solidarity in a Globalized World*, ed. Mario DeGiglio-Bellemare and Gabriella Miranda García (Geneva: World Student Christian Federation, 2004) 238.

9

U.S. Latina/o Theology

Challenges, Possibilities, and Future Prospects

Néstor Medina

CONTEXTUAL AND CULTURAL THEOLOGIES like U.S. Latina/o theology show that, as far as the task of theology is concerned, things are no longer business as usual. Influenced greatly by Latin American liberation theology (LALT), Latina/o theologians created what Orlando Espín has called their own "rebellious" hermeneutics. In doing so, they have sought to expose the ideological apparatus behind the marginalization of Latinas/os in the U.S., to name themselves, and to reclaim their own historical trajectory as a people.

Appropriately understood, U.S. Latina/o theology is a theological reflection on the praxis of the Latina/o people.[1] In positively engaging the social sciences, U.S. Latina/o theologians found that this approach has been useful in uncovering the ideological and racialized notions of cultural superiority from dominant Anglo theological approaches, and has helped in the theological framing of their struggle against conditions of social exclusion and poverty of Latinas/os in the U.S. As distinct from LALT, the writings of U.S. Latina/o scholars do not contain elaborations of anything like economic dependency theory or the explicit incorporation of Marxist

---

1. Roberto S. Goizueta, "Hispanic," in *Dictionary of Third World Theologies*, ed. Virginia Fabella and R. S. Sugirtharajah (Maryknoll, NY: Orbis, 2000) 212.

Part Two—Contextual and Constructive Proposals

analysis.[2] However, woven together with their theological articulations, one finds issues related to economics, race, class, gender, ethnicity, and culture. It is in this way that the social sciences are useful for Latina/o theologians, as they pertain to the sphere of the human.

There are debates as to how the social sciences are engaged by both LALT and U.S. Latina/o theologies. Both agree that the use and engagement of the social sciences are constitutive aspects of the theological task.[3] The intersection of these issues and debates, and the profound implications for theology and Christian life, characterize some of the interests and the life-long commitment to justice of Lee Cormie.

What follows is a brief summary of what I think are the main characteristics of Latina/o theology. I divide this paper in three sections. First, I explore some of the contributions that Latina/o theologians offer to the general discipline of theology. Here I focus on the particular way that they construct a unique theological method as a response to the social concerns of racism and marginalization of various kinds, the unique Latina/o hermeneutics, and the way they understand popular religious expressions. Second, I outline some of the challenges that Latina/o theology faces with

---

2. Although U.S. Latina/o theologians do not use Marxist analysis as explicitly as LALT, the fundamental questions, assumptions and concerns of a Marxist class analysis are found in their writings. It must be pointed out, however, that, for LALT theologians, engaging Marxist social analysis has to be understood within the use of the social sciences, as a means at understanding people's social reality. See Gustavo Gutiérrez, "Theology and the Social Sciences," in *The Truth Shall Make You Free: Confrontations*, trans. Matthew O'Connell (Maryknoll, NY: Orbis, 1991) 62–66. Similarly, in the writings of U.S. Latino theologians, one finds a wide range of scholars in the social sciences such as Gloria Anzaldúa, Walter Mignolo, David Abalos, Anthony Stevens-Arroyo, Chela Sandoval, Jorge Klor de Alva, Rafael Pérez Torres, Rudy Torres, and Ana María Díaz-Stevenz. These various scholars are drawn upon as a means to understand the U.S. Latina/o social reality.

3. Peter C. Phan, "Method in Liberation Theologies," *Theological Studies* 61 (2000) 45. I disagree with Clodovis Boff, for example, and his description of the use of the social sciences by LALT. While he rightly affirms that social-scientific data cannot replace "proper" theological reflection, he insists that the correct relation between the social sciences and theology is that "what for the sciences of the social is product, finding, or constructing, will be taken up in the theological field as raw material, as something to be (re)worked by procedures proper to theologizing, in such wise as to issue in a *specifically* theological product, and one so characterized" (Clodovis Boff, *Theology and Praxis: Epistemological Foundations*, trans. Robert R. Barr [Maryknoll, NY: Orbis, 1987] 31). In my view, Boff fails to acknowledge the fluid relation between the social sciences and theology. As I see it, theological knowledge cannot be placed in a state of "suspension," so that one can then proceed to engage the social sciences "objectively," only to later return and consider the data in theological terms. This, in my view, is a myth that needs to be deconstructed.

the present ethnocultural reconfiguration of Latina/o communities and the search for new language that more appropriately reflects this reality. Third, I try to imagine some of the aspects that Latina/o theologians will need to engage in order to broaden their theological horizons. I will argue that these three aspects find their coherence in the adoption and appropriation of the biological condition and cultural category of *mestizaje*.

Adoption of Mestizaje in Theology: Theological Category, Hermeneutical Key, and Popular Religion

There is some debate as to when U.S. Latina/o theology first emerged.[4] But it was not until the 1978 dissertation work of Virgilio Elizondo, *Mestizaje: The Dialectic of Cultural Birth and the Gospel*,[5] and its subsequent book-form publication in 1983,[6] that Latina/o theology began to be formalized as a theological discourse emerging from Latina/o communities.[7] Elizondo's

---

4. According to Orlando Espín, both Justo González and Virgilio Elizondo played a significant role in the early development and initial impetus of U.S. Latina/o theology. See Orlando O. Espín, "The State of U.S. Latino/a Theology: An Understanding," *Perspectivas: Hispanic Theological Initiative Occasional Paper Series* 3 (2000) 21. See also Justo L. González, *The Development of Christianity in the Latin Caribbean* (Grand Rapids: Eerdmans, 1969); Virgilio Elizondo, "Educación Religiosa para el México-Americano," *Catequesis Latinoamericana* 4/14 (1972) 83–86. Also, Juan González insists that the grievances of Latinos/as worsened after Mexican-American soldiers returned from WWII, some received Congressional Medals of Honor, but their communities continued to be neglected and discriminated, except that this time they were unwilling to accept it. See his *Harvest of the Empire: A History of Latinos in America* (New York: Penguin, 2000) 104. Similarly, Klor de Alva writes that "the black struggle for civil rights, the urban insurrections, the peace movements against the tragic Vietnam War, the widespread appeal of the anticapitalism espoused by the Neo-Marxists and the New Left, the ascent of feminist radicalism, and the anti-materialist challenge" made the moment ripe for Latino/a political protest; see J. Jorge Klor de Alva, "Aztlán, Borinquen and Hispanic Nationalism in the United States," in *Aztlán: Essays on the Chicano Homeland*, ed. Rodolfo A. Anaya and Francisco A. Lomelí (Alburquerque: Academia/El Norte Publications, 1989) 150.

5. Virgilio Elizondo, *Mestizaje: The Dialectic of Cultural Birth and the Gospel* (San Antonio: Mexican American Cultural Center, 1978).

6. Virgilio Elizondo, *Galilean Journey: The Mexican-American Promise* (Maryknoll, NY: Orbis, 1983).

7 For a fuller development of the use of *mestizaje* in Latina/o theology, see Néstor Medina, *Mestizaje: (Re)Mapping Race, Culture, and Faith in Latina/o Catholicism* (Maryknoll, NY: Orbis, 2009).

proposal for *mestizaje* was groundbreaking; even today his work continues to be a source of great inspiration for subsequent generations of Latina/o scholars.

As originally articulated by Elizondo, the condition of *mestizaje* means both the violent intermixture of indigenous and Spanish religious and cultural elements as a result of the Spanish conquest, and the added violent intermixture with the Anglo dominant culture of the U.S. after the Guadalupe-Hidalgo treaty of 1848.[8] Following Elizondo's original intuition of a double *mestizaje*, during the 1980s and into the 1990s, U.S. Latina/o theologians expanded the notion of *mestizaje* to include theological reflections on gender,[9] Christology,[10] pneumatology,[11] theological method,[12] hermeneutics,[13] and other areas. The image and language of *mestizaje*-intermixture quickly became the standardized frame for understanding Latina/o reality.[14] And today, no analysis of Latina/o theology can avoid engaging the various ways in which Latina/o theologians deployed the category of *mestizaje* in theology.

8. This is the way that Elizondo articulated his theological vision of *mestizaje*. For a more detailed development of Elizondo's theological method, see Néstor Medina, "*Mestizaje*: A Theological Reading of Culture and Faith: Reflections on Virgilio Elizondo's Theological Method," *Journal of Hispanic/Latino/a Theology* (forthcoming).

9. María Pilar Aquino, "Directions and Foundations of Hispanic/Latino Theology: Towards a *Mestiza* Theology of Liberation," *Journal of Hispanic/Latino Theology* 1/1 (1993) 5–21.

10. Luis Pedraja, *Jesus is My Uncle: Christology from a Hispanic Perspective* (Nashville: Abingdon, 1999).

11. Oscar García Johnson, "The Mestizo/a Community of Mañana: A Latino/a Theology of the Spirit," PhD diss., Fuller Theological Seminary, 2005.

12. Roberto S. Goizueta, "U.S. Hispanic Mestizaje and Theological Method," in *Migrants and Refugees*, ed. Dietmar Mieth and Lisa Sowle Cahill (New York: Orbis, 1993) 22–30.

13. Justo L. González, *Santa Biblia: The Bible Through Hispanic Eyes* (Nashville: Abingdon, 1996).

14. Although it can be argued that the character of U.S. Latina/o theology is Catholic as most Latina/o theologians are Catholics, this is not exactly true as Catholic and Protestants have been in conversation since the inception of Latina/o theology. Although not always successful, Latina/o theologians have gone to great lengths in order to work ecumenically. This has been one of the central characteristics of the Hispanic Theological Initiative. Another recent example of this "ecumenical" ethos is the meeting of Latina/o theologians that took place during June 3–6, 2007, in Los Angeles, under the auspices of the Academy of Catholic Hispanic Theologians of the United States (ACHTUS). They dealt with the general theme "Constructing a Latino/a Ecumenical Theology," and Protestant and Catholic scholars were invited to participate.

From the perspective of the first *mestizaje*, Latina/o theologians draw on the colonial rejection of mixed children because they were thought to be stained biologically with the blood of their "inferior" indigenous ancestors, and were seen as morally suspect for being the result of the "illicit" sexual relations between Spaniard men and indigenous women. From the perspective of the second *mestizaje*, they draw on the invasion-occupation of Mexico by the U.S., and the subsequent systematic attempts at erasing Latina/o culture, history, and ethnic identity, and their present conditions of social marginalization in the U.S.

U.S. Latina/o theologians used the multivalent character of *mestizaje* in five key ways: (1) to reclaim their mixed cultural heritage; (2) to identify their present condition of social exclusion and ethnocultural discrimination, and attitude of resistance against the dominant Anglo assimilationist monoculture of the country; (3) to describe the Latina/o experience of cultural in-betweenness in the complex process of identity formation as a people; (4) to name the characteristically mixed and complex religious world of Latinas/os, expressed in their religious symbols by weaving together indigenous, African, and Spanish-European elements; and (5) to find the divine legitimation for the existence of the Latina/o peoples. These areas are intertwined in the theological writings of U.S. Latina/o theologians.

Theological Category

U.S. Latina/o theologians redeemed the label of *mestizaje*. While during the sixteenth century *mestizaje* was used by the Spaniards in derogatory ways pointing to the "contaminated" existence, illegitimate status, and cultural and social "degeneracy" of *mestizo/a*-mixed children, Latina/o theologians turned it into a powerful subversive act of naming themselves and their struggles of resistance. Borrowing from the work of José Vasconcelos' *La raza cósmica*,[15] U.S. Latina/o theologians affirmed that the *mestizo* Latina/o people are a new race, a new breed that represent the future of humanity.[16]

---

15. José Vasconcelos, *La raza cósmica: Misión de la raza iberoamericana* (México DF: Litografía Ediciones Olimpia, S.A., 1983).

16. Admittedly these were assertions that Elizondo made concerning his own Mexican American community. But it was not before long that *mestizaje* was appropriated and further developed by other Latina/o theologians who do not identify themselves as Mexican Americans. See Virgilio Elizondo, *The Future is Mestizo: Life Where Cultures Meet* (Boulder, CO: University of Colorado Press, 2000).

Mestizaje was recast as the birth of a new people.[17] The condition of *mestizaje* makes concrete for Latinas/os the providential divine intent of creating something new out of the intermixture of disparate ethnic and cultural groups; it means reconciliation and inclusion.

The theological incorporation of *mestizaje* for Latinas/os opened new spaces for affirming their unique identity as a people. A key aspect here has been the rereading of history and reclamation of their historical agency. This was an attempt to uncover the "bad news" upon which the present has been constructed.[18] In other words, the history of *mestizaje* has remained absent from dominant versions of history and needs to be unearthed because it tells the story of the Latina/o people.

Here the dilemma intrinsic to *mestizaje* becomes visible among U.S. Latina/o theologians. The adoption of the condition of *mestizaje* shows the in-between existence that Latinas/os experience. This is not a version of a double-consciousness as articulated by W. E. B. Du Bois.[19] Latina/o consciousness can be defined more like a triple consciousness. They are conscious that they share much in common with, but many times are rejected by, Latin Americans. They are also conscious that they were born in the U.S. but are denied social participation by the dominant Anglo-European culture. Most importantly, they are conscious of their own ambiguous existence. They are both Latin Americans and North Americans, but they are also something else. In this way, U.S. Latina/o theologians have reinterpreted the condition of *mestizaje* and avoided essentialist air-tight identity labels by claiming a triple cultural ancestry.

This ambiguous existence is the cause of great pain, but is also the source of great creativity. The deployment and appropriation of the cultural category of *mestizaje* by U.S. Latina/o theologians provides the theologically based legitimation of their existence. They turned *mestizaje* into a discursive category to reflect theologically about the reality and faith

---

17. Elizondo, *Mestizaje*, 137.

18. María Pilar Aquino makes clear that the function is that of unearthing, unburying the bloody, violent history of marginalization, oppression, and social exclusion experienced by Latinas/os which has been intentionally covered-up by the dominant culture. So the Latina/o historical re-claiming is also a dis-covering. See her "The Collective 'Dis-Covery' of Our Own Power: Latina American Feminist Theology," in *Hispanic/Latino Theology: Challenge and Promise*, ed. Ada María Isasi-Díaz and Fernando Segovia (Minneapolis: Fortress, 1996) 240–60.

19. W. E. B. Du Bois, *The Souls of Black Folk* (1903; reprinted, New York: Dover, 1994).

experience of the Latina/o people. *Mestizaje*, as Elizondo claimed, is a *locus* of theological reflection.[20]

Contrary to the dominant U.S. Anglo-European culture of exclusion and segregation, the proposal of *mestizaje*-intermixture subverts notions that privilege biological or ethnocultural "purity" against miscegenation-intermixture as the corruption of what is "pure." For U.S. Latina/o theologians, the appropriation of *mestizaje*/mixing among cultural groups announces the divine act of creating an alternative new world of inclusion of other cultural groups by way of intermixture. Here they subvert the rules and categories of exclusion, and reinterpret intermixture-*mestizaje* as the discursive and social space where different voices, peoples, and cultures come together in the struggle for justice and inclusion. Stated differently, *mestizaje* is the lens through which one can see the divine at work among the Latina/o *mestizo/a* communities in the context of the U.S.

Hermeneutical Key

According to U.S. Latina/o theologians, the category of *mestizaje* provides a new optic for reading and understanding reality. Roberto Goizueta argues that by using *mestizaje* U.S. Latina/o theology has inaugurated a philosophical-theological shift away from modernity and postmodernity.[21] It goes beyond dominant modern binary oppositional categories; the condition of *mestizaje* provides a double lens with which to interpret reality. Latinas/os are not just either Latin Americans or "Americans"; they are both. Similarly, the U.S. Latina/o theological proposal of *mestizaje* is not a postmodern expression of the relative character of peoples, cultures, and traditions. By deploying *mestizaje* Latina/o theologians retrieve the possibility of mutual enrichment by way of intermixture. They do not uphold the postmodern notion of a multiplicity of realities. Rather, for them *mestizaje* is the expression of the dynamic interactive process by which different cultural horizons collaborate in interpreting reality.[22] According to them, in

---

20. See Virgilio Elizondo, "Mestizaje as a Locus of Theological Reflection," in *The Future of Liberation Theology: Essays in Honor of Gustavo Gutierrez*, ed. Marc H. Ellis and Otto Maduro (Maryknoll, NY: Orbis, 1989) 358–74.

21. Roberto S. Goizueta, *Caminemos con Jesús: Toward a Hispanic/Latino Theology of Accompaniment* (Maryknoll, NY: Orbis, 1999) ch. 6.

22. Orlando O. Espín, *Grace and Humanness: Theological Reflections because of Culture* (New York: Orbis, 2007) 17.

Part Two—Contextual and Constructive Proposals

mestizaje there is no hierarchy of cultural groups and no one cultural group is perceived to comprehensively understand or interpret reality. From the perspective of theology, no one cultural group has a monopoly of the divine self-disclosure. A fuller understanding of reality and God is only possible when cultural groups interact and mix with each other.

In proposing the alternative multiplicity of cultural horizons, U.S. Latina/o theologians have opened the door for possibilities of reading the Bible in creative new ways. This challenges the colonial approach that assumes one correct interpretation of the Bible story. For U.S. Latina/o theologians, reading the Bible is a dynamic exercise that cannot be reduced to the fusion of the biblical horizon with the horizon of the reader, as Gadamer would claim.[23]

This necessary re-reading of the Bible texts becomes a site of struggle. For U.S. Latina/o theologians, there is an operative hermeneutics of suspicion, as articulated by Segundo, and a resituating of culture as a key interpretive "tool." In light of this, besides being a religious document, the Bible is also conceived as a cultural product and, therefore, culturally bound. The Bible reflects the cultural milieu of the people of Israel in the Old Testament, and the sociocultural world of the historical Jesus in the New Testament. It reveals the sociopolitical and cultural dynamics of the time. Similarly, the readers are also culturally bound. They read the Bible through their cultural lenses, and their culture and social location inform the kinds of questions they ask and the answers they find in the Bible.[24] Here interpretation is necessary as the Bible is not perceived as containing literal mandates that ought to be followed unquestionably.

When reading the Bible from the perspective of *mestizaje*, U.S. Latina/o theologians claim that it says much about the condition of cultural intermixture/*mestizaje*, and those who are culturally mixed/*mestizo/as*. In the Bible mixed people were rejected during the times of the Old Testament. During the construction of the second temple, the people that eventually came to be known as the Samaritans were prevented from becoming part

---

23. Hans-Georg Gadamer, "Text and Interpretation," in *Dialogue and Deconstruction: The Gadamer–Derrida Encounter*, ed. Diane P Michelfelder and Richard E. Palmer (New York: SUNY, 1989) 41.

24. It is for this reason that Espín suggests that culture must be considered as a "necessary condition for revelation." See Orlando O. Espín, "Traditioning: Culture, Daily Life and Popular Religion, and Their Impact on Christian Tradition," in *Futuring Our Past: Explorations in the Theology of Tradition*, ed. Orlando O. Espín and Gary Macy (Maryknoll, NY: Orbis, 2006) 4.

of the people of Israel because they were mixed. However, despite being rejected, mixed people play a crucial role in the biblical story of salvation. This is illustrated by the important figures listed in Jesus' genealogy such as Rahab and Ruth. In fact, argues Justo González, mixed people are predominant in the biblical text. The apostle Paul would not have been able to go in his missionary journeys were he not a cultural *mestizo*.[25]

As would be expected, the most important figure of the New Testament, Jesus himself, is interpreted as culturally mixed-*mestizo*. Elizondo argues that Galilee was a place of significance in the New Testament both as the place Jesus grew up, and a place where merchants from different cultural backgrounds intersected and intermixed.[26] Jesus grew up in a context of great cultural diversity and, therefore, was culturally mixed. This is of great significance for Elizondo because God brought salvation through this particular Galilean *mestizo*.[27] This is the experience shared by Latinas/os as these *mestizos/as* epitomize the divine inauguration of a new world where diversity reigns supreme.[28] By interpreting the biblical Jesus as the divine *mestizo*, Elizondo elevates *mestizo*-Latinas/os to a messianic status embodying the promised reign of God for all peoples and all nations on the basis of intermixture.[29]

Popular Religion

By claiming the condition of biological and cultural *mestizaje*, U.S. Latina/o theologians have reclaimed the popular religious expressions of Latinas/os as epistemological sources. For them, the daily faith experiences and expressions of the people are the result of the condition of intermixture-*mestizaje*. This methodological shift by U.S. Latina/o theologians places the people at the center of the production of theological knowledge. In other words, the *fiestas patronales, la quinceañera, las prosesiones*, express concretely the people's own theological process. And the adoption of the category of *mestizaje* provides the framework for understanding these

---

25. González, *Santa Biblia*, 84.
26. Elizondo, *Galilean Journey*, 49–50.
27. Ibid., 50–53.
28. Virgilio Elizondo, "The New Humanity of the Americas," in *Beyond Borders: The Writings of Virgilio Elizondo and Friends*, ed. Timothy Matovina (Maryknoll, NY: Orbis, 2000) 276.
29. Elizondo, *Galilean Journey*, 53–64.

PART TWO—Contextual and Constructive Proposals

devotions, rituals, traditions, customs, and symbols. They display elements from their indigenous, African and Spanish ancestors.[30]

For Latina/o theologians, this version of *mestizaje* is particularly embodied in the apparition and subsequent development of the veneration of the Lady of Guadalupe. It is not difficult to see the numerous elements from Spanish Christian and indigenous religious traditions interlaced with the symbol of the Lady of Guadalupe.[31] As Goizueta puts it, the "divine is here revealed—of all things!—a mestizo Virgin, a woman of mixed blood, La Morenita . . . She is the Beauty of the mestizo, of the poor, a beauty rejected by the conquerors."[32]

Therefore, the condition of intermixture is pervasive in the popular religious expressions of faith of the Latina/o people. To speak of *mestizaje* as the defining characteristic of the Latina/o religious experience means that Latina/o theologians take seriously the theological value of popular religious expressions. For them, they are the truest expressions of Latina/o religious experience, and the well from which to draw theological knowledge.[33] U.S. Latina/o theologians challenge colonial notions that demonize different expressions and practices of faith as corruptions of one "true" Christian expression. Instead, they affirm that the Latina/o people's quotidian expressions of faith: rituals, feasts, traditions, and practices are legitimate ways of living the Christian faith.[34] At heart, one finds the categorical unmasking and denouncing of the absurdity behind ideas of "pure" or unmixed expressions of Christianity in the Latina/o appropriation of *mestizo/a* religious expressions. In other words, there is no one "true" "unmixed" expression of Christianity; and claims to "purity" are conceived as the residual ideological legacy of the colonial racialized destructive forces,

30. This is also true of the liturgy of many of the churches as they show a wide array of Latina/o cultural elements in the music, language, and art. For Chávez Sauceda, this kind of liturgy is quite literally the *work of the people* and, as such, it is a Latina/o "cultural product." See Teresa Chávez Sauceda, "Sacred Space/Public Identity," in *Handbook of Latina/o Theologies*, ed. Miguel De La Torre and Edwin Aponte (St. Louis: Chalice, 2006) 251.

31. For a detailed analysis and interpretation of the Lady of Guadalupe as a *mestizo* symbol, see Virgilio Elizondo, *Guadalupe, Mother of the New Creation* (Maryknoll, NY: Orbis, 1997).

32. Roberto S. Goizueta, "U.S. Hispanic Popular Catholicism as Theopoetics," in *Hispanic/Latino Theology: Challenge and Promise*, ed. Ada María Isasi-Díaz and Fernando F. Segovia (Minneapolis: Fortress, 1996) 282–83.

33. Ibid., 267–71.

34. Orlando O. Espín, "*Pasión y respeto*: Elizondo's Contribution to the Study of Popular Catholicism," in *Beyond Borders*, 103.

which fail to acknowledge the degree to which all expressions of Christianity have incorporated elements from other religious and cultural traditions.

CHALLENGES: IDENTITY DEFINITION, MULTICULTURALISM, AND RELIGIOUS PLURALITY

It needs to be made clear that Latinas/os in the U.S. continue to share the common experience of racialized discrimination, social marginalization, and resistance against dominant Anglo-cultural assimilationist pressures.[35] This is exacerbated by the stereotypical characterization of Latinas/os as perennial immigrants, foreigners in their own country. Despite the fact that most Latinas/os have been born in the U.S., the recent rhetoric of anti-terrorism and national security is effectively used as a mechanism of exclusion, and the sociopolitical and cultural landscape of the U.S. is perceived by Latinas/os as inhospitable and unwelcoming.[36]

Since the conditions that gave rise to Latina/o theology have changed, Latina/o theologians need to rethink what it means to speak about the reality and faith expressions of the Latina/o communities. This is a two-fold problematic: first, the need to create new language for speaking about the richness, diversity, and fluid character of identities among Latinas/os; second, the need to ground theological reflections in the ethnocultural and historical specificity of each of the groups that constitute the Latinas/os. On

---

35. According to Virgilio Elizondo, things have not changed much in more than 30 years. In 1971 he wrote that Latinas/os live with lack of work insurance, exploitation, appalling living conditions, no adequate housing, high rent rate, no vacation time, no union protection, poor or non-existent medical care, and poor education. The people are malnourished and sometimes only work seasonally. And university GRE and IQ tests are ethnically skewed. For him, all these amount to depriving Latinos/as from having equal opportunities because the structures are Anglo-centric. See his *Christianity and Culture: An Introduction to Pastoral Theology and Ministry for the Bicultural Community* (Huntington, IN: Our Sunday Visitor, 1975) 133. A more recent example of systemic discrimination against Latinas/os is found in the Anti-Ethnic Studies Bill, passed by the Arizona State Legislature in 2010, by which Mexican-American studies were effectively prohibited by law.

36. This has prompted many to rethink racialized popular notions of a ubiquitous black-white binary, but more like a black-white-foreigner social-cultural ethos that succeeds in making Latinas/os feel as foreigners in their own country. See Elizabeth Martínez, "Beyond Black/White: The Racisms of Our Time," in *The Latino Condition: A Critical Reader*, ed. Richard Delgado and Jean Stefancic (New York: New York University Press, 1998) 471; J. Jorge Klor de Alva, "Cipherspace: Latino Identity Past and Present," in *Race, Identity, and Citizenship: A Reader*, ed. Rodolfo D. Torres, Louis F. Mirón, and Jonathan Xavier Inda (Oxford: Blackwell, 1999) 169–80.

PART TWO—Contextual and Constructive Proposals

both counts, it is becoming increasingly necessary to negotiate the terms and limits of "Latina/o" identity, making it difficult to speak of Latinas/os using generalizing categories such as *mestizaje*. While the category of *mestizaje* has been very useful, it needs to be rethought, reconfigured, and qualified. I name four reasons why I think the label of *mestizaje* is becoming increasingly problematic for Latina/o theology.

First, with the present global patterns of migration, conflicts and interactions of masses of peoples are inevitable. These interactions show that what is happening is not the synthesizing of cultural groups in the direction of one global *mestizaje*.[37] Rather, we see a multiplication of syntheses and fusions and the creation of multiple new identities irreducible by rigid categories.

Second, because of the present reconfiguration of geopolitical actors and the proliferation of identities numerous groups the world over have resorted to use *mestizaje* to define their own identity, experiences, and struggles against sociopolitical and economic marginalization.[38] So *mestizaje* is not one thing, or one experience of intermixture shared by all peoples. *Mestizaje* must be seen in the plural sense, and qualified in light of the historical contexts from which they emerge.[39]

Third, U.S. Latina/o theologians borrowed the term from Latin America's long standing tradition of *mestizaje* discourses, but did not critically engage the racialized colonial configuration of the term. They failed to identify how in Latin America *mestizaje* functions as a whitening, exclusionary, and social structuring mechanism of the population, where indigenous peoples and African descendants are left outside of the debates and discourses of ethnocultural and national identity.[40] This is problematized

---

37. Virgilio Elizondo, "Transformation of Borders: Mestizaje and the Future of Humanity," in *Beyond Borders*, 176–86; Jacques Audinet, *The Human Face of Globalization: From Multicultural to Mestizaje*, trans. Francest Dal Chele (New York: Rowman & Littlefield, 2004); Vasconcelos, *La raza cósmica*.

38. See Élisabeth Delaygue, *Mestizo: Roman* (Paris: Présence Africaine, 1986); Leonard Blussé, *Strange Company: Chinese Settlers, Mestizo Women and the Dutch in VOC Batavia* (Riverton, NJ: Foris, 1986); Claudine Bavoux, *Islam et métissage: des musulmans créolophones à Madagascar: les indiens sunnites sourti des Tamatave* (Paris: L'Harmattan, 1990).

39. See Medina, *Mestizaje*, chapter 5.

40. Until now, U.S. Latino theologians have given little attention to volatile relationship that existed between *mestizos* and the indigenous peoples of the Americas. It is worth mentioning that in many places and at various moments in the history of Latin America *mestizos/as* were rejected by the indigenous peoples. This was the case because *mestizos/as* were a reminder, and at times continued the history of violation, rape and despoliation

by the number of diverse groups reclaiming the category of *mestizaje* as a suitable label to speak of their experiences of migration and struggle for social participation.[41] In Latin America, *Mestizaje* has become profoundly ambiguous and slippery sometimes used to subvert national and cultural assimilationist agendas, and in others as a sociological, ethnocultural, and ideological mechanism of cultural assimilation and conformity.[42] So it is necessary that U.S. Latina/o theologians engage the social context from where they borrowed and were inspired in using the label of *mestizaje*, and where, even in the present, *mestizaje* means the absence and historical erasure of indigenous and African descendants.

---

the indigenous suffered under Spanish rule. In fact, many *mestizo/a* males were repudiated because they had adopted their Spanish father's behavior by going into the *Reducciones* (reserves-like communities where the indigenous people were placed and were indoctrinated into Catholicism and Spanish culture) and raping indigenous women. So for many indigenous people, like Guaman Poma, the *mestizos* were a reminder and the continuity of the Spanish rapacious sexual behavior. See Phelipe Guamán Poma de Ayala, *La obra de Phelipe Guamán Poma de Ayala*, ed. Arthur Posnansky (La Paz, Bolivia: Editorial del Instituto "Tihuanacu" de Antropología, Etnografía y Prehistoria, 1944) 563.

41. See Marisol de la Cadena, "Reconstructing Race: Racism, Culture and *Mestizaje* in Latin America," *NACLA Report on the Americas* 34/6 (2001) 16–25; Ricardo Feierstein, "Todas las culturas, la cultura," in *Contraexilio y Mestizaje: Ser judío en latinoamerica*, Colección Ensayos (Buenos Aires: Editorial Milá, 1996) 109–59; de Lailhacar, *The Mestizo as Crucible: Andean Indian and African Poets of Mixed Origin as Possibility of Comparative Poetics* (New York: Lang, 1996).

42. In the history of Latin America there are repeated instances in which the discourse of *mestizaje* has been appropriated as emblematic of the grievances the subaltern groups may have against the dominant group. For example, in the sixteenth century Garcilaso de la Vega was the first person who appropriated the label of *mestizo* to define himself, which eventually led him to reclaim his indigenous heritage. And at the beginning of the nineteenth century Simon Bolívar also adopted the language of *mestizaje* in order to promote the struggle of independence from the Empire of Spain. For him, however, *mestizaje* was both the celebration of the *criollos*' double citizenship, Spanish and American (from the Americas), and the construction of a new body politic that pretended to construct the new Latin American societies independent from Spanish imperial intervention. Just recently, the indigenous people of the Cuzco market place have reclaimed *mestizaje* as a legitimate label to affirm their indigenous identity and culture, while at the same time rejecting the dominant *mestizo* culture that intends their assimilation. See Inca Garcilaso de la Vega, *Comentarios Reales de los Incas*, ed. Ángel Rosenblat (Buenos Aires: Emecé Editores, S.A., 1945) 2:ix–xxxi; Simón Bolívar, "Discurso pronunciado por el Libertador ante el Congreso de Angostura el 15 de febrero de 1819, día de su instalación," in *Simón Bolívar: Siete documentos esenciales*, ed. J. L. Salcedo Bastardo (Caracas: Edición de la Presidencia de la República, 1973) 65–98; Marisol de la Cadena, *indigenous Mestizos: The Politics of Race and Culture in Cuzco, Peru, 1919–1991* (Durham: Duke University Press, 2000).

Part Two—Contextual and Constructive Proposals

The complex reality of identity proliferation, construction, and definition among Latinas/os is a fourth and final reason. In attempting to find a sense of unity, U.S. Latina/o theologians painted a homogeneous picture of Latinas/os as *mestizos/as*. But defining Latinas/os as characteristically *mestizos/as* leaves out the other groups that reject the notion of *mestizaje* as a self-identifying category. Latinas/os and/or Hispanics are not a homogeneous ethnocultural collective.[43] On one hand, there are the three historical strands: Mexican Americans,[44] Puerto Ricans,[45] and Cuban Americans,[46]

---

43. Chávez-Sauceda points out very clearly that the diversity of the Latina/o communities goes beyond cultural differences. According to her, there are issues of language, generation, country of procedence, for many year of immigration into the U.S. education, gender, etc, all of which play an important factor in the diversity of the Latina/o communities. See Chávez Sauceda, "Sacred Space/Public Identity," 252–54. For a more recent discussion of the growing diversity of Latinas/os in the United States, see Edwin David Aponte, *¡Santo!: Varieties of Latina/o Spirituality* (Maryknoll, NY: Orbis, 2012).

44. For Mexican Americans the story of discrimination goes as far back as the Guadalupe-Hidalgo Treaty of 1848, when the entire States of California, Nevada, and Utah, and large portions of today's States of Colorado, Arizona, New Mexico, and Wyoming were ceded to the United States as a result of the latter's invasion of Mexico. The remaining parts of New Mexico and Arizona were later ceded under the 1853 Gadsden Purchase. Overnight the Mexican inhabitants of those regions became U.S. citizens but were not incorporated into the dominant Anglo social and cultural mainstream of the U.S. Justified by the Great Depression, in the 1930s over half a million Mexican Americans were forcibly thrown out from the U.S. and in the 1954 during Operation Wetback Countless many more were sent to Mexico under the excuse that they were seasonal workers who had overstayed their permits. For a more detailed description of the kinds of discrimination that Mexican Americans have endured in the regions of the Southwest of the U.S., see Juan González, *Harvest of the Empire*, ch. 5.

45. Among Puerto Ricans, the myth of Borinquen, the indigenous Taíno name for the island, was created as many relocated to continental U.S. Borinquen is the name which the indigenous Taíno gave the island and it means *La tierra del altivo Señor* (The land for the almighty Lord). The Taínos are generally considered to be part of the Taíno-Arawak group who traveled from the Orinoco-Amazon region of South America to Venezuela to the Caribbean Islands (2500 years ago). Starting around early 1940s, the massive migration of Puerto Ricans into continental U.S. was made possible by the Jones Act of 1917, by which Puerto Ricans became U.S. citizens. See Klor de Alva, "Aztlán, Borinquen and Hispanic Nationalism in the United States," 153–56. Many of those who relocated during the 1930s and 1940s carried the dream of returning to the land of their ancestors, the Taínos. Despite they were decimated into extinction by the Spaniards soon after their arrival to the Caribbean islands in 1493, for Puerto Ricans the spirit and culture of the Taíno's survives in the Puerto Rican cultural ethos. As Puerto Ricans arrived to continental U.S., and despite of being U.S. citizens, they were treated as foreigners and for years have remained invisible in U.S. society. See Juan González, *Harvest of the Empire*, ch. 4.

46. The first wave of Cuban refugees arrived to the U.S. as a result of the Cuban Revolution (1959), most of whom left because they were supporters of the dictator Fulgencio

with marked chronological, social, historical, and cultural differences, that for decades have constituted Latinas/os in the U.S.[47] And on the other hand, we have the multiple and diverse waves of immigrants (including millions of undocumented people) that have made the U.S. their home. Whatever we identify with the label "Latinas/os" refers to multiple ethnocultural groups that do not share the same experiences of migration, social exclusion, cultural marginalization, and religious affiliation in the same way; this is not to mention the tensions and differences that exist among themselves.[48]

The acknowledgement of the present proliferation of identities among Latinas/os highlights the reality of an intra Latina/o religious plurality. In my view this third challenge is one of the most important facing Latina/o theologians, as they are being forced to rethink the limits of theological reflection in relation to the plural non-Christian religious traditions that inform Latina/o religious and cultural practices. In other words, these theologians will have to go beyond "ecumenical" debates toward intra-Latina/o interreligious conversations.[49]

Batista. As Juan González puts it, the refugees from the 1960s and 1970s were largely from the upper and middle classes and brought with them considerable technical skills. They also received massive financial support by the federal government and quickly became the "country's most prosperous Hispanic immigrants." Considering themselves to be white, the first Cubans quickly assimilated into the dominant Anglo culture. Subsequent migrations of Cubans into the U.S. during the 1980s, the *marielitos* and 1994 *balseros* shattered the popular notion that Cubans were white. Mostly poorer and dark skinned these new waves of Cubans experienced discrimination and rejection by both White-Anglos and from among the members of their own community. According to González, because of their struggles in arriving to the U.S. and their experience of rejection and discrimination, the latest Cuban immigrants share much in common with other Latina/o immigrants. See Juan González, *Harvest of the Empire*, 109.

47. For a detailed analysis of the marked differences between Mexican Americans, Puerto Ricans and Cubans, see Juan González, *Harvest of the Empire*.

48. The history of each of these groups in the U.S. is so different that, according to Fernando Segovia, "it would be foolish to pretend that the most recent experience of Nicaraguans, Guatemalans, or Salvadorans fleeing for their lives in the midst of civil war is similar to that of the great migration of Puerto Rican families to the cities of the Northeast in the 1940s and 1950s, or that the massive exile of Cubans in the 1960s and 70s is similar to the situation of Mexican Americans born in the borderlands of the Southwest, of Puerto Ricans living on the islands" ("Two Places and no Place on Which to Stand: Mixture and Otherness in Hispanic American Theology," in *Mestizo Christianity: Theology from the Latino Perspective*, ed. Arturo Bañuelas [Maryknoll, NY: Orbis, 1995], 34). Another important element that is finally receiving its due attention is the discrimination against members of the Latina/o LGBT communities. See Espín, *Grace and Humanness*, ch. 2.

49. Latina/o Theologians are beginning to engage the plurality of religious traditions

Part Two—Contextual and Constructive Proposals

At stake is the theoretical need for the development of new language with which Latinas/os can identity the gaps, fissures, and absences in the U.S. Latina/o dominant discourses of identity and faith experiences using the category of *mestizaje*. This complicated self-critical process is necessary in order to engage the indigenous and African "Latinas/os" as theological dialogue partners. By "dialogue" I mean conversations that require that we learn to value the religious and ethnocultural universes of the indigenous peoples and African Latinas/os, but not as attachments to a larger *mestizo/a* identity. This is a cultural shift of enormous proportions, and requires that we take risks in the process of engaging Other "Latina/o" ethnocultural traditions, discounting any attempts to hide the tensions among Latinas/os and the irreducible differences that make Latinas/os in the U.S. multicolored, multi-cultural, and plurivocal communities. It is only in making room for Other fellow Latinas/os that we will move in the direction of retrieving their memories from a "forgotten pass," and reclaim their unique contributions to Latina/o societies and identities.

Future Prospects: Making the Connections

As I think about the future of U.S Latina/o theology, several things come to mind: First, despite its obvious limitations, and given our present reconfiguration of peoples, identities, national borders, and ideas, U.S. Latino/a theological discussions on *mestizaje* have much to offer to larger debates on intermixture and construction of "national," ethnocultural, and religious identities. Latina/o theologians have already gone far in demonstrating the complex and culturally colorful character of the faith experience of Latinas/os in the U.S. and in so doing have demonstrated that to speak of people's experiences it is necessary to work across disciplinary boundaries.

In engaging other disciplines, U.S. Latina/o theologians resist the fallacy of dominant attempts at keeping religious practices, faith experiences and expressions in the private sphere of life. They appropriately reflect on the praxis of the people, and they engage other disciplines to accomplish its task. In other words, religious life, and peoples' faith experiences have profound social, political, and economic repercussions.

---

among Latinas/os in the U.S. For example, Hjamil Martínez has published a study on Muslim Puerto Ricans, and Orlando Espín is finally making public his numerous engagements with the Lukumí Afro-Cuban religion. See Hjamil Martínez, *Latina/o y Musulmán: The Construction of Latina/o Identity Among Latina/o Muslims in the United States* (Eugene, OR: Pickwick Publications, 2009); Espín, *Grace and Humanness*, ch. 3.

Religious life and faith expressions are undeniably part of the complex and ambiguous social networks and the construction of meaning for human collectives. For Latina/o theologians, these concerns converge in the context of *lo cotidiano*,[50] where the false dualisms between the "secular" and the "sacred" become conspicuously evident. Latina/o theologians contradict erroneous dichotomies that render ethnic and cultural identity and expressions of faith as belonging to the private sphere.[51] From this vantage point, it can also be stated that for Latina/o theology interdisciplinarity is also constitutive of the theological task.

Second, in deploying *mestizaje* Latina/o theologians have affirmed the centrality of culture in religious experience and expressions. They have discerned God's activity among the Latina/o peoples. In other words, for them the people's religious activities and expressions are a legitimate *locus* of divine self-disclosure. This brings serious challenges to rigid traditional approaches that view revelation as one historical event in the person of Jesus. These theologians affirm the continuing divine disclosure in the people's everyday practices of faith.[52] This goes beyond stating that all theological affirmations are contextual. U.S. Latina/o scholars affirm the historical, social, political, and economic contextual limitations of their theological assertions. But the real contribution to theology is the proposal that the very intellectual structures and logic of understanding God are culturally bound. All theological assertions reflect the cultural universe from which

---

50. As María Pilar Aquino states about women and *lo cotidiano*: daily life is where real transformations take place. Daily life has to do with the totality of life. It produces, reproduces, and multiplies the totality of social relationships. In it anyone can clearly discover the concrete exercise of male power. Asymmetrical relationships occur in repetitive and continuous form in both the public and private arenas, because this is how they acquire daily character. In this sense, life has a fundamental political and religious role in the theological task of women. Its importance is even greater from the standpoint of the Christian faith, since theological reflection seeks to contribute to the creation of new models of social relationships" (Aquino, "The Collective 'Dis-Covery' of Our Own Power," 257).

51. This dichotomy, argues Ada María Isasi-Díaz, has contributed greatly in the oppression of women. See Ada María Isasi-Díaz, "Un poquito de justicia—A Little Bit of Justice: A Mujerista Account of Justice," in *Hispanic/Latino Theology: Challenge and Promise*, ed. Ada María Isasi-Díaz and Fernando F. Segovia (Minneapolis: Fortress, 1996) 338.

52. This is also exemplified in the more recent collection of articles on the diverse portraits of Christ among the Latina/o communities. These portraits reveal the broadening of the understanding of the divine disclosure even in the person of Jesus. See Harold Recinos and Hugo Magallanes, eds., *Jesus in the Hispanic Community: Images of Christ from Theology to Popular Religion* (Louisville: Westminster John Knox, 2009).

PART TWO—Contextual and Constructive Proposals

they come. Hence their theology is Latina/o theology![53] This is not about placing specific characteristics that distinguish a given theological affirmation as Latina/o from others that are not. Rather, it is the deliberate affirmation that there are no universal theological articulations that transcend all cultural groups, because there is no such thing as a universal culture.

U.S. Latina/o theology breaks away from "universal-objective" claims. In affirming their plural ethnic and cultural identities and traditions as the epistemological sources and *loci* of theological reflections, it rejects notions of value-free, objective, neutral theological articulations. Such affirmations debunk the fallacy of theological traditions claiming universal applicability. Again, this is not just a postmodern affirmation absolutely relativising any claims to truth. Rather, the U.S. Latina/o rejection of universal claims relates more to the affirmation that Latinas/os are legitimate producers of theological knowledge. Their knowledge, however, is intricately connected and bound to their history of discrimination and marginalization, and their mixed ethnic and cultural identity and tradition. It is from the vantage point of marginalization that Latina/o people claim to have encountered the divine. But, as Espín has argued, Latinas/os can only experience God in Latina/o ways and it could not be otherwise. "God" as experienced by Latinos/as is necessarily culturally and socially contextualized in ways "possible only to them and expressive of the language, symbols, understandings, and image(s) of the divine shaped by *their* culture, and by *their* social place."[54]

Third, the critiques of *mestizaje* demand that we re-appropriate the notion of viewing the faith experiences of the people as a necessary condition for theological reflections; this time it means recognizing the multiple

---

53. Identity has become an issue of serious debate among Latinas/os in the U.S. The limits of theological affirmations are being reconfigured and challenged as Latinas/os move into the public sphere. For some, questions of cultural identity have become an impediment in the degree to which U.S. Latina/o theology shifts its attention toward more public fora. For me, however, cultural identity is not something one is divested from, nor is it something contained or a finished product. Identity is far more fluid and porous. Theological affirmations are part of the public arena precisely because they emerge from culturally located spaces of identity. To claim otherwise would mean to engage in an abstract ahistorical intellectual space which runs the risk of claiming universality. See Benjamin Valentín, *Mapping Public Theology: Beyond Culture, Identity, and Difference* (New York: Trinity, 2002); Harold Recinos, ed., *Wading Through Many Voices: Toward a Theology of Public Conversation* (Lanham, MD: Rowman & Littlefield, 2011).

54. Orlando O. Espín, "Popular Catholicism: Alienation or Hope?" in *Hispanic/Latino Theology: Challenge and Promise*, 115; Orlando O. Espín, "An Exploration Into the Theology of Grace and Sin," in *From the Heart of Our People: Latino/a Explorations in Catholic Systematic Theology*, ed. Orlando O. Espín and Miguel H. Díaz (Maryknoll, NY: Orbis, 1999) 134.

diverse religious experiences of Latinas/os. This is not just a cultural shift but an epistemological one as well. Theologically speaking, the challenge to engage ourselves, especially those outside the dominant discourse of *mestizaje*, results in the broadening of our epistemological horizons. It helps us realize the as yet untapped universes of African Latina/o and indigenous cosmologies and cosmogonies that can shed light on the ways we conceive reality, the world, nature, and the mystery of the divine. In a sense, then, it is necessary that we go back to "drinking from our own wells," and from that intellectual and theological space rethink our theological articulations.

Fourth, in my critique of *mestizaje* I have emphasized the importance of engaging the indigenous and African traditions and forms of wisdom and knowledge. So in drawing from the wisdom and religious traditions of these communities Latina/o theologians gain a tremendous reservoir of material knowledge for constructing an ecological theology. I venture to say that the lack of recognition of and conversation with indigenous and African forms of wisdom and knowledge is linked to the fact that ecology is one of the least developed areas of Latina/o theology. To my knowledge no U.S. Latina/o theologian has systematically addressed some of the theological implications of the present environmental crisis we are experiencing.

Nevertheless, I believe that Latinas/os are in the unique position to articulate a theology of creation with profound ecological underpinnings for two fundamental reasons: first is the issue of "environmental racism." Any struggle against racialized forms of discrimination goes hand in hand with issues related to the environment. In the U.S. the majority of environmentally hazardous material ends up stored in areas populated by African Americans, Latinas/os, and Native Americans. Even worse is the fact that the great polluting corporations of the U.S. have taken the world as their dump site. So the struggle against the dominant forces of assimilation and racism in the U.S. are of global proportion, as toxic waste ends up being dumped in countries populated with people of color. In the words of James Cone: "If toxic waste is not safe enough to be dumped in the United States, it is not safe enough to be dumped in Ghana, Liberia, Somalia nor anywhere else in the world."[55] Thus U.S. Latina/o theologians should be front and center on issues and struggles concerning the environment. "What good is it to eliminate racism if we are not around to enjoy a racist free environment?"[56] And second, U.S. Latina/o theologians cannot avoid becoming intimately

---

55. James H. Cone, "Whose Earth Is It Anyway?" *Cross Currents* 50/1–2 (2000) 41.
56. Ibid., 42.

PART TWO—Contextual and Constructive Proposals

involved in issues related to the environment because of the wisdom and knowledge within the indigenous and African traditions.

Drawing from the wisdom and knowledge of these communities can provide Latina/o theologians with key theological insights as to how to conceive human existence in relation to the world, nature, and the environment. Attitudes of maintaining balance and coexisting with and depending on nature are not aspects outside of our traditions, and so we can only benefit from engaging our fellow indigenous and African Latinas/os. Notions of domination and exploitation must be considered foreign to the Latina/o imaginary, and must therefore be abandoned. All this to say that there is need for U.S. Latina/o theologians to address environmental concerns, and draw from their own reservoir of knowledge to address such concerns.

Instead of a Conclusion

Consistent with the initial intuitions of LALT, U.S. Latina/o theologians have engaged the social sciences and opened new horizons for understanding the social reality and faith experience of the Latina/o communities. Despite of the profound limitations in the use of the term, by deploying *mestizaje* U.S. Latina/o theologians have affirmed the centrality of culture in religious experience and expressions and discerned God's activity among the Latina/o peoples. It is in this way that they came to affirm the people's religious expressions as a legitimate *locus* of divine self-disclosure.

As they embarked in their own theological journey and in order to give language to the experience of faith of the Latina/o communities in the U.S., Latina/o theologians engaged these communities and found their own sources of theological knowledge. By engaging other disciplines and the social sciences, these theologians created their own theological method in which people's ethnocultural identity is conceived as central to the task of doing theology. This tendency to cross disciplinary boundaries continues to be a major characteristic of Latina/o theology as it engages other intellectual schools and remains relevant for the present social, political and theological climate. In considering ethnic and cultural identity as central to theology, U.S. Latina/o theologians go beyond contextual theologies so as to put into question even the intellectual edifice of the theological traditions they inherited.[57]

---

57. This self-reflective task is already taking place as Latinas/os look toward the future. See Néstor Medina, "Tongue Twisters and Shibboleths: On Decolonial Gestures in Latina/o Theology," *Journal of Hispanic/Latino Theology* 18/2 (2013) 3–19.

10

Chi and Holy Spirit

Towards a Korean North American Theology

GRACE JI-SUN KIM

THE EMPIRE THAT THE United States has built needs to reexamine its role, its policies and its own theology. If Christian theology is to contribute to empowering the powerless, be a force to extend justice to humankind, and provide moral-intellectual grounds to share and preserve creation's resources, then it is imperative for Christian theology to include every appropriate cultural dimension possible. The necessity for such efforts has been underscored dramatically by the emergence of the hegemonic dominance of the U.S. over the world's political, military, societal and even cultural structures and institutions. At the same time, the world is becoming globally interdependent, inter-woven, integrative, and dangerous. Samuel Huntington's "clash of civilizations"[1] may become a dreaded reality unless deliberate action, including a theological response, is taken. I offer here a Korean North American perspective to move that response to action. I propose that a Korean North American hybrid understanding of the Asian concept of *Chi* and the Christian understanding of the Holy Spirit is an excellent model of an intercultural and global pneumatology.

---

1. Samuel Huntington, *The Clash of Civilizations* (New York: Touchstone, 1996).

Part Two—Contextual and Constructive Proposals

Postcolonial Context

As background to the core proposal about *Chi* and the Spirit, I will consider in survey form the postcolonial context. Postcolonial studies offers ways of examining and understanding the human situation, which in turn help us understand the divine and ourselves. Postcolonialism describes the modern history of imperialism, beginning with the process of colonialism, through the struggles for political independence, the attainment of independence, and to the contemporary neocolonialist realities. This definition emphasizes the connection and continuity between the past and the present between the colonizer and the colonized. Postcolonialism is not about dwelling on the crimes of the past and their continuation, but about seeking transformation for liberation.[2] Colonialism seeks to define people in ways that facilitate exploitation.[3] Postcolonial theory provides concepts and terms that are valuable in analyzing and reconceptualizing our past and present context. It speaks against the past colonial and current neocolonizing tendencies that continue to exert influence even after territorial and political independence have been accomplished.[4] Postcolonial theory is concerned with the effects of unequal power relations between groups of people[5] that still exist even though the territorial divisions are not that clear.

> Postcolonialism is about a set of measures worked out by diasporan Third World intellectuals in order to undo, reconfigure and redraw contingent boundaries of hegemonic knowledges. Postcolonialism points not towards a new knowledge, but rather towards an examination and critique of knowledges.[6]

Postcoloniality is another name for the globalization of cultures and histories. It pursues a post-national reading of the colonial encounter by focusing on the global amalgam of cultures and identities consolidated by

---

2. Musa W. Dube, *Postcolonial Feminist Interpretation of the Bible* (St. Louis: Chalice, 2000) 15.

3. Deane Curtin, *Environmental Ethics for a Postcolonial World* (Lanham, MD: Rowman & Littlefield, 2005) 59, 166.

4. R. S. Sugirtharajah, *The Bible and the Third World: Precolonial, Colonial and Postcolonial Encounters* (Cambridge: Cambridge University Press, 2001) 250.

5. Revathi Krishnaswamy, "The Criticism of Culture and the Culture of Criticism: At the Intersection of Postcolonialism and Globalization Theory," *Diacritics* 32 (2002) 106.

6. Sugirtharajah, *Bible and the Third World*, 246.

imperialism. It uses a variety of conceptual terms and categories of analysis that examine the corruptive relationship between colonizer and colonized.[7]

> Postcolonialism provides a space in which to choose voices to construct interpretations that may have decolonizing effects in the contemporary world. Postcolonial study must be informed by class analysis if it is to succeed at its academic task of describing the effects of colonization or its ethical goal of decolonization in today's world.[8]

A part of this process leads to anti-colonial reading. Postcoloniality begins when subjects find themselves thinking and acting in certain ways. It goes beyond the binary notions of colonized and colonizer and lays weighty emphasis on critical exchanges and mutual transformation between the two. Postcolonialism does not mean that the colonized are innocent whereas the former colonizers are all innately greedy and responsible for all social evils. Not only is such a notion an invented form of colonialism but it also absolves the third-world elite from their patriarchal and vassalizing tendencies. The current postcolonialism tries to emphasize that this relationship between the ruler and the ruled is complex, full of cross-trading and mutual appropriation and confrontation.[9]

Postcolonial theory offers a space for the once-colonized. It is an interpretative act of the descendents of those once subjugated. In effect it means a resurrection of the marginal, the indigene and the subaltern. It is an act of reclamation, redemption, and reaffirmation against the past colonial and current neocolonizing tendencies that continue to exert influence even after territorial and political independence has been accomplished. "It means finding ways of operating under a set of arduous and difficult conditions that jeopardize and dehumanize people."[10]

A task of postcolonial criticism is to engage in constructive theological discourse. It rereads biblical texts from the perspective of postcolonial concerns such as liberation struggles of the past and present and be sensitive to subaltern and feminine elements embedded in the texts. "It will interact with and reflect on postcolonial circumstances such as hybridity,

---

7. Leela Gandhi, *Postcolonial Theory: A Critical Introduction* (New York: Columbia University Press, 1998) 129.

8. Jon L. Berquist, "Postcolonialism and Imperial Motives for Canonization," *Semeia* 75 (1996) 29.

9. Sugirtharajah, *Bible and the Third World*, 249.

10. Ibid., 250.

fragmentation, deterritorialization, and hyphenated, double, or multiple identities."[11] Furthermore, the religious landscape is so complex that reading a text through one single religious view may not yield much these days when cultural identities and religions coalesce. Postcolonial reading will also investigate interpretation that contested colonial interests and concerns. "It will bring to the fore how the invaded, often caricatured as abused victims or grateful beneficiaries, transcended these images and wrested interpretation from the invaders, starting a process of self-discovery, appropriation, and subversion."[12]

Postcolonial criticism seeks to dismantle hegemonic interpretations and does not hesitate to offer prescriptions and make moral judgments while acknowledging the perils of such decisions. Postcolonialism as an offshoot of postmodernism, while it collaborates with it, distances itself from its errors and unsavory aspects. Postcolonialism understands the Bible and biblical interpretation as a site of struggle over its efficacy and meanings. Postcolonialism is guarded in its approach to the Bible's serviceability as it sees the Bible as both a safe and an unsafe text, and as both a familiar and a distant one.[13] Liberation theology works with the binary notions of Christian and non-Christian and sees religious pluralism as an exception rather than a norm. "Postcolonialism on the other hand, is able to draw on a larger theological pool and is not confined to a particular religious source."[14] Liberation for the postcolonial subject is not imposing a pre-existing notion, but working out its contours in responding to voices within and outside the biblical tradition.

> Postcolonial space refuses to press for a particular religious stance as final and ultimate. As a point of entry, individual interpreters may have their own theological, confessional, and denominational stance, but this in itself does not preclude them from inquiring into and entertaining a variety of religious truth claims. It is the multi-disciplinary nature of the enterprise that gives postcolonialism its energy.[15]

---

11. Jean-Pierre Ruiz, *Reading from the Margins: The Bible and People on the Move*, (Maryknoll, NY: Orbis, 2011) 88.
12. Sugirtharajah, *Bible and the Third World*, 252, 257.
13. Ibid., 259.
14. Ibid., 262.
15. Ibid., 269.

What postcolonialism will argue for is that the idea of liberation and its praxis must come from the collective unconscious of the people. It sees liberation not as something hidden or latent in the text, but rather as born of public consensus created in democratic dialogue between text and context. Postcolonialism recognizes a plurality of oppressions. Postcolonialism does not perceive the other as a homogenous category, but acknowledges multiple identities based upon class, sex, ethnicity, and gender.[16] "Postcoloniality is about acquiring a new identity. One of the legacies of colonialism is an intermingling of people and cultures and the result is a hybridized identity."[17] This hybridity is a key term for postcolonialism as it brings into the forefront the complexities of the human context and situation. It is a difficult situation for humanity to be in as the difficulties of the political, cultural, and historical situation make an impact on the situation.

The postcolonial situation informs the identity of a person. The identity is crucial to understand how one understands God and does theology. Postcolonial criticism has given tools to understand the hybrid situation of immigrants and in particular to Korean North Americans as it accentuates their complex situation and context. Korean North Americans have experienced colonialism while living in Korea under Japanese rule. Certainly Koreans understand colonialism and its detrimental effects. For such immigrants it is important to examine their hybrid situation to get a better glimpse of how they are to do theology.

Hybridity

Korean North Americans are interested in assessing Christianity's role in supporting colonialism and patriarchy, because political independence for many of them happened only a generation ago.[18] The term hybridity needs further elaboration and is an essential tool that Korean American theologians are turning to to help describe this situation of instability and create new spaces and places of discourse. Essentially hybridization is a mixture of two things as it brings together, fuses, but also maintains separation. Hybridity makes difference into sameness and sameness into difference, but in a way that makes the same no longer the same, the different no longer sim-

16. Ibid.
17. Ibid., 6.
18. Kwok Pui Lan, *Postcolonial Imagination and Feminist Theology* (Louisville: Westminster John Knox, 2005) 152.

Part Two—Contextual and Constructive Proposals

ply different.[19] Hybridity is a way to conceptualize porous religious, ethnic, and cultural boundaries. Christianity has been hybrid and syncretistic from its beginnings, emerging from subjugated Palestine, where Judaism intersected with Greco-Roman cultures. Throughout its history, Christian thinkers and leaders have adopted and assimilated cultures and values of their own and of their neighbors.[20]

Hybridity works in different ways at the same time, according to the cultural, economic, and political demands of specific situations. It involves processes of interaction that create new social spaces to which new meanings are given.[21] Thus, as Asians immigrate to North America, they are displaced in many ways. They are displaced from their motherland, their families, their familiar social and religious groups. As they are displaced, hybridity helps to define new spaces so that they can build new identities and understandings. Hybridity works to bring in new possibilities of religious communication so that they can find peace and solace in their place of displacement and transformation.

What hybridity does is to shift the conceptualization of identity as identity is no longer a stable reference point. It moves to a different paradigm in which it is liminality, instability, impurity, movement, and fluidity that inform the formation of identities. "Hybridity is not about the dissolution of differences but about renegotiating the structure of power built on differences."[22] Thus when hybridity is brought into the Christian realm, there will be many differences and these differences will interact to bring forth a new way to do theology. The hybridity makes one question about the traditional ways of doing theology and understanding God. It makes us recognize that there are so many complexities that inform theology. There are distinctive contributions to North American Christianity and through it the world in adapting Korean insights based on Asian perspectives and Christian views of the Spirit. It is a genuine interpenetration and not superficial. This concept of hybridity is different from multicultural and integration models. As Koreans immigrated to North America, they left

19. Robert J. C. Young, *Colonial Desire: Hybridity in Theory, Culture and Race* (London: Routledge, 1995) 22, 26.

20. Rita Nakashima Brock, "Pacific and Asian Women's Theologies," in *Feminist Theologies: Legacy and Prospect*, ed. Rosemary Radford Ruether (Minneapolis: Fortress, 2007) 47.

21. Robert J. C. Young, *Postcolonialism: A Very Short Introduction* (Oxford: Oxford University Press, 2003) 79.

22. Sugirtharajah, *Asian Biblical Hermeneutics and Postcolonialism*, 125, 126.

their Asian context and entered a hybrid context that contested their Asian identity and belongingness.

IMMIGRATION, THE OTHER, AND RACISM

Since the early nineteenth century, Asians have been migrating worldwide but especially to the United States and Canada. At the height of the United States' westward expansion (across the Indian lands and Mexican territory to a new Pacific frontier) and the building of its economy, Asians provided cheap and abundant labor. Their first area of destination was Hawaii and over three hundred thousand Asians entered the islands between 1850 and 1920. The U.S. government and private companies ordered Asian labor as if it was a commodity and the Chinese were among the first as they worked in the sugar industry in Hawaii. These laborers helped transform the sugar industry into a big industry and helped themselves earn income, while at the same time displacing the Native Hawaiians.[23]

Korean immigration patterns were not the same as other Asian groups as many Koreans initially did not want to immigrate to the West. Missionaries played an active role and Koreans eventually overcame the initial resistance to the idea of immigration. A number of missionaries persuaded members of their congregations to go to Hawaii, a Christian land.

> As a result of the active role that missionaries played, an estimated 40 percent of the 7,000 emigrants who left the country between December 1902 and May 1905 were converts. Moreover, unlike the Chinese and Japanese who came from geographically confined areas, Korean emigrants originated from many places, especially seaports, and their vicinities. Furthermore, fewer of the Korean emigrants than Chinese or Japanese came from agricultural backgrounds. Of the 7,000 Koreans taken to Hawaii, about 1,000 eventually returned home, while another 1,000 proceeded to the mainland.[24]

---

23. Eleazar S. Fernandez, "American from the Hearts of a Diasporized People," in *Realizing the America of Our Hearts: Theological Voices of Asian Americans*, ed. Fumitaka Matsuoka and Eleazar S. Fernandez (St. Louis: Chalice, 2003) 256. Parts of this section are excerpts from cited by Grace Ji-Sun Kim, "Asian American Feminist Theology," in *Liberation Theologies Primer*, ed. Anthony Pinn and Stacey M. Floyd-Thomas (New York: New York University Press, forthcoming).

24. Sucheng Chan, *Asian Americans: An Interpretive History* (New York: Twayne, 1991) 15.

Part Two—Contextual and Constructive Proposals

However, as immigrants come into the West, there are problems of prejudice, racism and lack of religious tolerance for the immigrants. Racism is a system that promotes domination of the vulnerable by a privileged group in the economic, social, cultural, and intellectual spheres.[25] "We live in a society in which racism has been internalized and institutionalized and is woven deeply into a culture from whose inception racial discrimination has been a regulative force for maintaining stability and growth and for maximizing other cultural values."[26] Racism is the manifestation of the deeply entrenched determination to maintain the existing dominant culture and group. Only a full awareness of this disturbing reality leads to a new insight into what is possible. "The nation cannot redeem what has not been established."[27]

Immigrants live with racism. Racism is prejudice and discrimination. Racism is due to Westerners' act of racializing immigrants. Racialization is a Western construct to further separate and dominate the Other. As immigrants try to assimilate into the dominant culture they experience more alienation as there appears to be an invisible boundary that prevents them to become part of the mainstream White culture. Thus, many are living in this hybrid location, which is not stable and needs to be negotiated. Korean North Americans exist in this hybrid location. In this location, they are often viewed as the Other. The Other who is inferior, weak, and less intelligent. The Other becomes the one who needs to be dominated. In this process of becoming the Other, they become powerless. They need a theology that is empowering and works towards eliminating the understanding of the Other. There is some creativity that can take place in this hybrid location. It is where one can think outside of the mainline theological perspective and get a closer glimpse of the theological truth. It is important to understand that the Korean immigrants exist here and it is here that their theological growth occurs. It is the sacred hybrid location where they can begin to understand themselves and God. It is here that they recognize that they are worthy and are not to be understood as the Other as many Westerners have already categorized them as.

---

25. Fumitaka Matsuoka, *The Color of Faith: Building Community in a Multiracial Society* (Cleveland: United Church, 1998) 3.

26. Grace Ji-Sun Kim, "Asian American Feminist Theology," in *Liberation Theologies in the United States: An Introduction*, edited by Anthony Pinn and Stacey M. Floyd-Thomas (New York: New York University Press, 2010), 143.

27. Matsuoka, *The Color of Faith*, 95.

"Orientalism expresses and represents that part culturally and even ideologically as a mode of discourse with supporting institutions, vocabulary, scholarship, imagery, doctrines, even colonial bureaucracies and styles."[28] The Orient came to designate a number of peoples and their spaces, and this designation carries negative stereotypes. These stereotypes are used, then, to support or justify colonial endeavors.[29] Orientalism has been used by Europeans and North Americans as a way of dominating the East and having self-ascribed authority over the East. European culture gained in strength and identity by setting itself off against the Orient as a sort of surrogate and even underground self.[30] The Other are usually understood to be people from the East who are thought of as inferior, lesser, less intelligent, and exotic.

As Korean North Americans experience oppression through racism, discrimination and multiculturalism, they also have to endure the consequences of Orientalism and the experience of being treated as the Other. The Other is viewed as inferior and powerless. The Other is weaker, less intelligent, or a nuisance to society.[31] The Other remains the Other in many ways. They are "incorporated" into the world of Christianity but they do not own theology, they just rent it. The Other never becomes equal to but is incorporated as marginal and as such fulfills a useful role.[32] The Other becomes a necessity and a useful commodity for those who are the majority and the dominators. Therefore, it is necessary to dispel the category of the Other and continue to dialogue so that Korean Americans are not placed in that role.

Within this postcolonial world, where there are so many divisions and power dynamics, people are struggling to survive. They are trying to understand the power dynamics that may exist between those who hold and exercise power and those who do not. Therefore it is necessary to work towards removing these barriers. A possible step to removing them is to

28. Edward W. Said, *Orientalism* (New York: Vintage, 1979) 2.

29. Eric Bain-Selbo, "Understanding the Other: The Challenge of Post-Colonial Theory to the Comparative Study of Religion," *Religious Studies and Theology* 18 (1999) 62.

30. Grace Ji-Sun Kim, "What Forms Us: Multiculturalism, the Other and Theology," in *Feminist Theology with a Canadian Accent: Canadian Perspectives on Contextual Theology*, ed. Mary Ann Beavis et al. (Ottawa: Novalis, 2008).

31. Bain-Selbo, "Understanding the Other," 64.

32. Marcella Althaus-Reid, "Grace and the Other: A Postcolonial Reflection on Ideology and Doctrinal Systems," in *The Bright Side of Life*, ed. Ellen van Wolde (London: SCM, 2000) 67.

Part Two—Contextual and Constructive Proposals

understand the Other and understand the commonalities and similarities between people of different cultures, histories, and religion. As the world becomes smaller and more inter-related and inter-reliant, it is important to recognize the commonalities between the people to understand the binding characteristic that keeps people together. One such fact is the understanding of the spirit. The Spirit is part of most cultures and societies, and it may be the binding factor among people as many religious experiences of the Spirit are found around the world. Christianity and the West[33] have monopolized the understanding of the Spirit, and have not allowed the East to help define, understand and experience the Spirit. An examination of the Asian concept of *Chi* can be a source of entry for interreligious dialogue that can help move towards a new theology of world peace and tolerance. An understanding of *Chi* will help illustrate how the Korean North American hybrid identity affects their theological discourse, as their Christological and pneumatological understandings are interstitial and hybrid.

Chi-Spirit

In the present postcolonial context and in their hybrid situation, it is important to search for a new way of understanding the Spirit that is liberating and empowering. Asian thought stresses balance and harmony as compared to Western thinking based in contrasts and separations. An intercultural perspective of spirit from the Asian concept of *Chi* is a helpful tool for Korean North Americans as they search for a new method of pneumatology. In Eastern thought, *Chi* is the life force or spiritual energy that is part of everything that exists. It is what makes one alive, as it is the life force energy that makes one a living being. The Spirit becomes the essence of all things as all things exist because of the Spirit as *Chi*. *Chi* is the ultimate reality and is imminent in all things, and all things in the universe consist of Chi. Therefore, no being can exist apart from *Chi*.[34] This notion of the

---

33. When I speak of the West, it is Western Christian formulations that have been used to dominate other cultures. The Western intellectual social stances based on separation, division, destruction not harmony. The Western view of progress is tilted towards domination and destruction of the Other.

34. Jumsik Ahn, "Korean Contextual Theology as Related to *Ch'i*: An Assessment of the Theology of Jung Young Lee," PhD diss., Trinity Evangelical Divinity School, 2002, 162, 305.

Spirit as *Chi* reaffirms the idea of divine immanence or Immanuel.[35] This allows one to recognize that everything exists in God and because of God.

A study of *Chi* characters illustrates this. Western language translations of *Chi* include: air, wind, vapor, breath, gas, vital spirit, anger, appearance, intelligence, vital fluid, energy, material force, vital force, and subtle spirits.[36] The Chinese language is pictographic and to understand the original intent of the word *Chi*, we need only analyze the components of the ideogram. One of the earliest characters for *Chi* consists of the word for "sun" and "fire," suggesting that *Chi*, like sunlight, is a source of warmth and is essential for life. A living body is warm; cold slows down the movement of *Chi* and leads to death. This concept of vital heat is maintained in a specialized ideogram for *Chi* used exclusively in Daoist literature. "The upper part of the character, a picture of a man clearing the land of trees, means 'negation.' The wood is gone, hence 'negation, wanting, lacking, without.' The lower part of the character consists of four sparks from a flame."[37] As a whole, the character seems to mean "no fire." Just as extreme cold slows down the *Chi* and is too yin, so excess fire over-stimulates and is too yang. *Chi* requires a moderate, balanced polarity: passive and active, cold and warm. If the *Chi* is healthy, then the energy does not go to extremes.[38]

The *Chi* ideogram has strong metaphysical, spiritual, and psychological connotations and is unique to Daoist writings. The most common character for *Chi*, which appears throughout qigong, medical, and popular literature, represents such everyday concepts as "weather" (sky *Chi*), "balloon" (*Chi* sphere), "customs" (habitual *Chi*), "arrogant" (*Chi* high), "oxygen" (nourishing *Chi*), and the "healing exercises" of *qigong*. According to the ancient *Shu Wen Jie Zi* (Dictionary of Chinese Etymology), the three lines at the top of the character mean steam or vapor; the character for rice is on the bottom. Thus *Chi* means "vapor or steam rising from cooking rice." Some texts substitute the character "fire" for rice. In either case, the implication is that for water to boil and produce steam, there must be fire. *Chi* then can be defined as the energy produced when complementary, polar opposites are harmonized. Vital energy, *Chi* arises when opposites are

---

35. Jung Young Lee, *The Trinity in Asian Perspective* (Nashville: Abingdon, 1996) 98.

36. Lee Rainey, "The Concept of *Ch'i* in the Thought of Wang Ch'ung," *Journal of Chinese Philosophy* 19 (1992) 263.

37. Kenneth S. Cohen, *The Way of Qigong: The Art and Science of Chinese Energy Healing* (New York: Ballantine, 1997) 31.

38. Ibid., 30–31.

Part Two—Contextual and Constructive Proposals

unified: fire and water, heavenly (the steam) and earthly (the rice). Other yin/yang polarities include: mind and body, conscious and subconscious, self and environment. In the same way that an electric circuit requires the positive (yang) and negative (yin) pole, so a strong current of *Chi* requires a balance of opposites.[39]

Chi is commonly understood as a generic term for life energy. Just as a medical scientist thinks of healing as multifaceted, including chemical, psychological, electromagnetic, and environmental components, so *qigong* practitioners compartmentalize the concept of *Chi* into several different categories. There are three main sources of *Chi*: breath, food, and constitution. Air or breath (*zong Chi*) and food (*gu Chi*, literally "grain Chi") mix to form the "nutritive Chi" (*ying Chi*) that travels through the acupuncture meridians to all the tissues of the body. Whereas breath and food are acquired *Chi*, the third source of *Chi* is inborn and called *yuan qi*. Original *Chi* accounts for our constitution and inherited tendencies toward health or disease. A child with weak original *Chi* may have birth defects, be subject to frequent colds and infections, or in an extreme case, fail to thrive.[40] Therefore, it is important to have a good balance of *Chi* in one's body to maintain good health and energy.

Just as *Chi* does, the Old Testament *ruach* and the New Testament *pneuma* carry the same ambiguity of multiple meanings.

> The word *ruach* has its etymological origin in air, which manifests itself in two distinctive forms: that of wind in nature and that of breath in living things. Because God as the Spirit manifests herself as wind or *ruach*, she is also *Chi*. Wind symbolizes the power of life in nature, while breath symbolizes the power of life in the living.[41]

Without *Chi*, life does not exist, and similarly, if there is no Spirit, nothing living can exist.

If the Asian concept of *Chi* is found to be similar to and largely the same as the Christian concept of the Holy Spirit, there will be a stronger basis for arguing that what the Other believes and understands to be God is quite similar to the Western understanding of God. There is an undeniable recognition of the similarities between *Chi* and the Holy Spirit and

---

39. Ibid., 32.
40. Ibid., 32.
41. Grace Ji-Sun Kim, "Exploring Holy Spirit, Chi and the Other," in *A New Day: Essays on World Christianity in Honor of Lamin Sanneh*, edited by Akintunde Akinade (New York: Lang, 2010), 293.

this is the first step to the understanding that there is more commonality than differences between the East and the West. The Other may in fact have more similarities that were perceived and developed in different parts of the world and in a variety of cultures. These particular similarity should make each culture more willing to accept the views of and help the acceptance of the Other.

As we recognize the similarities between *Chi* and the Holy Spirit, it makes us question the separation that has existed between those two intimately tied terms. Is this separation the West's concern for power and authority over the East, or is this separation the West's way of monopolizing the idea of the Spirit and limiting the understanding of the Spirit as it pertains to Christianity? Whatever reason it may be, it is crucial to recognize and accept the similarities and commonalities that are found between people all over the world. With this recognition, it is then crucial to accept and welcome the Other. In particular, the racialized[42] immigrants who come to the West to begin a new life with many hopes and visions. It is important not to make them the Other or have power and authority over them, but to embrace and empower one another. The power of *Chi* can help build bridges between the East and the West, and bridge the gap created by ignorance and dominance. The destructive powers of separation can be overcome through *Chi*. We need to realize that *Chi* is the Spirit that is in all things. Whether called *Ruach*, *Pneuma*, or *Chi*, this Spirit is the selfsame Spirit of God. If God dwells within us, it makes a difference in how we live, treat others, and treat nature. Thus, it is important to acknowledge that *Chi* is necessary for our livelihood.

There is much to learn from the East and from one another. The East cannot be easily dismissed or ignored as their concept of *Chi* can add richness and new dimension to the Christian concept of God. In Christianity, there needs to be a stronger awareness of the Spirit within us. It is this Spirit that gives us life and it is this Spirit that maintains our life. As Westerners, we do not take good care of our Spirits. It is important to recognize the importance of the Spirit within our daily lives. If we give greater attention to this spirit, we would live this life differently. We may be more welcoming and more likely to embrace the Other if we recognize the commonalities

---

42. Everyone living in this world is racially ethnic. As immigrants enter the West, they are suddenly understood to be racially ethnic minorities. This process can be understood as people becoming racialized.

Part Two—Contextual and Constructive Proposals

that exist between the two. This is important as we live in a global village where cultural divides between people are becoming increasingly smaller.

Through the understanding of *Chi* as the Spirit of God, perhaps racism and prejudice can be eliminated from society. People can begin to welcome and embrace the Other. It is important to recognize the life-giving spirit that is found in *Chi*. This is crucial in how one treats others and how one is treated in return. This recognition is important in a globalized and postcolonial world that wants to destroy and conquer the Other, making sure that the Other will be kept in their place. Developing a deep life-giving understanding of the Spirit is crucial in those who oppress the Other. This emphasis on common ground in the shared Spirit of God will make a difference in how immigrants live in the Western world. The understanding that God is in all will help us to treat one another with love and respect. As immigrants face hardships and oppression, the understanding of the Spirit as life-giving will be an empowering concept.

Hence, Spirit/*Chi*[43] is essentially what keeps humanity alive as it is the life-giving force within us that sustains us and keeps us in harmony with nature and the world. The West builds polarities of rich/poor, white/black etc.; *Chi*/Spirit will help white Christians to grow away from the separation modality to an inclusion of all humans. Those who think they are powerless can gain a new vision of themselves through *Chi*. Spirit/*Chi* embraces life and makes it full. Spirit/*Chi* is crucial to Asian American women's theology as it emphasizes the Spirit/*Chi* power within all of us to make a difference in this world. Spirit/*Chi* is salvific and negotiates a space to save those who are living in the liminal spaces between us.

As we recognize the undeniable similarities between *Chi* and the Holy Spirit, we must question the separation that has existed between those two intimately tied terms. Is the separation due to the West's concern for power and authority over the East or is it the West's source of monopolizing or colonizing the idea of the Spirit as a way to limit the understanding of the Spirit as it pertains to Christianity? Whatever the reason, it is crucial to recognize and accept the similarities and the commonalities that are found between people all over the world. With this acceptance, it is then crucial to accept and welcome the Other, in particular the racialized immigrants who come to the U.S. It is important not to make them exotic or to have power and authority over them, but to really embrace and empower them.

---

43. Due to the similarity between *Chi* and Spirit, it seems appropriate to combine the words to write Spirit/*Chi*.

Conclusion

This chapter examined the colonial context in which we live in the present world. Koreans who have immigrated to North America within the last one hundred years have dealt with living in the diasapora, and as a consequence, racism and living as the Other. The hybridity of these immigrants put a dividing factor between themselves and the dominant culture. However, it is within this hybrid space that the Spirit can maneuver and make changes within people. The U.S. empire can be challenged and dismantled as the West begins to open itself to the East and Eastern ideas.

The Eastern concept of *Chi* and the Western Christian understanding of the Holy Spirit have a striking resemblance to one another. This similarity opens the door for greater communication and dialogue about the Other. It leads to a deeper understanding of God and spirituality as it provides a wider plane for religious discourse. It will sustain us and keep us aware of our interconnectedness and inter-reliance. The Spirit understood as *Chi* in many parts of the world is within us and gives us life. This *Chi* that exists within our bodies will bring healing to our physical bodies as well as our spiritual bodies. Therefore, it is essential to recognize the Spirit/*Chi* as a new way to do pneumatology that will be liberating for Korean North Americans.

Spirit/*Chi* will also help and maneuver our task of welcoming and accepting the Other. Everyone possesses *Chi*, so it is important that we recognize this and name it. This *Chi* will help us overcome the burden of racism and being objectified as the Other. With a combined understanding of Spirit/*Chi*, a new pneumatology will be developed that the Church can embrace to help strengthen its role in the world today. This proposed pneumatology will allow the West to recognize that the Spirit is a worldwide concept found in many religions.

11

Fossil Fuels and Apocalypse

Theology for "A New Dark Age"

Harold Wells

Predictions of the future are always precarious, since no one knows the future and history is full of surprises. Yet any theologian or preacher who wishes to be "contextual" must be alert to the soothsayers among us. In the urgent matter of climate change, theological reflection cannot proceed without close attention to the relevant science. The venerable British geo-physicist James Lovelock warns in apocalyptic tones of "a new Dark Age later in this century" because of drastic global warming, the portents of which are already evident.[1] Eminent because of his original discoveries in the field of ozone depletion, Lovelock should be taken seriously as a pioneer in the field of climate science.

Perhaps every epoch of history has been "dark" for some segments of humanity. Jane Jacobs, who also writes of "a dark age ahead," speaks of "countless Dark Ages and extinctions suffered by cultural losers."[2] Eras of darkness are about profound evil and suffering, as well as cultural loss. If we think of the brutal military conquests, mass enslavements, and crucifixions of the Roman and other ancient empires; of the tyrannies and

---

1. James Lovelock, *The Revenge of Gaia: Earth's Climate in Crisis and the Fate of Humanity* (London: Lane, 2006) 11.

2. Ibid., 161.

deadly plagues of the medieval period; then in modern times, of centuries of African slavery, the world wars, and holocausts of the twentieth century—we might regard most of human history as dark indeed. All of the indigenous cultures faced with European invasions experienced Dark Ages. Reaching much further back into pre-history, we learn from paleo-climate science that humans became almost totally extinct in a sudden cooling of the earth some 70,000 years ago—reduced perhaps to a mere 1,000 couples—the probable result of the eruption of the Toba supervolcano.[3] So, it is not only the conflict of human cultures that brings about Dark Ages.

Talk of impending darkness is not wildly popular in our optimistic society. It is true that bright and wonderful things, too numerous to name, were accomplished in the twentieth century to overcome pain, poverty, and oppression. Yet a broad literature has appeared warning of multiple crises confronting us in the decades ahead. Can theology have relevance to a time of impending disaster? Since millions of people still gather in churches weekly, church leaders surely have a role to play in preparing people to face a time of troubles in coming decades. Times of calamity also raise questions of theodicy and the kind of God that may be credible in a Dark Age. But, first, I shall consider the most dangerous feature of the context that we need to address.

Context: The Burning Planet

We live with growing awareness of multiple crises now facing humanity. Basic to these is the burgeoning human population, now exceeding seven billion; competition for costly energy resources and scarcity of fresh water; acidification of the seas, eroding soils, food shortages; and underlying most of these, climate change.[4]

---

3. Tim Flannery, *Here on Earth: A Natural History of the Planet* (Toronto: HarperCollins, 2011) 122.

4. Lester R. Brown, *World on the Edge: How to Prevent Environmental and Economic Collapse* (New York: Norton, 2011).

PART TWO—Contextual and Constructive Proposals

Glimpses into Climate Science

An almost universal consensus among climate scientists now affirms the fact of global warming.[5] Here we can only glimpse some of its main features. The highly respectable and quite conservative Intergovernmental Panel on Climate Change (IPCC), made up of more than 2,000 climate scientists from all over the world, warn that the planet is warming at a rate dangerous to life and human societies. This warming is mainly human caused, by emissions of carbon dioxide (CO_2) from the burning of fossil fuels—coal, oil, gas—which trap heat in earth's atmosphere. Australian climate scientist Tim Flannery tells us that even if we ceased burning fossil fuels today it would take several centuries for the CO_2 to dissipate.[6] Besides the observation of present conditions and computer models projecting climatic trends, paleo-climate records found in layers of ice and deep-sea sediment cores reveal much about planetary history, providing ample evidence of the power of CO_2 (produced in the past by natural processes over very long periods of time) to force climate change. The NASA climate scientist James Hansen asserts that, while there exist other "climate forcings" (tilting of the earth, variability of the earth's orbit, heat from the sun, volcanoes) the burning of fossil fuels today totally dominates other forcings.[7] The unprecedented rapidity of climate change is exacerbated by the mass destruction of forests, which serve to absorb carbon, and by agriculture, especially the clearing of land for the raising of animals (and their methane emissions).[8]

Global average temperatures have increased by .8 degree Celsius since pre-industrial times. While this may seem trivial, we note that this is an average of the whole surface of the earth, including the oceans, which are relatively cooler than the land.[9] Increases in land temperature vary and are much greater at the polar regions than elsewhere, where we see rapid melting of the Arctic, and the beginnings of the melting of the Greenland ice

---

5. For a dissenting view, contrary to the overwhelming majority of climate scientists, see Patrick J. Michaels, Robert C. Balling Jr., *Climate of Extremes: Global Warming Science They Don't Want You to Know* (Washington, DC: Cato Institute, 2011).

6. Flannery, *Here*, 196.

7. James Hansen, *Storms of My Grandchildren* (New York: Bloomsbury, 2009) 6–7, 49.

8. Ibid., 119. See Peter Singer's argument against raising cattle, in his essay "No More Excuses," in Tim Flannery, *Now or Never: Why We Must Act Now to End Climate Change and Create a Sustainable Future* (Toronto: HarperCollins, 2009) 131–42.

9. Hansen, *Storms*, 70–72.

sheet and West Antarctica. The melting of Arctic ice suddenly accelerated in 2007, so that in 2008 both the Northwest and Northeast passages were open for the first time in human history.

A factor not thoroughly dealt with by the IPCC is that of amplifying feedbacks. The Arctic is the most important refrigerator that keeps the planet cool, reflecting light and heat back into space (the "albedo effect"). The reduction of ice is an important feedback factor causing the earth to absorb more of the sun's heat. A further feedback is the melting of methane deposits in the Arctic tundra. Methane, like CO_2, is a greenhouse gas, and even more potent than CO_2, though it dissipates more quickly. Moreover, huge deposits of methane are found on the floor of the oceans, which, with the warming of the seas, could bubble forth, greatly accelerating the greenhouse effect: "Think of a nasty belch—it would release a tremendous amount of methane into the atmosphere that could prove such an assault . . . that it could represent a tipping point."[10]

Hansen identifies "tipping points" for "runaway" climate change: (1) the collapse of the West Antarctica or Greenland ice sheets, melting now at a rate of 100 cubic kilometers per year, which bodes ill for sea level and storms; (2) growing accumulation of carbon dioxide in the atmosphere, which has increased from c. 270 parts per million in the pre-industrial era to c. 387 ppm. (in 2009)—a level not seen on Earth for three million years![11] Hansen, Flannery, and others argue that we need to reduce that to no more than 350 ppm. One degree celsius of additional warming would probably mean 450 ppm, a certain recipe for climate disaster; (3) massive discharge of methane deposits, either from tundra or the sea. Any or all of these could produce a runaway greenhouse effect that would be beyond human control.[12]

Sea level rise is one of the worst consequences of global warming, threatening to flood coastal regions, including hundreds of large cities all over the world. Water expands when it warms, and with the dumping of trillions of tons of melting ice the seas are already rising at a rate of 3.4 centimeters per decade. While this seems harmless, it is already being felt by low lying islands in the Pacific and is likely to increase incrementally as glaciers and ice caps melt and feedbacks take effect. Flannery warns of "sea-level rise that would be a catastrophe for much of East and South Asia, the

---

10. Alanna Mitchell, *Sea Sick* (Toronto: McClelland & Stewart, 2009) 96–97.

11. Flannery, *Here*, 196.

12. Hansen, *Storms*, 276, 140–42, 164–66.

east coast of the US and parts of Europe." It could be dramatic indeed, even several meters higher, "if a large ice shelf collapses and melts."[13]

The health of the ocean is immensely important to the well-being of all life on the planet. Oceans cover 70 percent of the earth's surface,[14] and like the forests, are an important carbon sink, absorbing carbon dioxide best when cold. Hansen explains that when it becomes colder it absorbs more CO_2; when it warms, it releases CO_2 and methane. Moreover, as CO_2 increases in the air, the ocean dissolves more carbon dioxide and becomes more acidic. Acidification of the ocean is now killing the coral reefs and other marine life. A huge decline in fishing stocks and marine bio-diversity is a result partly of this acidification.[15]

Global warming also carries the implication of more violent and extreme weather, which has already been observable in recent years. Hansen explains that this is because the amount of water vapor that air can hold is a function of temperature; atmospheric water vapor increases rapidly with only a small rise of temperature. This can cause heavier rain and flooding. Greater heat can also result in more frequent and more intense hurricanes, tornadoes, and typhoons. Increased heat causes rapid evaporation, drought, desertification, reduction of fresh water supplies, forest fires, and unendurable temperatures.[16] Recently we have seen extraordinary examples of these phenomena. Thus, climate change is already bringing hardship to millions of humans, as well as many other species. All of our major informants on climate science agree that the burning of fossil fuels, and most especially the burning of coal to produce energy, must urgently come to an end.

The Energy Debates

Debates are ongoing about sources of the energy that drive our modern technological world. Given the rapid industrialization of parts of the developing world, will there be sufficient supply of the fossil fuels that make possible modern industry, transportation, agriculture, and heating? Will our use of fossil fuels so impact the earth's climate that we will perpetrate an apocalypse, drastically endangering our very survival on the planet?

13. Flannery, *Here*, 197; Hansen, *Storms*, 256.
14. Mitchell, *Sea Sick*, 7.
15. Hansen, *Storms*, 165–66; Flannery, *Here*, 198, 227; James Lovelock, *The Vanishing Face of Gaia* (London: Lane, 2009) 79.
16. Hansen, *Storms*, 253.

Peak Oil, or Oil Plateau?

Considerable debate exists about the future of oil, the main energy source for the modern world as we know it, and a major contributor to global warming. "Peak oil" refers to the assertion of many experts in the fields of petroleum geology that world oil production has peaked, i.e., that approximately half of all the available oil has already been used over the last century or so. The situation is complicated by the enormous growth in oil consumption in such developing nations as China and India. The alarm about peak oil was sounded in the 1970s by the Club of Rome in their famous book *Limits to Growth*.[17] Even earlier, M. King Hubbert, a petroleum geologist, accurately predicted in 1956 the peak of U.S. oil production in the early 1970s. Geologist Kenneth Deffeyes used Hubbert's methods to date global peak oil in the first decade of the new century[18]—not that oil would run out, but that much of the remaining oil would not be economically recoverable even if prices rose very high. Oil prices have already begun to fluctuate wildly, as economic recessions reduce the price temporarily within a general upward trend.

Enforced cutbacks in oil consumption would be painful, but could be good news if it diminished the dangers of climate change and forced the development of renewable energy (wind, solar, geo-thermal, biomass, etc.). Hubbert and Deffeyes were evidently right about the oil peak from the "low hanging fruit" of conventional sources. However, it has been precisely this oil peak that has pushed the industry to search for fossil fuel in the most unlikely places and to sink enormous investment into methods and sources once considered exorbitantly expensive. The debate about peak oil has now shifted, as new technologies have allowed for a greatly increased oil production.

Economist Daniel Yergin tells us that deep sea oil resources which were previously not accessible are now available because of sensors that provide clarity of information and digital communication between field and technology centers.[19] Growth of production from the deep water sector has grown from 1.5 million barrels a day in 2000 to 5 million by 2009, and by 2009 underwater wells in the Gulf of Mexico were supplying 30 percent

---

17. Donnella Meadows et al., *Limits to Growth* (Nwe York: Universe Books, 1972).
18. Kenneth S. Deffeyes, *Beyond Oil* (New York: Hill & Wang, 2005) xiii–xvii.
19. Daniel Yergin, *The Quest* (New York: Penguin, 2011) 227–41.

Part Two—Contextual and Constructive Proposals

of U.S. production.[20] The oil resources of the Arctic, increasingly accessible because of the melting of polar ice, is another potential source, with major development especially off the northern shore of Russia.[21] Canada, the U.S., and other Arctic powers, too, are eying large potential for deposits there. Yergin also points out new production of shale oil, recoverable from shale and other kinds of rock widely found in the U.S. and Canada. Horizontal drilling and hydraulic fracturing has enabled growth in production from 10,000 barrels per day in 2005 to 400,000 in 2010.[22]

Production of "dirty oil" from the bitumen (a sticky molasses-like substance) of the tar sands, is slated to be transported by new pipelines from Alberta to Texas and to the Pacific coast. Tar sands production has more than doubled, from 600,000 barrels per day in 2000 to 1.5 million in 2010.[23] Environmental journalist Andrew Nikiforuk writes that "Bitumen is what a desperate civilization mines after it's depleted its cheap oil. It's a bottom-of-the-barrel resource, a signal that business as usual in the oil patch has ended."[24] Sadly, one barrel of bitumen (after it has undergone a pollution-heavy process of recovery using much cleaner natural gas) requires the consumption of three barrels of fresh water from the Athabasca River. Thus, he writes, "Every day, Canada exports one million barrels of bitumen to the United States and three million barrels of virtual water."[25]

The fact that a great deal of additional oil is obtained in these ways does not negate the fact that oil resources are finite and will eventually go into decline. Yergin suggests that rather than "peak" we should imagine a "plateau" of oil discovery and production. He writes: "The world has decades of further production growth before flattening out into a plateau—perhaps sometime around midcentury—at which time a more gradual decline will begin."[26]

20. Ibid., 246.
21. Ibid., 41.
22. Ibid., 261.
23. Ibid., 256.
24. Ibid., 15.
25. Ibid., 3.
26. Ibid., 226–27.

Natural Gas: New Sources

It has been common also to hear of shortages of natural gas. In 1978 the U.S. Congress enacted a ban on the use of natural gas for the generation of electricity. However, Yergin informs us that new discoveries of natural gas, together with the new technologies, have greatly increased the supply not only in North America, but in such places as Qatr, Australia, Siberia.[27] Most dramatic is the enormous growth in the production of shale gas, widely present in North America, and newly accessible because of the technology of hydraulic fracturing, which uses large amounts of water and chemicals to extract gas from shale rock. While shale gas was just 1 percent of natural gas supply in 2000, by 2011 it accounted for 25 percent of gas production, transforming the natural gas market. World gas consumption has tripled over the last thirty years and, according to Yergin, is "the fuel of the future."[28]

Continuing Use of Coal

Coal is "exceedingly dirty stuff," says Hansen, producing arsenic and mercury pollution to air and water.[29] It accounts for 40 percent of the world's electricity generation and is plentiful and easily accessible in many places. In 2011 about twenty-five coal-fired plants were under construction in the United States.[30] Coal accounts for three quarters of CO_2 emissions in both China and India. Until recently China was adding a new coal fired power plant every week or two, though this rate of growth has declined recently because of increased investment in renewables, in which China has become a leader. Still, 65 percent of new Chinese capacity is from coal. An "Asian brown cloud" floats above south Asia, especially India, because of thousands of coal-burning power stations, tens of thousands of factories, and millions of open cooking fires.[31] Germany, too—though it has made impressive progress toward renewable energy from wind—has committed to phasing out nuclear power, and will resume the building of coal fired plants.[32]

27. Ibid., 332–35.
28. Ibid., 329–32, 340.
29. Hansen, *Storms*, 176.
30. Ibid., 400.
31. Mark Lynas, *The God Species* (London: Fourth Estate) 184–85.
32. Hansen, *Storms*, 179–81.

Part Two—Contextual and Constructive Proposals

The continuing availability of fossil fuels is bad news from the perspective of climate change. Deep sea oil spills (most dramatically the Gulf of Mexico in 2010) renders our fragile oceans ever more vulnerable. Oil pipelines too are notorious for breaking and spilling. Great amounts of water needed to extract oil from tar sands and from shale also diminishes scarce sources of fresh water at a time of diminished rivers and depleted aquifers. The use of relatively cleaner natural gas for the extraction of dirty oil from tar sands is also deplorable. Since concern about peak oil and peak natural gas has declined, there is less incentive to develop all-imporant energy alternatives.

Nuclear?

The question of nuclear energy as a power source for electricity is fiercely debated. Since nuclear energy production emits very little CO_2, Hansen, Lovelock, and Lynus all argue persuasively for the necessity of further and rapid nuclear development as the only adequate source of energy for a transitional period prior to the full development of renewable energies. But others point out the huge expense of building, maintaining, and eventually replacing nuclear power plants, as well as the waste disposal difficulties and potential danger to populations arising from nuclear accidents, earthquakes, or terrorism.[33] It seems wise to avoid the casual optimism that alternative conventional energy sources, including nuclear, will solve the problem.

Widespread agreement exists that the elimination of the use of coal is indeed urgent. Hansen declares that "coal emissions must be phased out as rapidly as possible or global climate disasters will be a dead certainty"; if coal is rapidly phased out, "the climate problem is solvable."[34] Gas and oil could then be phased out more gradually until replaceable by renewables.

There is not space here to discuss renewable sources of energy that produce no CO_2: wind, solar, geo-thermal, biomass, carbon neutral fuel from algae, etc. Many argue that conservation, plus renewables, could be entirely sufficient.[35] Others argue that development of renewables will not be adequate for the foreseable future to supply the needs of modern tech-

---

33. See also Kristin Shrader-Frechette, *What Will Work* (Oxford University Press, 2011).
34. Hansen, *Storms*, 172–73.
35. Brown, *World*, ch. 9.

nological societies. What is obvious is that enormous public investment in research and development of renewable sources of energy is essential. Such innovation may be the key to a viable future civilization. The question is whether the political will exists to accomplish this in time. So far politicians barely dare to raise the issue at election time for fear of losing public support. A "tipping point" of public awareness will be necessary before political leaders have the courage to stand against powerful fossil fuel industries, and act decisively.

Lovelock discusses possibilities for "geo-engineering" (e.g., using technology to reflect back into space the heat of the sun; injecting aerosauls into the air to produce global dimming, etc.).[36] But he is not optimistic that such desperate experiments would be successful, or even agreed upon by a divided humanity. He is not hopeless, but is not optimistic that humanity will have the wisdom to take the steps necessary to cool the burning planet. He imagines a much hotter world, where humans, after many predictable catastrophes, including perhaps nuclear wars,[37] will be reduced to about 10 percent of its present population, confined to polar regions like Greenland and Antarctica, the northern regions of Canada, Scandinavia, Siberia, and certain islands, like Japan and New Zealand. He fears a return to much more violent, barbarous, and pre-modern levels of civilization. Hansen bemoans the low level of public awareness of the dangers confronting us, of the lethargy of governments, which actually gag and persecute scientists who publicize climate science research.[38] He envisages a truly apocalyptic scenario reminiscent of the book of Revelation: the "Venus syndrome," wherein life on a burning planet Earth could become as impossible as it is on the planet Venus, which early in its history suffered a runaway greenhouse effect from natural causes. He declares that if the fossil fuel industries prevail, and fossil fuels are used as they are now, this will certainly happen as we pass the tipping points and reach a point of no return.

It is obvious that, at root, this is an ethical and spiritual matter, to which faith and theology must have something to say.

---

36. Lovelock, *Vanishing*, 92–104.

37. For imaginative projections into the future, see Gwynne Dyer, *Climate Wars* (Toronto: Vintage, 2009).

38. Hansen, *Storms*, esp. chap. 3.

Part Two—Contextual and Constructive Proposals

Where Is Theology in All of This?

It will be difficult to convince most people that theology has any relevance at all to the multiple crises facing humanity, including climate change. Will preachers have anything to offer beyond moral platitudes about excessive consumerism and the virtue of sharing? What will Christians have to offer, first to resist and reverse the present situation, or to live well as a new Dark Age unfolds? What manner of theology and faith will provide hope and direction in the years ahead?

Possibly a time of encroaching disaster will evoke an upsurge of popular religion. While many would, understandably, turn to atheism, many others would turn to religion for comfort and direction. Would this religion be constructive, life-giving, and liberating? Or would it be fearful, harsh, xenophobic, and judgmental? James Kunstler imagines a "Christianity inflamed"—a stronger religion, fundamentalist, and apocalyptic, severe in its moral judgments, harsh in its punishments. The civilized tolerance of liberal theologies might find little place in the face of widespread panic, want, and fear.[39]

I suggest that much can be learned from the theologies of the twentieth century, which have reflected deeply on the realities of evil and suffering. Specifically, I suggest that a marriage of the "theology of the cross" with ecological theology will offer guidance and hope for the struggles that lie ahead.

Theology of the Cross

The genre of Christian thought known as "theology of the cross" became prominent during and after World War II. In a Dark Age this theology speaks profoundly of the suffering of God in the suffering of creation. Some of the most important theologies of the twentieth century have attempted to address this suffering in terms of a *theologia crucis*—a mode of thought with roots in Hebrew prophetic faith, in Jesus of the New Testament, especially the event of the cross itself, and in the theology of Paul; then explicitly in Luther. In the twentieth century, theology of the cross is found in such contextual theologians as Bonhoeffer, Moltmann, Sobrino, Hall, and

---

39. James Howard Kunstler, *The Long Emergency: Surviving the Converging Catastrophes of the Twenty-first Century* (New York: Atlantic Monthly Press, 2005), 287–89.

Johnson.[40] We need not reinvent the wheel, having much to build upon in the insights of twentieth-century theology.

A theology of the cross is centered in God's suffering love in Christ. Because for Christians Jesus Christ is supremely God's own presence and self-revelation, the incarnation of God's Word in his life, death, and resurrection is the bottom-line norm of Christian truth. At the same time, ecological theology, emphasizing respect for God's creation, will become more essential in a context of climate change. As the social sciences have been important dialogue partners with liberation theologies, so now ecological theology needs to be in dialogue with the sciences of energy and environment. Particularly the "option for the poor," founded in the praxis of Jesus himself, must be a basic hermeneutical tool for theology and ethics, for the sake of the victims of global warming, but now extended to include all the myriads of non-human species disappearing as a result of human environmental destruction.

The Doctrine of God

By "God," I mean the Ultimate Source, the Ultimate Meaning and Destiny of all things. "God" is that which we finally worship, love, and trust. Christians find the self-disclosure of God pre-eminently in the crucified Christ. Thus the God we proclaim, according to a *theologia crucis*, will be fundamentally determined by the event of the cross, for there God is revealed as the One who reigns through gentleness and love. The nonviolent God of the cross has entered, in Christ, into physical pain but also into the anguish of abandonment and despair, enduring humiliation and death. Luther declared that "it is not sufficient for anyone, and it does him no good to recognize God in his glory and majesty, unless he recognizes him in the shame and glory of his cross."[41] He contrasted a theology of the cross with a "theology of glory," which emphasizes the power and majesty of God, but also glories in human good works, human reason, and loves the trappings of a glorious, rich, and powerful church. Luther drew inspiration from Paul's poignant words: "The foolishness of God is stronger than human strength, and the weakness of God, is wiser than human wisdom" (1 Cor 1:25). The manger

---

40. See my discussion of this: "Theology of the Cross and the Theologies of Liberation," *Toronto Journal of Theology* 17/1 (2001) 147–66.

41. Martin Luther, *Heidelberg Disputation*, in *Luther's Works*, vol. 31, ed. H. J. Grim (Philadelphia: Muilenberg, 1957) 52–53.

and the cross speak to us of a God of gentleness and humility and of inexhaustible grace, a God of power, but not of brute force or domination.

If we believe that self-giving Love is the highest and deepest reality, and that "God is Love" (1 John 4:8), we do not speak easily of God's almighty power. When we consider the randomness of the evolutionary process, the disasters to vulnerable creatures that result from volcanic eruptions, meteorites, earthquakes; when we experience the non-intervention of God in the most extreme circumstances of human evil—slavery, concentration camps, torture—we surely lament the "foolishness and weakness of God." A credible doctrine of God for a Dark Age will not speak of the "Almighty" as one who controls the world and all that happens within it. It can only speak of a God of *kenosis*, a self-emptying God, who, in Christ, has "emptied himself, taking the form of a servant . . . [who] being found in human form humbled himself and became obedient unto death, even death on a cross" (Phil 2:7–8). This, then, is "the Crucified God."[42]

Dietrich Bonhoeffer stated it most starkly, writing from a Nazi prison just before his execution: "The God who is with us is the God who forsakes us (Mk. 15:34). . . . Before God and with God we live without God. God lets himself be pushed out of the world on to the cross. He is weak and powerless in the world, and that is precisely the way, the only way, in which he is with us and helps us."[43] Emphatically, for Bonhoeffer (aware that no supernatural rescue was in store for the Jews), God is no *deus ex machina* descending supernaturally to fix up human affairs. Nor should we today expect a supernatural intervention that will fix our climate change problem, eradicate carbon dioxide from the atmosphere, or halt the hurricanes. God provides no guarantee that human beings will not destroy themselves, whether in nuclear wars or global warming.

A doctrine of God according to a theology of the cross will continue to be trinitarian. This is the God who in Christ entered deep into the darkness in order to be fully immersed in the life of the world, and remains present with us now, inspiring and empowering, through the Spirit.

The theology of the cross can be highly congenial with recent ecological theologies if it is *pan-en-theistic* (all things in God, God in all things). God lives within creation as Spirit and as immanent, indwelling Wisdom. Creation, then, is not merely profane, for the divine Spirit lives within it.

---

42. Jürgen Moltmann, *The Crucified God*, trans. R. A. Wilson and J. Bowden (London: SCM, 1974).

43. Dietrich Bonhoeffer, *Letters and Papers from Prison*, trans. and ed. E. Bethge (London: SCM, 1953) 360–61.

This is a passionate deity, who suffers the vulnerability of love and can be loved in return. The prophet Isaiah already knew that God is "afflicted in all our afflictions" (Isa 63:9) and is integrally related to creation. We note that major theological figures such as Moltmann, Johnson, and Boff share the panentheistic emphasis on God's immanence, and have been notable as pioneers of ecological theology, linking trinitarian thought to ecological concerns.[44] Boff finds the communal life of the triune God reflected in the intimate connectedness of the structures of creation: "If God is communion and relationship, then the entire universe lives in relationship, and all is in communion with all at all points and at all moments."[45]

But the question remains: Is this God powerless? Is God overwhelmed by the power of darkness and finitude? Most traditional theology taught the impassibility (the incapacity for suffering) of the omnipotent God who "can do anything," who can only act and cannot be acted upon. But since the unspeakable calamities of the twentieth century it has been impossible for most people to love or worship an impassible God. "Only a suffering God can help," said Bonhoeffer in prison.[46]

Yet a powerless God cannot help either. This God, after all, is the Creator, the *Alpha and Omega*, the eternal source of all power, who raised Jesus from the dead, against whom no power can ultimately prevail. This is the Lord of a universe of unimaginable immensity, of billions of planets and infinite possibilities, the holy One for whom a thousand years is but as yesterday. God's limitation against evil can only be *self-limitation* or *kenosis* (self-emptying), not only in the Incarnation in Christ, but also in the very act of creation. The kenotic God whom we meet in Christ is the self-limiting Creator, who allows creation to exist in its own autonomy and freedom. Thus, by the very act of creation, God makes space for vulnerable creatures to live and to love. Moltmann writes that "in the divine act of self-humiliation we also have to respect an act of God's omnipotence . . . God never appears mightier than in the act of his self-limitation, never greater than in the act of his self-humiliation."[47]

---

44. Jürgen Moltmann, *God in Creation*, trans. M. Kohl (London: SCM, 1985); Elizabeth A. Johnson, *Women, Earth and Creator Spirit* (Philadelphia: Fortress, 1985).

45. Leonardo Boff, *Cry of the Earth, Cry of the Poor*, trans. P. Berryman (Maryknoll, NY: Orbis, 1997) 156–57.

46. Bonhoeffer, *Letters*, 361.

47. Jürgen Moltmann, "God's Kenosis in the Creation and Consummation of the World," in *The Work of Love*, ed. John Polkinghorne (Grand Rapids: Eerdmans, 2001) 148.

Part Two—Contextual and Constructive Proposals

The paradox of God's weakness and God's power only makes sense in view of Jesus' resurrection. The resurrection means that God the Creator will ultimately reign over the powers of evil, darkness and death. The raising of the crucified Jesus is the unique intersection of eternity and time, our preview (*prolepsis*) into the eschatological future breaking into time and history. It is not a forceful, coercive event, but hidden to all but the eyes of faith. Because of the resurrection, a theology of the cross, especially in a Dark Age, will be a theology of hope. The risen Jesus gifts us with a glimpse into the eternal Kingdom of God, which promises a "new heaven and a new earth" (Rev 21:1), transcending history, time, and space as we know it.

Implications for Ethics and Church

It matters in practical terms what content people put into the word "God." If God is the capricious, all-powerful monarch of the universe, ruling all by his inscrutable will, believers may be inclined to domination—over one another and over the natural realm. According to such a theology, whatever disasters occur, they will be seen as God's will. But if God is the eternal communion of Love, and if, through the Spirit, we are gifted here and now and beyond death, with a share in the eternal life of God, we will surely learn to love community and equality in human relations, and learn to live gently with the natural world around us.

Moving beyond the Constantinian establishment of the church as a rich, powerful institution, we can learn to be a servant church, not merely reflecting the marketing strategies of the world around us in search of success and mastery, institutional status and prestige. Canadian theologian Charles Fensham suggests that we can learn from the monastic tradition, which flourished and served in other dark times. He envisages a future Christian *ecclesia*—not in withdrawn celibate cloisters, but in vowed communities—that would pursue prayer, offer hospitality, preserve scholarship, and participate in God's mission of justice, peace, and wholeness.[48] In the decades ahead this will include a degree of asceticism and an ethic of self-limitation. Modest life style and "greening" will be basic to the church's integrity if we wish to live as stewards of God's creation in a time of great deprivation. Living with respect for God's good creation, we will have to be less concerned with grand buildings and learn to practice reverence for all

---

48. Charles Fensham, *Emerging from the Dark Age Ahead: The Future of the North American Church* (Ottawa: Novalis, 2008) 171.

living things and the earth's delicate ecological balance.[49] Church leaders, many of whom have long been preoccupied with issues of sexual morality, need instead to challenge the people with questions about their automobiles, heating arrangements, and use of electricity, their air flight and use of plastics and imported food. The Spirit, we may believe, is providentially at work, striving among people and movements, both religious and secular, to bring wholeness to creation.

How should Christians live politically in light of the self-giving God? Surely we will have to put our weight politically behind structures of social solidarity. If we are committed to the "option for the poor," we can learn from looking again at the tradition of Christian Socialism in the nineteenth and early twentieth centuries, in its many forms—communalism, cooperativism, social democracy—seeking justice in economic relations. We need to be open also to local organic farming and to green business entrepreneurs. Politicians need public support to impose taxes on carbon emissions and to reward green economic development. Why would Christians, called to live with respect in God's creation, not be at the forefront of movements and campaigns to meet the challenge of climate change?

Despite the lack of establishment, or because of it, the churches are still in a position to inspire great numbers of people, providing opportunity for reflection, for public education, and prophetic action. It is difficult to imagine most of our churches, flawed as they are, playing such a role. But churches have played a revolutionary role in the past, and can do so again. It is difficult to think of any other *locus* in society that is comparable in its (unrealized) potential to challenge those forces that lead us toward a new Dark Age.

---

49. Ross L. Smillie, *Practicing Reverence* (Kelowna: Woodlake, 2011).

Index

Abalos, David, 142
Academy of Catholic Hispanic Theologians of the United States (ACHTUS), 144
Ad Gentes, 133
Adorno, Theodor W., 68, 70
agency, moral, 29, 33–36, 37–38, 40
Aichele, George, 8
Airhart, Phyllis, 55
Ali Modad Aguilar, Felipe J., 133
Allen, Richard, 42–44, 48
Allende, Salvador, xii, 114
Althaus-Reid, Marcella, 107–8, 169
Alvarez, Sonia, 81–82
Andraos, Michel, 129–31, 137, 138
Antony, Wayne, 83
Anzaldúa, Gloria, 39, 142
Aponte, David Edwin, 150, 154
Arroyo, Gonzalo, 114
Atleo, Shawn, 102
Aubry, Andrés, 131
Audinet, Jacques, 152
Aune, David E., xi
Avakumovic, Ivan, 46

Backhouse, Roger E., 51
Badham, Roger A., 37
Bain-Selbo, Eric, 169
Banta, Martha, 51
Bañuelas, Arturo, 155
Barber, Michael, 129
Barnes, Michael H., 29
Barr, Robert R., 110, 142
Bauckham, Richard J., xi

Baum, Gregory, 26, 119
Bavoux, Claudine, 152
Belo, Fernando, 6
Benjamin, Bret, 81
Benjamin, Don, 7
Berquist, Jon, 163
Berryman, Phillip, 114, 188
Bessette, Alfred, 114
Bland, Salem, 42, 54
Blond, Phillip, 67
Blondel, Maurice, 65–67, 69
Blount, Brian, 6
Blussé, Leonard, 152
Boff, Clodovis, 142
Boff, Leonardo, 188
Bounds, Elizabeth M., 25, 28, 30
Brazil, 22, 80–81, 85
Brittain, Christopher, 58
Broad, Robin, 80
Brown, Lester R., 177
Brubaker, Pamela, 25
Brueggemann, Walter, 6, 105
Bush, George W., 11

Cadorette, Curt, 113
Callahan, Allen D., 6
Campbell, Douglas F., 53–54
Campbell, Colin, 47
Canadians, 36, 46, 51, 55–56, 105, 108
Candelaria, Michael R., 115
capitalism, vii, 42–3, 51–52, 58, 81, 124
Carter, Warren, 7

193

Index

Cassidy, Richard, 6
Cauthen, Richard, 43
Cavanaugh, William T., 62
Ceresko, Anthony, 6
Chamberlain, Mary, 94
Charlton, Thomas L., 96
Chi, vi, xvi, 161–63, 165, 167, 169–75
Chile, xii, 113–16
Chopp, Rebecca, 33
Christ, xi–xii, 9, 12, 60, 67, 123–26, 133, 157, 186–89
Christian, William, 47
Christian Right, 22
Christianity, iv, 44, 47, 52–53, 61, 67, 71–72, 76, 116, 143, 150–51, 166, 169–70, 173–74
church, v, vii–ix, xi–xiii, 4–5, 9–12, 19, 21–24, 27–28, 32–35, 37, 42, 45, 48, 54, 56–57, 59–60, 63, 73–75, 79, 82, 111, 114–17, 119–20, 125, 128–40, 150, 175, 177, 187, 190–91
class, 10, 12–13, 28, 34, 36, 45, 105, 122, 142, 165
Clevenot, Michel, 6
Cohen, Kenneth S., 171
Cole-Arnal, Oscar L., 55
Coleman, John A., 29
Collins, John J., 8
colonialism, 80, 102, 105, 107, 136, 162–63, 165
community, 14, 18–20, 25, 28, 32–33, 39, 74, 95, 97–99, 104, 119, 132, 134–35, 137, 143, 153, 155, 160
Comte, Auguste, 53
Cone, James, 159
Conway, Janet, 83
Cook, Guillermo, 111
Cormie, Lee, iv, vii–ix, xii–xiii, xvii, 3–4, 9, 24–26, 29, 40, 58, 63, 77–79, 85–86, 88–89, 129, 140, 142

creation, 53, 86, 89, 99, 104, 120, 122, 135, 152, 157, 159, 186, 188–91
cross, 116–17, 134, 186–89
Curtis, Susan, 42–45, 47–48
Cyrus, King, 13

Davis, Charles, 66
D'Costa, Gavin, 72
de Alva, Jorge Klor, 142–43, 151, 154
Deffeyes, Kenneth S., 181
DeGiglio-Bellemare, Mario, 63, 78, 117, 118, 140
Delgado, Richard, 151
Díaz, Miguel H., 111, 158
Dillard, Annie, 10
disciples, 11–12, 17–19, 23
diversity, 32, 34, 36, 80, 82, 84–85, 87, 151, 154
Dobson, James, 11
Dorrien, Gary, 44
Downey, John K., 4
Dupré, Louis, 59
Durkheim, Emile, 53
Dussel, Enrique, 128–29, 136

ecological theologies, 114, 159, 186, 188
Ekblad, Robert, 6
Elizondo, Virgilio, 143–47, 149–52
Elliott, John H., 7, 24
Elliott, Neil, 6
Ellis, Marc H., 147
Ellison, Marvin, 30
Ellwood, Charles A., 54
Enlightenment, v, 50, 58–65, 67, 69, 71, 73, 75–76, 96, 129
Espín, Orlando O., 111, 141, 143, 147–48, 150, 155–56, 158
Ethics, Christian, v, xiii, xix, 25–29, 31, 33, 35, 37, 39–40, 79
Evans, Christopher H., 42

Index

experience, religious, 44, 120, 127, 139, 150, 157, 159–60, 170

Fabella, Virginia, 141
Fazio, Carlos, 132
Feierstein, Ricardo, 153
First Nations, xv, 93–99, 102–3, 109
Fisher, William F., 88
Fixico, Donald L., 99, 101
Flanagan, Tom, 98
Flannery, Tim, 177–80
Floyd-Thomas, Stacey M., 167–68
Foucault, Michel, 64
Fowkes, Ben, 69

Gaillardetz, Richard, 129, 138
Gaiser, Frederick, 15
Gay, Peter, 59
Goizueta, Roberto S., 141, 144, 147, 150
González, Juan, 143–44, 149, 154–55
Gottwald, Norman, 4–5, 7
Grossberg, Lawrence, 98
Gutiérrez, Gustavo, xv, 59, 63, 76, 110–12, 114, 117–18, 127, 142, 147
Gwyther, Anthony, 7

Hammock, Clinton, 13
Hancock, Carol L., 48
Hansen, James, 178–80, 183–85
Hanson, John, 4, 7
Haraven, Tamara, 94
Harper, Stephen, 102
Harrison, Beverly W., 31
Harvey, Jennifer, 28
Hauerwas, Stanley, 59, 62, 74, 76
Hawthorne, Gerald F., xi
Hennelly, Alfred, 3
Hirst, Paul, 100, 104
Hodgson, Jim, 85
Holland, Janet, 97

Holy Spirit, vi, xvi, 123, 161, 163, 165, 167, 169, 171–75
Horkheimer, Max, 69–70
Horner, Tom, 15
Horsley, Richard, 4–5, 7, 9
Howard-Brook, Wes, 7
Hubbert, King, 181
Hullot-Kentor, Robert, 68
Humphrey, Ted, 58
Hunter, Frederic, 70
Huntington, Samuel P., xvi, 151, 161
Hutchison, William R., 44
hybridity, xvi, 36, 117, 163, 165–66, 175

incarnation, 74, 135, 186, 189
indigenous cultures, v, 104, 128–29, 131, 133, 135, 137, 139, 177
indigenous peoples, xv–xvi, 26, 93, 95–101, 104–5, 107–8, 117, 128–32, 136–37, 139–40, 152–53, 156
Insole, Christopher J., 75
Irarrázaval, Diego, v, xv, 110–11, 113–27
Isasi-Díaz, Ada María, 146, 150, 157

Jacobs, Jane, xvii, 176
Jakobsen, Janet R., 34–35
Jay, Martin, 69
Jesus, vii, xi–xii, 4–7, 9–12, 15–21, 24, 34, 49–50, 52, 59–60, 86, 124, 144, 149, 157, 186, 189
Johnson, Elizabeth A., 186, 188
justice, viii–ix, 4–5, 11, 14, 24, 26, 29, 34–35, 38, 45, 48, 50, 54, 72, 74, 81, 93, 104–6, 122, 129, 136–37, 142, 147, 157, 161, 190–91; racial, 10, 32, 35
justice-love, xiv, 29–30, 32, 40

Keesmaat, Sylvia C., 7
kenosis, 66, 187, 189
Kierkegaard, Søren, 67–68

195

Index

Kim, Grace Ji-Sun, 167, 168, 169, 172
Kinsler, Gloria, 5
Kinsler, Ross, 5
Klaiber, Jeffrey, 117
Kunstler, James, 186
Laarman, Peter, 23
Lang, Bernhard, 7
Latin America, xii, 3, 5, 58, 63, 75, 81, 107, 110–18, 120, 122, 130–32, 152–53
Latina/o peoples, 141–42, 143, 145–47, 150–51, 154–60
Latina/o theologians, xvi, 141–57, 159–60
Latina/o Theology, v, xvi, 141–45, 147, 149, 151–53, 155–60
Lemert, Charles, 35
liberation, xiii, xvii, 5–6, 34, 63, 76, 79, 85, 114–15, 117, 119, 124, 126–27, 135, 144, 162, 164–65, 186
liberation theologies, viii–ix, xiii, xvii, 3–5, 8, 59–60, 63, 69, 74–76, 79, 81, 85, 111–12, 115, 119, 124, 147, 168, 186
Lincoln, Abraham, 10, 95
Lind, Christopher, 129
Lomelí, Francisco A., 143
Lora, Carmen, 134
Lovelock, James, xvi, 176, 180, 184–85
Lowery, Richard, 5
Lugones, Maria, 39
Luther, Martin, 186–87

MacDonald, Fiona, 103
MacEoin, Gary, 132
Macy, Gary, 148
Maduro, Otto, 147
Magallanes, Hugo, 157
Maguire, Daniel, 26
Maldonado-Torres, Nelson, 96
Malik, Faris, 15

Malina, Bruce, 7, 9
Maracle, Lee, 108–9
marginalization, 37, 86, 130, 141–42, 146, 158
Marshall, Christopher, 5
Martínez, Elizabeth, 151
Marx, Karl, 5, 50–52, 69–70
Marzal, Manuel, 123
Matovina, Timothy, 149
Matthews, Victor, 7
Maya-Christian Spirituality and Theology, 139
McClung, Nellie L., 41–42, 48–49
McFague, Sallie, 30
McGovern, Arthur, 4
McNaught, Kenneth, 54, 57
Medina, Néstor, 143, 144, 152, 160
Meeks, Wayne, 7
mestizaje, xvi, 143–50, 152–54, 156, 159
mestizos, 145, 150, 152–53
Mexican Americans, 145, 154–55
Mexico, xv, 128–29, 131–32, 137, 139, 145, 154
Michaels, Patrick, 177
Mignolo, Walter, 142
Mihevc, Joe, 129
Milbank, John, v, xiv, 58–76
Miranda, Jose, 5
Mirón, Louis F., 151
missionaries, 131, 134, 167
Mitchell, Tom, 48, 179
modernity, v, 61, 86, 96, 128–29, 136, 147
Moltmann, Jürgen, 186, 188–89
Morrison, Daniel, 83
Morrow, Ray, 26
Munger, Theodore, 44
Myers, Ched, 7, 21, 23

Nelson, Cary, 98
Nelson, Susan, 23
Noël, Alan, 103
Nolan, Albert, 6

Index

Oakman, Douglas, 5, 7
oral traditions, xv, 93–99, 101, 108
Owen, Robert, 42

Palmer, Richard E., 148
Pasewark, Kyle A., 106
Pedraja, Luis, 144
Penner, Norman, 46
Perú, 110–14, 117–18, 120–21, 125
Phan, Peter C., 142
Philcox, Richard, 96
Pilch, John, 7
Pinn, Anthony, 167–68
Pippin, Tina, 8
Pixley, George, 4
Polkinghorne, John, 189
Ponniah, Thomas, 88
popular religion, xv–xvi, 110–23, 126–27, 143, 148–49, 156–57, 185
Portelli, Alessandro, 94, 96–97
Posnansky, Arthur, 153
Postcolonialism, 36, 162–66
power, xiii, 6–7, 9, 14, 16, 20, 22, 26, 30, 34–35, 38, 51, 61, 63–64, 83–85, 96, 99, 103, 105–7, 110, 121, 127, 139, 146, 157, 166, 173–74, 178, 187, 189
Putnam, Hilary, 30

racism, viii, xvi, 6, 28, 36, 39, 142, 151, 153, 159, 167–69, 174–75
Rahner, Karl, 65
Rainey, Lee, 171
Ramazanoğlu, Caroline, 97
Rauschenbusch, Walter, 41–42, 44, 51–53
Recinos, Harold, 157–58
religion, ix, xii, xix, 4, 7, 13, 38, 45, 55, 61, 66, 72, 88, 103, 110, 112, 116–17, 119, 122, 124, 132–33, 139–40, 169–70, 175, 185–86

Rhoads, David, 22
Richard, Pablo, 111, 113–14, 116
Rieger, Jorg, 9
Ringe, Sharon, 5
Robb, Carol S., 29
Robles, Ricardo, 139
Rohr, Richard, 23
Rohrbaugh, Richard, 7
Rose, Gillian, 73, 75
Rowland, Christopher, 5
Ruiz, Jean-Pierre, 134, 164
Ruiz, Samuel, xv, 130–35, 137

Said, Edward W., 169
Salm, Luke, 29
salvation, 34, 44, 59, 65, 73, 123, 133, 135, 149
Samuelson, Les, 83
Santiago, Jorge S., 130–31
Scripture, vii–viii, xiii, 3, 5, 8–9, 14, 16, 49, 118
Segovia, Fernando F., 6, 33, 146, 150, 155, 157
Sharpless, Rebecca, 96
Shrader-Frechette, Kristin, 184
Silber, Stefan, 85
Skidmore, Thomas E., 122
Smillie, Ross L., 190
Smith, A. E., 41, 48–49
Smith, Adam, 51
Smith, Mel, 98
Smith, Peter H., 122
Sobrino, Jon, xii, 6, 186
Social Gospel, v, xiv, 9, 41–45, 47–57
socialism, 46–7, 81–2, 111, 114–16, 124; Christian, 124, 191
sociology, xiv–xv, xix, 4, 6–7, 28, 41–42, 45, 48, 53–54, 56–57, 119–20
Stefancic, Jean, 151
Stevens-Arroyo, Anthony, 142
Strong, Josiah, 55
Sugirtharajah, R. S., 8, 111, 141, 162–64, 166

Index

Swartley, Willard, 5

Taylor, Graham, 51
Temple, William, 42
Thompson, Paul, 94
Tillich, Paul, xv, 105–6
Tolbert, Mary, 33
Torres, Rodolfo D., 142, 151
Torres, Sergio, 114
Townes, Emilie M., 34, 36
transformation, 30, 33–34, 37, 55, 116, 136, 138, 162, 166

United States, 42, 95, 101, 143, 154, 156, 159, 161, 167–68, 182–83
Uyede-Kai, Kim, 32, 37

Valentín, Benjamin, 158
Vansina, Jan, 94–95, 101
Vargas, Javier, 133–35
Veblen, Thorstein, 50–52
Viertel, John, 68
Vincent, John, 23

Walsh, Brian J., 7
Warne, Randi, 48
Weaver, J. Denny, 5
Weber, Max, 53
Wells, Samuel, 62
West, Gerald O., 6
West, Traci, 28
Whitaker, Francisco, 81–85
Wilson, Nancy, 15, 100, 188
Wink, Walter, 6
women, viii, 15, 17, 26, 28, 46, 48–49, 113, 118, 157, 188
Woodsworth, J. S., 41–43, 54–57
World Social Forum, v, ix, xiii–xiv, 26, 77–88

Yee, Gale, 8
Yergin, Daniel, 181–83
York, Geoffrey, 74
Young, Robert, 35, 100